Voices in Translation

TRANSLATING EUROPE
Series Editors: Gunilla Andeman, *University of Surrey, UK*
Margaret Rogers, *University of Surrey, UK*

Other Books in the Series
In and Out of English: For Better for Worse
    Gunilla Anderman and Margaret Rogers (eds)
Incorporating Corpora: The Linguist and the Translator
    Gunilla Anderman and Margaret Rogers (eds)

Other Books of Interest
A Companion to Translation Studies
    Piotr Kuhiwczak and Karin Littau (eds)
Contemporary Translation Theories (2nd edition)
    Edwin Gentzler
Constructing Cultures: Essays on Literary Translation
    Susan Bassnett and André Lefevere
Cultural Encounters in Translation from Arabic
    Said Faiq (ed.)
Frae Ither Tongues: Essays on Modern Translations into Scots
    Bill Findlay (ed.)
Identity, Insecurity and Image: France and Language
    Dennis Ager
Literary Translation: A Practical Guide
    Clifford E. Landers
Politeness in Europe
    Leo Hickey and Miranda Stewart (eds)
The Pragmatics of Translation
    Leo Hickey (ed.)
Theatrical Translation and Film Adaptation: A Practitioner's View
    Phyllis Zatlin
Time Sharing on Stage: Drama Translation in Theatre and Society
    Sirkku Aaltonen
Translating Milan Kundera
    Michelle Woods
Translation, Linguistics, Culture: A French-English Handbook
    Nigel Armstrong
Translation, Power, Subversion
    Román Alvarez and M. Carmen-Africa Vidal (eds)
Translation and Nation: A Cultural Politics of Englishness
    Roger Ellis and Liz Oakley-Brown (eds)
Translation and Religion: Holy Untranslatable?
    Lynne Long (ed.)
Words, Words, Words. The Translator and the Language Learner
    Gunilla Anderman and Margaret Rogers
Written in the Language of the Scottish Nation: A History of Literary Translation into Scots
    John Corbett

For more details of these or any other of our publications, please contact:
Multilingual Matters, Frankfurt Lodge, Clevedon Hall,
Victoria Road, Clevedon, BS21 7HH, England
http://www.multilingual-matters.com

TRANSLATING EUROPE
Series Editors: Gunilla Anderman and Margaret Rogers
University of Surrey

Voices in Translation
Bridging Cultural Divides

Edited by
Gunilla Anderman

MULTILINGUAL MATTERS LTD
Clevedon • Buffalo • Toronto

Library of Congress Cataloging in Publication Data
Voices in Translation: Bridging Cultural Divides / Edited by Gunilla Anderman.
Translating Europe.
Includes bibliographical references and index.
1. Translating and interpreting. 2. European literature–History and criticism.
I. Anderman, Gunilla M.
PN241.V583 2007
418'.02–dc22   2007000081

British Library Cataloguing in Publication Data
A catalogue entry for this book is available from the British Library.

ISBN-13: 978-1-85359-983-5 (hbk)
ISBN-13: 978-1-85359-982-8 (pbk)

Multilingual Matters Ltd
UK: Frankfurt Lodge, Clevedon Hall, Victoria Road, Clevedon BS21 7HH.
USA: UTP, 2250 Military Road, Tonawanda, NY 14150, USA.
Canada: UTP, 5201 Dufferin Street, North York, Ontario M3H 5T8, Canada.

Copyright © 2007 Gunilla Anderman and the authors of individual chapters.

All rights reserved. No part of this work may be reproduced in any form or by any means without permission in writing from the publisher.

The policy of Multilingual Matters/Channel View Publications is to use papers that are natural, renewable and recyclable products, made from wood grown in sustainable forests. In the manufacturing process of our books, and to further support our policy, preference is given to printers that have FSC and PEFC Chain of Custody certification. The FSC and/or PEFC logos will appear on those books where full certification has been granted to the printer concerned.

Typeset by Wordworks Ltd.
Printed and bound in Great Britain by the Cromwell Press Ltd.

Bill Findlay

11th June 1947 – 15th May 2005

In Memoriam

Contents

Acknowledgements ix

Contributors: A Short Profile x

Introduction
Gunilla Anderman 1

1 Voices in Translation
  Gunilla Anderman 6

2 From Rouyn to Lerwick: The Vernacular Journey of
  Jeanne-Mance Delisle's 'The Reel of the Hanged Man'
  Martin Bowman 16

3 Speaking the World: Drama in Scots Translation
  John Corbett 32

4 Staging Italian Theatre: A Resistant Approach
  Stefania Taviano 46

5 The Style of Translation: Dialogue with the Author
  Joseph Farrell 56

6 Chekhov in the Theatre: The Role of the Translator in
  New Versions
  Helen Rappaport 66

7 The Cultural Engagements of Stage Translation: Federico García
  Lorca in Performance
  David Johnston 78

8 To Be or Not To Be (Untranslatable): Strindberg in Swedish
  and English
  Gunilla Anderman 94

9 Mind the Gap: Translating the 'Untranslatable'
   Margaret Jull Costa 111

10 Alice in Denmark
   Viggo Hjørnager Pedersen and Kirsten Nauja Andersen. 123

11 Little Snowdrop and The Magic Mirror: Two Approaches to
   Creating a 'Suitable' Translation in 19th-Century England
   Niamh Chapelle and Jenny Williams 134

12 From Dissidents to Bestsellers: Polish Literature in English
   Translation After the End of the Cold War
   Piotr Kuhiwczak. 148

Acknowledgements

Our thanks must first of all go to Bill Findlay's wife, Jessica Burns, and their daughters, Hannah and Martha, for agreeing to let us dedicate *Voices in Translation: Bridging Cultural Divides* to his memory. When planning this volume we were in contact with Bill about making a contribution, only to learn after production of the volume had begun that sadly he would be unable to contribute. Dedicating this volume to his memory seemed the obvious way of acknowledging Bill Findlay's work in the field of Translation Studies and the contribution he was unable to make to this book. Once this decision was taken, speed of completion had by necessity to be sacrificed to our concern to include as many as possible of those who wished to pay tribute. A debt of gratitude is owed both to those contributors who endeavoured to meet the tight deadline and to those who patiently waited to see the finished volume, including the publisher, Multilingual Matters, to whom we would also like to express our thanks. Last, but certainly not least, we would like to thank Gillian James whose commitment to the project and creative input helped *Voices in Translation: Bridging Cultural Divides* see the light of day.

Gunilla Anderman
Guildford, October 2006

Note added in proof

The current volume – *Voices in Translation* – was generously dedicated to the memory of Bill Findlay, a pioneer in the field of dialect translation, by our friend and colleague Gunilla Anderman. Tragically, Gunilla herself did not live to see this rich edited collection of papers reach its final stages. As an accomplished translator of drama, as well as a distinguished scholar in Translation Studies, Gunilla would have delighted in the final publication of a volume that highlights and celebrates the role of the translator as a skilful and creative cultural mediator. Her own contribution to this volume illustrates this better than any further commentary. Let the volume be a fitting tribute to Gunilla's outstanding work in this field.

Margaret Rogers
Guildford, July 2007

Contributors: A Short Profile

Gunilla Anderman was Professor of Translation Studies at the University of Surrey, where she taught translation theory, translation of drama and translation of children's literature – fields in which she had published and lectured widely in the UK as well as internationally. She was also a professional translator, with translations of Scandinavian plays staged in the UK, USA and South Africa. Her most recent book was *Europe on Stage: Translation and Theatre* (2005).

Kirsten Nauja Andersen, MA, is Deputy Head of the Translation Centre, Copenhagen University. She also works as a subtitler, translator and lexicographer. In 1994 she was awarded Copenhagen University's gold medal for her thesis on the Danish translations of Lewis Carroll's *Alice*.

Martin Bowman was born and raised in Montreal of Scottish parentage and educated at McGill University and Université de Montréal where he gained his PhD. With Bill Findlay he co-translated into Scots eleven plays by four Quebec playwrights, and with Wajdi Mouawad he has co-translated two plays, *Trainspotting* and *Disco Pigs*, into French. Now retired from teaching, he is presently engaged in translating the work of Jeanne-Mance Delisle.

Niamh Chapelle gained her PhD from Dublin City University, entitled *The Translators' Tale: A Translator-Centred History of Seven English Translations (1823–1944) of the Grimms' Fairy Tale 'Sneewittchen'*. Before moving back to Ireland to work in the localisation industry, she was employed as an in-house translator in Germany. More recently, she has been working as a freelance translator. Her fascination with fairy tales and the history of translation continues.

John Corbett is Professor of Applied Language Studies in Glasgow University's Department of English Language. Among his publications on the use of Scots in literature are *Language and Scottish Literature* (1997) and *Written in the Language of the Scottish Nation: A History of Literary Translation into Scots* (1999). He is also the editor of *Language and Intercultural Communication*.

Joseph Farrell is Professor of Italian Studies in the University of Strathclyde, in Glasgow. His main research interests are in the fields of Sicilian culture and Theatre History. He is the author of *Leonardo Sciascia* (1995), and

Dario Fo and Franca Rame: Harlequins of the Revolution. (2001). The *History of Italian Theatre*, which he co-edited with Paolo Puppa of Ca' Foscari University, is soon to be published. In addition, he has edited volumes on Carlo Goldoni, Dario Fo, Primo Levi and on the Mafia. His translations include novels by Sciascia, Consolo and Del Giudice, as well as plays by Fo, Baricco, De Filippo and Goldoni.

Viggo Hjørnager Pedersen, D.Phil, is Associate Professor of English at Copenhagen University. His research is in the field of Translation Studies and Literature. His recent book, *Ugly Ducklings? Studies in the English Translations of Hans Christian Andersen's Tales and Stories* (2004) is a monograph on English translations of Hans Christian Andersen's tales. He is editor of the 3rd and 4th editions of the *Vinterberg & Bodelsen Danish-English Dictionary* (1990 and 1998). His literary translations include novels by E.M. Forster and William Golding.

David Johnston is Professor of Spanish and Head of the School of Languages, Literatures and Performing Arts at Queen's University Belfast. He has published on Spanish culture, theatre, and translation, including *Stages of Translation* (1996). He is currently completing *Translation and Performance: The Practice of Theatre*, to be published in 2007. An award-winning translator for the stage, his versions of plays by Valle-Inclán and Lorca have been produced by BBC Radio 3 and Radio 4, and in 2003–2004 his *The Dog in The Manger* by Lope de Vega was performed by the Royal Shakespeare Company. More recently he has also translated contemporary Mexican and Argentine plays for the Royal Court in London and for the Ohio International Theatre Festival respectively. A number of his own plays have been produced on stage including, in 1988, his version of *Don Quijote*.

Margaret Jull Costa has translated a number of Spanish, Portuguese and Latin American writers including Eça de Queiroz, Fernando Pessoa, Javier Marías and José Régio. She was joint winner of the Portuguese Translation Prize in 1992 for the *Book of Disquiet* by Fernando Pessoa. More recently she has been noted for her work in translating the novels of José Saramago, her translation of *All the Names* winning the 2000 Weidenfeld Translation Prize. In 2006, she won the Premio Valle Inclán 2006 for her translation of Javier Marías's *Your Face Tomorrow: Fever and Spear* (2005).

Piotr Kuhiwczak, PhD, lectures in the Department for Translation and Comparative Cultures at Warwick University and is Deputy Chair of the advisory board of the British Centre for Literary Translation, and the Chair of the editorial board of *The Linguist*. With Dr Karin Littau of the University of Essex, he has recently completed an edited volume of essays, *A Companion to Translation Studies*, to appear in May 2007. His major research project is concerned with the study of the impact of translation on the reception of Holocaust memoirs and testimonies and the impact of censorship on writing and translation, particularly in Central and Eastern Europe.

Helen Rappaport graduated in Russian Special Studies from Leeds University, after which she took up an acting career, as well as working as a Russian translator for the National Theatre, the Royal Shakespeare Company, the Almeida and Donmar Warehouse theatres. Since 1976 she has worked with major British playwrights such as David Lan, Nick Wright, Kevin Elyot, Frank McGuinness, Trevor Griffiths and David Hare on new versions of plays by Chekhov, Ostrovsky and Gorky. She has translated all seven of Chekhov's extant plays, most notably for director Katie Mitchell. In addition to her work as a translator, she is increasingly concentrating on her writing career as a specialist in 19th-century women's history, as in her 2007 publication *No Place for Ladies: The Untold Story of Women in the Crimean War.*

Stefania Taviano who holds a PhD in Translation Studies from Warwick University, now lectures in English at the University of Messina, Italy. She is the author of *Staging Dario Fo and Franca Rame: Anglo-American Approaches to Political Theatre* (2005) and of a number of articles on Italian modern dramatists as well as Italian American theatre and performance art. She has also translated Italian contemporary playwrights, such as Spiro Scimone, and contributed to the translation of Dario Fo's *Johan Padan and the Discovery of the Americas.*

Jenny Williams, Associate Professor and Head of the School of Applied Language and Intercultural Studies at Dublin City University, has published in the fields of German and Translation Studies. Her most recent book (with Andrew Chesterman) is *The Map: A Guide to Doing Research in Translation Studies* (2002). Her translation works include a poetry anthology from German into English: Sabine Lange *The Fishermen Sleep,* with an introduction by Mary O'Donnell (2005).

Introduction

GUNILLA ANDERMAN

This volume focuses on two problems that face the translator of European fiction: voices speaking across cultural borders and the difficulty of transferring the social, cultural and political milieu in which these speakers are rooted.

The volume opens with 'Voices in Translation' in which Gunilla Anderman discusses the importance of providing speakers of other nations and cultures with an authentic voice in translation. Following an exposé of the reasons why awareness of the importance of speakers communicating across cultural divides in voices of their own has been slow in coming, tribute is paid to the work of Bill Findlay in Scots dialect translation. Particular attention is given to his imaginative re-creation of Gerhart Hauptmann's *The Weavers*, a milestone in the development of modern European drama, and *Bairns' Brothers*, his dialect version of *Enfantillages* by Raymond Cousse, a contemporary play written in standard French. Mention is also made of Findlay's work with co-translator Martin Bowman on the translation of the plays by Michel Tremblay, which have made the Quebec playwright the most frequently performed foreign-language playwright in Scotland for the past 16 years.

In Chapter 2, 'From Rouyn to Lerwick: The Vernacular Journey of Jeanne-Mance Delisle's *The Reel of the Hanged Man*', Martin Bowman tells of another Quebec playwright whose work he and Findlay brought to the stage. The play's first production proved to be a difficult ride, due to a large extent to the sensitivity of the subject – Delisle deals with the topic of incest. In this chapter the author introduces us to the Quebec playwright as well as to her play, pointing to the importance of vernacular theatre beyond its original culture.

John Corbett's contribution, 'Speaking the World: Drama in Scots Translation' pays tribute to Bill Findlay, drawing on the experience of co-editing with him the anthology *Serving Twa Maisters: Five Plays in Scots Translation*. While the non-standard urban argot of Scots has been linked to the conditions of class oppression (as in the writing of Irvine Welsh and James Kelman), this chapter sets out to redress the balance by exploring the uses of Scots in English plays translated over the second half of the 20th century.

Chapter 4, Stefania Taviano's contribution, also has a strong Scottish link. The Italian stagings discussed in 'Staging Italian Theatre: A Resistant Approach' include a joint production of *The Odyssey* by the Italian theatre group Stalker and the Glasgow-based Working Party, a project funded by the Scottish Arts Council that formed part of a month-long season of theatre, and literary events in Glasgow between October and November 2002. Taviano argues that the use of non-standard language and the commitment of theatre collectives to physical acting form the central elements of a *resistant* approach that distinguishes itself by its challenging interpretation of foreign theatre. She suggests that a resistant approach to the staging of the work of foreign playwrights subverts strategies centred on the 'exotic' nature of foreign plays by focusing instead on their political role.

In 'The Style of Translation: Dialogue with the Author', the contribution from Joseph Farrell, Italy and Scotland similarly figure prominently. 'The words may belong to language but the voice belongs to the artist', Farrell observes, and proceeds to discuss the style of Sicilian writer Vincenzo Consolo. In the context of the discussion of how to convey in translation the impact created by the distinctive style of a writer, Farrell approaches the issue of dialect translation. He also broaches the issue of the function and status of dialects in different languages, notably Scots and Italian.

While Farrell is adamant on the point of withholding the role of 'second creator' from the translator, an increasingly popular way of attracting the interest of British theatre-goers is attempting to bridge the cultural divide between source and target language and culture by 'domesticating' the foreign text. In Chapter 6, 'Chekhov in the Theatre: The Role of the Translator in New Versions', Helen Rappaport discusses the emergence over the last few decades of new versions or adaptations of European plays by contemporary British playwrights, in particular the four major plays by Anton Chekhov. Following a discussion of strengths and weaknesses inherent in the writing of new 'versions' of Chekhov by playwrights who are not speakers of the source language and possess limited knowledge of 19th century rural Russia, Rappaport asks the legitimate question: Whose work is it anyway? Is it the star dramatist who often leaves his signature on the work produced by the literary translator, or the foreign playwright?

According to David Johnston in 'The Cultural Engagements of Stage Translation: Federico García Lorca in Performance', in order to bridge the cultural divide between the receiving culture and Lorca's systemic patterns of imagery, with their characteristically powerful interplay between animate and inanimate elements drawn from the everyday world of rural Spain of the past, the translator may employ the same tactics normally used to transfer culture-specific items. It is important, however, Johnston argues, that the translator does not allow Lorca's encyclopedia of reference to push the translation process towards a merely linguistic exercise. The aim of

Lorca's theatre is to reframe experience, which means that the translation of culture-specific items in his writing is governed by rhetorical and stylistic considerations as much as by any external referencing. The author concludes that to translate Lorca for performance requires a clear-sighted view of how to provide him with a voice on stage, how to write towards his plays' potential in order to engage an audience and charge the air in the theatre.

Writing about rural Spain, Lorca would frequently draw on flower symbolism; the Spanish writer is not, however, the only writer to employ this form of imagery; flora as well as fauna are used as symbols in many languages. At the end of Act 2 of Ibsen's *Little Eyolf*, it is through flowers that Asta says a last farewell to her brother Alfred. The flowers are water lilies, their beauty suggesting purity; through the symbolism of their use, Alfred's obsession is shown as something more than just a weakness, something beautiful in its own way, but a beauty that, like the water lily, has reached the surface from the deep bottom.

As symbols, the languages that flowers speak are many and varied. At the time of Strindberg, hyacinths were associated with death and funerals in Sweden, as illustrated by the ailing girl in the Hyacinth Room in *The Ghost Sonata*. Lilacs, on the other hand, in Sweden stand for light and early summer, as in *Miss Julie*, where they preside prominently on the kitchen table when Julie and Jean meet, but in Italy they reportedly represent envy. And in some English villages, a lilac branch may also signify a broken engagement, potentially applicable to the situation of the protagonist of *Miss Julie*. Flower images figure prominently in Strindberg's writing, and the choice of flower is rarely random. The selection of the flower image is often sensitive to the fabric of the individual play, as discussed by Gunilla Anderman in Chapter 8, 'To Be or Not to Be (Untranslatable): Strindberg in Swedish and English'.

In Strindberg's *Easter*, the daffodil represents the coming of light after a winter of physical and spiritual darkness. If replaced by a lily, as has often been the case in English-speaking productions of the play, the change in flower also means a change in the language it speaks: a white lily with its associations of funerals speaks a language different from that of a sun-soaked daffodil. According to Anderman, aspects such as flower and bird symbolism need to be left intact in translation even if what they stand for is 'untranslatable'. Other aspects of the Swedish playwright's work may also present obstacles, Anderman argues, but these problems need not defy translation if the translator or creator of 'new versions' makes sure to dig beneath the surface.

For a professional translator of fiction, on the other hand, a solution always has to be found to what might at first sight appear untranslatable. In 'Mind the Gap: Translating the Untranslatable', Margaret Jull Costa, a literary translator from Spanish and Portuguese, acknowledges that she cannot afford to believe in the 'untranslatable'. It is the translator's job to translate everything, knowing that there might be some loss in translation but, as Jull Costa points out, there might also be some gain. Among the problems she has had to solve in attempting to bridge the cultural divide between the world inhabited by the writers whose books she has translated and the English-speaking world, Jull Costa chooses to discuss first the words used to name phenomena in the physical world, then linguistic obstacles such as puns, idioms and proverbs, and, in conclusion, historical, geographical and cultural references. As an example of a translation problem belonging to the first category, she discusses the translation of *queijadas*, tartlets filled with a mixture of sugar, cinnamon, egg and fresh cheese, a unique speciality of Sintra, the fashionable summer retreat just outside Lisbon. As 'cheese cakes' conjure up the wrong associations, Jull Costa, who is still working on the translation as this volume goes to press, is choosing between 'cheese tartlets' and 'cheese pastries'. In the case of the translation of puns, she acknowledges that they are too, in a sense, untranslatable but others may be created to replace them as long as they are in keeping with the tone and the tenor of the original. The last problem with which Jull Costa is concerned is the rendering of geographical and historical references. Not favoured by publishers of foreign fiction, footnotes do not figure prominently in her translations, although she acknowledges that, in her translation of Luís Cardoso's *The Crossing: A Story of East Timor*, the unfamiliarity to the reader of place names, personal names and terminology made it necessary to include a glossary.

References to food similarly constitute a problem for the translator of Lewis Carroll into Danish, as discussed in 'Alice in Denmark'. In this chapter, Viggo Hjørnager Pedersen and Kirsten Nauja Andersen compare Danish translations of *Alice in Wonderland* (1865) which originate at different points in time, spanning the period from 1875 to 2000. Among stumbling blocks for the translator such as style, related linguistic problems and allusions, the untranslatability of culinary references figure prominently. For example, Alice compares the taste of one of her magic potions to '... custard, pineapple, roast turkey, toffy and buttered toast', but at the time of the early translations some of these well-known English delicacies were unknown in Denmark – even 'turkey', the functional equivalent of which, according to the authors, is likely to have been *andesteg* ('roast duck'). In conclusion, the translations examined in this chapter are declared to be failing to live up to the original, in part because of the unwillingness of the translators to take on the challenge of cultural adaptation. In order to succeed, it is argued, the translations would have had to depart more from the source text, substituting Danish jokes and word play. But then, as the authors admit, the story might not have been about Alice, but about Marie, a different girl, a strategy attempted by only one of the translators.

The difference in approach favoured by translators is also discussed by Niamh Chapelle and Jenny Williams, who examine the use of different strategies adopted by two translators for bridging the same cultural divide. In Chapter 11, 'Little Snowdrop and the Magic Mirror: Two Approaches to Creating a "Suitable" Translation in Nineteenth-century England', they examine two translations of the same 1857 edition of the Grimms' fairy tale *Sneewittchen* (*Snow White*), which appeared within no more than 11 years of each other. Both translators were translating for young people, and in the prefaces they were at pains to explain that they had tried to ensure that the translations were suitable for their audience in terms of style and content. Still, the resulting translations turned out to be very different. The reasons for the difference between *Little Snowdrop* (1863) and *The Magic Mirror* (1871–4), the authors conclude, is to be found in the translators' radically different definitions of 'suitability' and their attitude toward the target audience.

In the concluding contribution to the volume, Piotr Kuhiwczak points to yet another factor that bears on translation: the political and economic life of a nation may affect the relationship between original and translated literature. In his contribution, 'From Dissidents to Best Sellers: Polish Literature in English Translation After the End of the Cold War', Kuhiwczak discusses the role played by politics prior to the 'velvet revolutions' when the process of selection of literature to be published in the Eastern Bloc was controlled by the state apparatus – the Marxist-Leninist regime considered literature an important part of dogma. Using Poland as the country of exemplification, Kuhiwczak shows how poetry, previously in a dominant position, was replaced by other new genres of literature, introduced through a steady growth of translation from English into Polish. Outside Poland a similar change made itself known: UK publishers began to apply to Polish literature the same criteria as they did to the literatures of other countries. In particular a new interest began to develop in Polish writing concerned with the ethnic and political dilemmas of Poland's past.

For writers from this part of Europe it took turbulence and political change to help bridge the cultural divide and provide them with a voice in translation.

Chapter 1
Voices in Translation

GUNILLA ANDERMAN

Introduction

An enlarged European Union, the rapid growth of electronic communication and the emergence of English as the lingua franca of Europe are now providing Europeans with easy access to the cultural and literary heritage of a multitude of other nations. But while the citizens of Europe are beginning to experience different cultures at first hand, many social and cultural concepts that they are now encountering will remain unknown outside national borders and, as a result, lack lexical designation in other languages. How, for example, does a translator render in another language the information that speakers convey when they engage in a dialogue, the way in which English dialect and sociolect interact to make language a unique indicator of class and education? As Bernard Shaw famously remarked 'it is impossible for an Englishman to open his mouth without making some other Englishman despise him.' Although different factors may come into play in other languages spoken in other countries, speakers still have a voice of their own for which writers have a finely attuned ear. And when the work of the writer reaches the translator responsible for transferring it into another language, a voice has to be found in the new language that closely resembles that of the original. It is equally difficult for the translator to find appropriate means of expression in another language for what speakers may engage in dialogue about: flora and fauna and cultural customs, as well as the social and political conventions that are little known to anyone outside the country in which they form part of everyday life.

This volume focuses on two problems that face the translator of European fiction: voices speaking across cultural borders, and the means of expression to convey the social and cultural milieu in which the speakers are rooted. In particular, attention is given to the work of Bill Findlay – to whom this collection of essays is dedicated.

Speaking across Cultural Borders

For a playwright aware of the importance of the uniqueness of the voice of each character on stage, recognising the problems facing the translator is but a short step, as evidenced by Ibsen's comments in relation to the translation of *The Wild Duck*:

> [...] consistently every character in the play has their particular, individual way of expressing themselves, through which the degree of their culture and education is manifested. When for example Gina speaks we should hear immediately that she never learnt any grammar and that she was born into a lower, social class. And the same applies to all the other characters. The task of the translator is, in other words, not an easy one.[1] (Ibsen, 1891)

Equally attuned to the different voices of his characters is the Spanish poet and playwright Federico García Lorca. While attending a performance of *Doòa Rosita the Spinster,* Lorca's cousin Mercedes Delgado García immediately recognised that the protagonist's speech derived from Asquerosa, Lorca's home town (Gibson, 1989: 406). In Brecht's play about the ravages of the Thirty Year War, *Mother Courage and Her Children*, the protagonist speaks in a language strongly coloured by her Bavarian dialect. And in his commentary to his translation of *The Cherry Orchard* by the Russian playwright Anton Chekhov, Michael Frayn points out that each of the characters speaks in their own distinctive voice, revealing their education (or lack thereof), place of birth and social class (Frayn, 1995: xxxix–xi). Failure to capture the difference in the speech of the Chekhov characters through simply translating their language into Standard English has resulted, as famously remarked, in creating the impression that all his Russian peasants live in the vicinity of Sloane Square.

Giving each character a voice of his or her own requires, however, that the translator first has an awareness of where the characters live, their social position and their own, personal idiosyncrasies in the source culture, and also the ability to find the lexical and grammatical means of matching expressions in the target language. Dialect in translation, however, is more frequently than not rendered into the standard variety, often as a result of the way translation used to serve as a means of language teaching and learning. Although the last few decades of Modern Language teaching have embraced the so-called communicative approach, pedagogy has long been influenced by the methodology favoured in the instruction of the classical languages.

Spoken Versus Written Language

In the instruction of Greek and Latin, translation was used as a means of ensuring that new vocabulary had been acquired: often students were worried that too creative an effort would be penalised with a bad mark and would settle for as close to a word-for-word translation as possible. In similar fashion, many translators would also simply replace one word in the foreign language with the equivalent written word in the target language. And with spoken varieties of the classical languages no longer in existence, limited attention was given to difference in genre and the fact that people rarely speak the way they write.

The lack of knowledge about the spoken mode of language was, however, not of crucial importance in the theatre, as the speech of ordinary people was not considered to be appropriate language for use on stage. When, in 1914, Shaw's *Pygmalion* first opened at *His Majesty's Theatre* in London with Herbert Beerbohm Tree as Professor Higgins and Mrs Patrick Campbell as Eliza Doolittle, the *Daily Express* took a Charing Cross flower girl, Eliza Keefe, along to the *Haymarket*, loftily reporting her reactions to the amusement of its readers: 'Well, I've never 'ad such a night in all me natural ... '. What offended the papers was not the social inequity but the use of bad language on stage, especially 'not bloody likely', spoken in Act 3. Indignantly the *Daily Sketch* headline pronounced: 'Mrs Patrick Campbell swears on stage and cultured London roars with laughter' (Butler, 2001).

As Bernard Shaw's passion with reforming English society grew, so did his interest in reforming language. In the early 1880s he had met Henry Sweet (1845–1912) whose interest in spoken language resulted in the publication of *A Handbook of Phonetics* in 1877. Adapted in 1890 as *A Primer of Spoken English*, it became the first scientifically-based description of educated London speech or Received Pronunciation (RP). In the preface to *Pygmalion*, which in the character of Professor Higgins contains obvious touches of Sweet, Shaw refers to Sweet's 'satanic contempt for all academic dignitaries and persons in general who thought more of Greek than phonetics' (Butler, 2001). The study of speech sounds was further advanced by Daniel Jones (1881–1967) who, in 1921, became the first professor of Phonetics at London University. Influential in spreading the use of the International Phonetic Alphabet (IPA) throughout the world, his efforts provided the mechanism for the use of transcription of speech sounds. By the time of his retirement in 1949 Daniel Jones had created a department with a worldwide reputation.

With the interest in the written mode long pre-dating the study of spoken language, it is hardly surprising that, in the teaching of foreign languages, translation paid scant attention to linguistic variation and that texts were routinely translated into the standard variety of the target language. As a result, in the transfer from source to target language, the specific characteristics of the individual voices disappeared and a new blander text emerged, devoid of the force and colour of the original.

Geographical and Historical Re-location

In the case of a play performed on stage, the linguistic as well as the cultural obstacles encountered in the transfer from one language and culture to another are sometimes most easily overcome by transporting the play, either in time, by placing it in a different historical period, or geographically, by finding a different location. Examples of transposition through geographical and/or historical re-location of modern European drama are numerous. In the Yale Repertory Theatre's production of *The Cherry* Orchard in 2005, the characters wore late-19th century clothes for the first half of the play, then were transposed a century ahead to 2005 fashion, language and music. One of the songs they danced to was the Rolling Stones's 'Start Me Up'. An example of a French play transposed to an English setting is the 1996 National Theatre production of Victor Hugo's *Le Roi s'amuse*, titled *The Prince's Play* in a verse translation by Tony Harrison that was set in an English music hall. A similar example of complete acculturation of an Italian play would be British playwright Mike Stott's relocation of Eduardo de Filippo's *Natale in casa cupiello* (*Christmas at the Cupiellos*) to Yorkshire under the title *Ducking Out*. An example from Spanish theatre is provided by the 1993 production of *Bohemian Lights*, where David Johnston replaced the 1920 Madrid of Valle-Inclán with Dublin in 1915, the year before the Easter rising. The permutations are many and varied; in *The Blue Room,* David Hare transported Schnitzler's *fin de siecle* Vienna in *Reigen* or *La Ronde*, to the end of the 20th century and changed the original location of the play into an unspecified, global metropolis. In contrast, by transplanting the same play to present-day Belfast, Carlo Gebler's *10 Rounds,* at the Tricycle theatre in the autumn of 2002, succeeded in providing the sense that the original had of an entire society being eroded, a feature arguably missing in the Hare/Mendes version at the Donmar, with its anonymous urban location (cf. Anderman, 2005, in particular Chapter 1).

In addition to relocation, there are other options available to make 'foreignness' in translation less of an obstacle for English theatre audiences. There is, in virtually all drama translation, some degree of 'acculturation' applied to the final product (Aaltonen, 1996). This process may not be total, but may simply take the form of neutralisation through toning down what is deemed to be too 'foreign' – a practice extending as far back in history as the Romans. Translated from Greek into Latin, the Roman comedies retained their Greek setting and it was made perfectly clear early on in the play that the characters clad in the Greek mantle lived in a Greek city. The action was usually set in Athens, the city that Roman audiences apparently considered to be more Greek than any other location. According to Plautus, the successful Roman adaptor of Greek comedies into Latin: 'Now writers of comedy have this habit: they always allege that the scene of action is Athens, their object being to give the play a more Grecian air' (Gilula, 1989: 102).

Translation into Scots

Whether re-located or just 'acculturated,' the characters of a foreign play or work of fiction still need to retain their individual voices in order to retain the interest of audiences and readers. And this is how Bill Findlay's work as a translator, often together with Martin Bowman, marks an important step forward in Translation Studies. Findlay finds individual voices for the source-language characters by drawing a distinction between English and Scots-speaking characters and by using different Scots linguistic varieties to reflect more subtle distinctions in their approach and personalities. In his translation for the stage, Bill Findlay lifted the language of the characters from the page and gave them a voice of their own.

Little had been written about drama dialect translation until Bill Findlay and Martin Bowman started to discuss the process from the perspective of their work as translators. Together the two brought the plays by playwright Michel Tremblay into Scotland by translating the *joual* French dialect of Quebec in which they are written, into Scots. Findlay's own translations include his version of *Die Weber* (1892) by Gerhart Hauptmann, the 1912 recipient of the Nobel Prize for Literature. Consistent with Hauptmann's aim to convey socialist ideas in a naturalist setting was the need for *The Weavers* to be written in the language actually spoken in the region in which the action took place, and the German original was written in the distinctive dialect of Silesia. The first version of the play, called *De Waber*, was written in uncompromising dialect, but once the stage première of this version was prohibited, Hauptmann set to work on a new version, now called *Die Weber*. Although Hauptmann's play about the real-life uprising of Silesian handloom weavers in the 1840s appeared in print in 1892, working conditions had largely remained unchanged, and the appearance of the play aroused a storm. When finally performed in 1893, the play became a literary sensation. If transferred into a Standard English medium, however, Hauptmann's original Silesian is likely to become diluted to the point of failing to make credible the social position and working conditions of his weavers. The problem of capturing the robustness of the original dialect in English translation is compounded by the fact that the events described took place a long time ago, and unless the language of the characters is in keeping with the period, there is the potential danger of anachronism. A further linguistic problem for the translator is Hauptmann's German, which is 'masterly handled'; and his reproduction of everyday speech with its subtlest nuances is 'unsurpassed', including the different mixtures of local dialects, colloquial talk and several layers of High German

(Grimm, 1994: xiv). In fact, it has been suggested (Maurer, 1982: 50) that 'even the most talented and experienced translator with a perfect command and knowledge of German (including not only several dialects but, in addition, various sociolects and idiolects too) will never succeed in rendering Hauptmann's naturalistic texts entirely satisfactorily'. Part of Hauptmann's talent lies in his ability to imbue all of his characters with distinct, individual voices. 'Each speaks in his own characteristic language with distinctive dialectical inflections, idiomatic peculiarities, syntax, speech rhythm and melody and even gestures' (Maurer, 1982: 50). Hauptmann's plays have been described as not dependent 'primarily on subject matter theme or even location: the stuff of his drama is language' (Skrine, 1989: 19).

As pointed out by Findlay (1998), the particular feature whereby all but the most peripheral of Hauptmann's characters generate and communicate their personalities and shifting social relationships through linguistic variation is a feature also found in Scottish writing. In a position to draw on a varied linguistic resource embracing Standard English, Scottish Standard English and Scots dialect, Scottish writers are able to style-shift between these different linguistic varieties as they see fit. As a result, the numerous linguistic options made use of by Hauptmann can find their match in Scots dialect, offering a number of flexible choices; it can be urban or rural, regional or standardised, historical or contemporary.

In a play such as *The Weavers* on the theme of worker/management conflict, clear linguistic signals are obviously needed to highlight differences in occupation and/or class. To this end, Findlay made the decision to draw a basic distinction between Scots and English-speaking characters. He then took the process a step further, using a stiff variety of Standard English to help reinforce an attitude of inflexibility in some characters and their concern to uphold the status quo as reflected in their reactions to the weavers' action. Unmoved by their plight, Pastor Kittelhaus shows little understanding or sympathy, which in turn is reflected in his use of a pompously correct and sanctimonious English:

> PASTOR KITTELHAUS: When a man has delivered sermons from the pulpit fifty-two Sundays a year for some thirty years – and that's not counting the Holy Days in the calender – of necessity he acquires a sense of proportion. (Findlay, 1998: 97)

In contrast, Surgeon Schmidt is a more sympathetic character who is able to relate to the weavers and their suffering. In order to show that this is his attitude, Schmidt makes use of a more conversational tone, generously peppered with Scotticisms, as for instance when he speaks to the little girl Mielchen:

> SCHMIDT: Here Mielchen, come and have a lookie in my coat pocket. (*Mielchen does so.*) The ginger snaps are for you – but don't wolf them all at once ... In fact, I'll have a song first! 'The tod run off ... wi the bubbly, bubblyjock, bubbly, bubblyjock ... oh, just you wait, young lady! (Findlay, 1998: 97)

In the case of Dreissiger, the manufacturer, the choice of language was not, however, as clear cut. While apparently voicing a degree of compassion, Dreissiger retreats to his office, referring the weavers to Pfeifer, his manager. At best Dreissiger can be described as ambivalent, at worst as hypocritical. Still, for Dreissiger simply to have been English-speaking would have polarised his relationship to the weavers to the point of turning him into a caricature of a capitalist. To avoid creating such a stark black-and-white distinction, Findlay's version has Dreissiger use a Scots similar to the weavers while, at the same time, making it sufficiently differentiated and less dense to leave us in sufficient doubt whether he is good or bad, humane or exploitative. First an exchange between Pfeifer, formerly one of the weavers himself, and the weavers as he is inspecting the cloth they have made, dismissing their efforts:

> PFEIFER: (*to the weaver standing before him.*) If ah've tellt ye wance ah've tell ye a hunner times! Yuv goat tae redd up yir wabs better nor this! Look at the state o'this claith! Hit's fu o'durt, bits o'strae as lang's ma finger ... a'kinna muck an fulth.
>
> WEAVER REIMANN: Ah canna help stoor gittin intil it.
>
> APPRENTICE: (*has weighed the cloth*) The wecht's shoart an a'. (Findlay, 1998: 98)

And here is Dreissiger, when the starving weaver laddie faints, in his Scots tempered by English, allowing him to veer between familiarity and superiority:

> DREISSIGER: It's a doonricht disgrace. The bairn's jist a skelf, thurs nuthin o'him. Hoo onybody kin ca' thumsels a mither an faither an treat thir bairns that wey ah jist don't know ... (Findlay, 1998: 99)

Through a cruel twist of irony, old Hilse, the only weaver to remain faithfully at his loom, becomes the arbitrary victim of a bullet. Reflecting his individualism in his use of language, Hilse's conversational Scots is, in Findlay's version, made more restrained than that of the other weavers; it is also suffused with religiosity in the form of references to God, the Lord, the Day of Judgement and vengeance. Through the inclusion in his speech of 'biblical English', sprinkled with Scots items, a language is created, distinctive of someone God-fearing and resigned to the life God has meted out to him, which sets him apart from the other weavers whom he declines to join in their stand against authority. Here, at the opening of Act 5, he recites a family prayer:

> HILSE: Our Father, we offer up our thankfulness that in Thy almighty grace and goodness Thou have this nicht cast your benevolence upon us. We offer our thankfulness too, that this nicht Thou have protected us from misfortune. Lord, Thy grace is infinite: we stand here before you, poor hummle sinners ... (Findlay, 1998: 101)

Through the creative use of dialect varieties available in another language, Hauptmann's play, which defies transfer into Standard language has been recreated in translation. Too frequently, the weavers of Hauptmann's Silesian play have been bereft of a voice in English translation. Findlay's achievement is to provide an imaginative version of the dialect-coloured essence of a little-known German play, written by one of the leading representatives of modern European drama.

In *The Weavers* Findlay transferred the dialect of the source language into a target language dialect. In *Bairns' Brothers*, his translation of Raymond Cousse's *Enfantillage* (Findlay, 2000), a contemporary play written in Standard French, he also eschews Standard English in favour of a Scots dialect version, this time in order to capture the language of a special social group at a given period of time.

Enfantillages is set in a country village in the 1950s and takes the form of a monodrama with one actor playing Marcel, a young boy of working class origin. There is also a multitude of other characters, both children and adults, whose voices are heard, relatives as well as members of the village, all mediated by the boy. The number of characters provides a good degree of scope for incorporating contrasting speech varieties. Findlay first establishes an obvious contrast between the Scots speech of the local villager and the English spoken by the sprinkling of 'professionals' who speak Standard English, such as the teacher, the priest and the vet. An exception to this broad distinction between the Scots-speaking villagers and English-speaking 'professionals' is the boss of the undertakers. Arriving at the family of the bereaved, his occupational role demands that he speaks semi-formally. To this end, in certain situations Findlay has him speak rather stiff English: this is for example the case in Scene 9, 'The Death of Marcel' where he first addresses the family:

> Good day ladies and gentlemen we apologise for disturbing you we've come for the box ... (*to his men*) Kindly bring forward the box, gentlemen, and don't forget your nails, Gaston. (Findlay, 2000: 43)

Here the undertaker addresses his men as well as the family of the bereaved and, as a result, there is a note of formality to his language. This differs, however, from the way he speaks directly to his men; now he is at ease and his language is more natural:

> That's us Gaston doon a wee bit oan your side
> straightforrit at that. (Findlay, 2000: 43)

And when Marcel's sister tries to cling to the coffin, he is very gentle with her, something that shows in his language:

> Come on now lass you mustnae get yourself intae a state like this you're young you've yir haill life in front of you. (Findlay, 2000: 43)

While the words in Scots are fatherly and informal, fulfilling the function of showing his sympathy and kindness to the young girl, there is still a note of restraint in his speech as he is speaking to a member of the bereaved family. Hence he is speaking in a modified form of Scots. Had he spoken in a fully fledged register, Findlay points out, he is more likely to have said:

> Come oon noo lass ye mustnae git yirsel aw wrocht up
> lik this young ye've yir haill in front ae ye. (Findlay, 2000: 44)

As in *The Weavers*, in his translation of *Enfantillages* Bill Findlay gives a voice to a group of speakers living at a particular point in time. Together with Martin Bowman, he gave the characters of Quebec playwright Michael Tremblay, living in Montreal, a language with which to speak in translation. For the first performance at the Tron stage in Glasgow in 1989, *The Guid Sisters*, their version of Tremblay's play *Les Belles-soeurs*, went on the following year to Toronto and the next year to the Edinburgh Festival Fringe before taking the stage in Montreal itself. It was the first of eight Findlay-Bowman 'trans-creations' of Tremblay's plays, including *A Solemn Mass in Summer*, seen in Glasgow, Perth and Edinburgh as well as London, Toronto and New York. Findlay also worked with Bowman to translate from Québecois into Scots Jeanne-Mance Delisle's *The Reel of the Hanged Man* (see Chapter 2, this volume).

It is to be hoped that, following Bill Findlay's example, more translators and Translation Studies scholars will help bridge cultural divides and give speakers of other languages and countries voices that 'sing' in translation.

Note
1. Unless otherwise indicated, translations throughout are my own.

References
Aaltonen, S. (1996) *Acculturation of the Other: Irish Milieux in Finnish Drama Translation*. Joensuu: University Press.
Anderman, G. (2005) *Europe on Stage: Translation and Theatre*. London: Oberon Books.

Butler, R. (2001) *George Bernard Shaw: My Fair Lady*. National Theatre performance programme.
Findlay, B. (1998) Silesian into Scots: Gerhart Hauptmann's The Weavers. *Modern Drama* XLI, 90–104.
Findlay, B. (2000) Standard into dialect. Missing the target? In C-A. Upton (ed.) *Moving Target* (pp. 35–46) Manchester: St Jerome.
Frayn, M. (trans.) (1995) *Anton Chekov: The Cherry Orchard*. London: Methuen.
Gibson, I. (1989) *Federico García Lorca: A Life*. London: Faber and Faber.
Gilula, D. (1989) Greek drama in Rome: Some aspects of cultural transposition. In H. Scolnicov and P. Holland (eds) *The Play Out of Context* (pp. 99–109). Cambridge: Cambridge University Press.
Grimm, R. (ed.) (1994) *Plays by Gerhart Hauptmann*, New York: Continuum Publications.
Ibsen, H. (1891) Letter to Victor Barrucand, 6 March.
Maurer, W. (1982) *Gerhart Hauptmann*. Boston: Twayne Publishers.
Skrine, P. (1989) *Hauptmann, Wedekind and Schnitzler*. London: Palgrave Macmillan.

Chapter 2

From Rouyn to Lerwick: The Vernacular Journey of Jeanne-Mance Delisle's 'The Reel of the Hanged Man'

MARTIN BOWMAN

Introduction

On 29 March 2000 at the Traverse Theatre in Edinburgh, Stellar Quines, an Edinburgh-based company focusing on works by and about women, premiered their production of Quebec playwright Jeanne-Mance Delisle's *The Reel of the Hanged Man*. The translation into vernacular Scots of *Un «reel» ben beau, ben triste* was commissioned from translators Martin Bowman and Bill Findlay, best known for their Scots translations of Michel Tremblay. Over the next five weeks, the production was given 14 performances: in Edinburgh, Lerwick, Glasgow, Stirling and Paisley. This was the play's European premiere and its first translation into any language. Unlike many Quebec plays, including Delisle's *A Live Bird in Its Jaws* (*Un oiseau vivant dans la gueule*), for which she received The Governor-General of Canada's Award for best play in French in 1987, *Un «reel» ben beau, ben triste* has never been produced in English in Canada. In Quebec, however, the play, regarded as an important work in Quebec dramaturgy, has been produced several times. It premiered at the Théâtre de Coppe in Rouyn, Abitibi in 1978 and was toured the following year in another production to eight venues throughout the region of Abitibi-Témiscamingue, including Barraute, where Delisle was born and raised. Among other important productions were those presented at the Théâtre du Bois de Coulonge, Quebec City, in 1979; the Théâtre du Nouveau Monde, Montreal, in1981; and the Théâtre de la Bordée, Quebec City, in 1993.

The production in Edinburgh of the Scots translation almost did not happen. Its choice by Stellar Quines led to a much-publicised internal difference of opinion that culminated, in November 1999, in the resignation of co-founder Gerda Stevenson and board member Janet Paisley. The Scottish press had a field day covering the story, which had a second life in

February 2000, when Colin Marr, the director of the Eden Court Theatre in Inverness, cancelled the only scheduled performance in the Highlands. The story was even covered by the *National Post* in Canada, which published a short article on 17 November 1999 under the headline, 'Quebec play causes Scottish drama' (Brown, 1999). When Steve Cramer (2000) reviewed the production in *The List*, he dismissed what had happened as a 'hullabaloo'; Joyce McMillan's (2000) review in *The Scotsman*, however, under the headline 'Searing light on a family's dark secret' said that *The Reel of the Hanged Man* was 'one of the most controversial plays to be staged in Scotland for years'.

When I was invited to contribute an article to this collection of essays dedicated to the memory of my collaborator and friend, Bill Findlay, I suggested to the editors that I write something about the translation of Delisle's *Un «reel» ben beau, ben triste*. I did so, not because of the controversy that haunted its pre-production days in Scotland, but because the play allowed us to explore new territory as far as the translation of plays into vernacular language is concerned. Bill and I had a great deal of success with the plays of Montreal playwright, Michel Tremblay. From 1989 to 2003, eight of our Scots translations of his plays were produced in Scotland by the following companies: Tron Theatre, Glasgow (*The Guid Sisters*, *The Real Wurld?* and *Hosanna*); Traverse Theatre (*The House among the Stars* and *Solemn Mass for a Full Moon in Summer*); Perth Theatre (*The House among the Stars*); LadderMan Productions (*Forever Yours, Marie-Lou*); Clyde Unity (*Albertine, in Five Times*), and Royal Lyceum Theatre, Edinburgh (*If Only...*). It is no exaggeration to say that these translations received the attention of some of the most accomplished theatre artists in Scotland. Bill and I were always as surprised as we were delighted to have a real career in the theatre, basking as translators in the glory of Michel Tremblay's wonderful plays.

We were also, it must be said, frustrated in our dream of bringing other Quebec playwrights to the Scottish stage. Very early on, we had translated Dominic Champagne's *La Répétition* (*The Rehearsal*) and Michel-Marc Bouchard's *Les Feluettes* (*The Skelfs*), but neither has been produced.[1] Much has been written about the Scots translations of Michel Tremblay but, as far as I know, *The Reel of the Hanged Man*, apart from the press coverage and reviews in 1999 and 2000, has received no attention at all. Theatre critics and academics alike have examined with zeal the success of Tremblay in Scotland. Most famously, Tremblay was dubbed 'the greatest playwright Scotland never had (Fisher, 1992) and one of his plays in Scots, *The House among the Stars* (*La Maison suspendue*), was described as a work 'which speaks intimately to the Scottish soul' (Linklater, 1992). In its own way, it can be said that *The Reel of the Hanged Man* struck a nerve in the collective Scottish psyche as well. For us translators, the play offered the opportunity to widen our experiment through the translation of a play by a writer who is seen in

Quebec as writing in a dramatic register different from Tremblay's.[2] Robert Lévesque (1992: 53), for a time the dean of Quebec theatre critics and latterly less sympathetic towards Tremblay than he had been, in a turn-of-the-century article said of Delisle that 'she has a unique voice ... as poetic as it is dramatic ... where one finds a nobility of character, a grandeur, an eroticisation of the soul that reduces the dramaturgy of Tremblay to a simplification of the world ...' (Levesque,1999: 53).[3] Without in any sense agreeing with Lévesque's latter-day turning away from the master of Quebec theatre (Levesque,1992: A4),[4,5] Bill and I saw in his assessment of Delisle an insight into an essential aspect of her work where vernacular language is taken to a level beyond the quotidian to something that Delisle herself identifies as atavistic and ritual: 'I am fascinated by primitive beings. I would like to go back to the source. I would like to penetrate the secret of primordial beings' (Delisle, 2001: 101).

The Genesis of the Project

For Bill and me, the *raison d'être* of our work as translators was to explore to what degree the Scots language could carry plays written in a vernacular language, specifically in the case of our collaboration, the various vernacular forms of French that can be found in Quebec. In Tremblay's case, we were translating not only *joual*, the urban dialect of working-class Montreal, but also in *The House among the Stars* a dialect with rural roots in the language spoken by the 1910 characters (the play is set in three times: 1910, 1950 and 1990). In Michel-Marc Bouchard's *The Skelfs*, most of which is set in the northern Lac St. Jean town of Roberval in 1912, we had another regional variety of Quebec French. *The Reel of the Hanged Man* afforded us another intriguing possibility, for the play is set in the 1960s in remote Abitibi, several hundred miles northwest of Montreal, in a rural area settled in the 1930s by urban transplants from the St Lawrence Valley who brought their urban dialect with them. In other words, Delisle's characters speak an urban demotic in a far-distant rural region unlike any other in Quebec, a place, in European terms at least, with almost no history. Abitibi, which only became part of the province of Quebec in 1898, is certainly a place with no exact equivalent in Scotland where there is, for example, no Scots-speaking enclave of recent establishment in the Gaelic-speaking Highlands. Additionally, Delisle uses Quebec fiddle music as an intrinsic part of the play. The fiddle speaks another kind of vernacular as it were, and one derived from the Scots-Irish folk music tradition. Bill and I were intrigued to see how this musical language of the people might return to its Scottish roots in a play whose very structure is derived from the form of the reel. Furthermore, in eschewing a naturalistic mode for her play, Delisle challenges certain assumptions about the nature of plays written in vernacular language as she moves beyond realism into another mode, an innovation that might be called, for want of another term, vernacular ritual. In other words, there were at least three important and distinct reasons why Bill and I wanted to make a Scots translation of *Un «reel» ben beau, ben triste*. I must stress here that we were dedicated to translation, and not in any way to adaptation into a Scottish cultural milieu. Some commentators have written about the Scottish appropriation of the plays we have translated, but we were always convinced that such appropriation was in the ear of the beholder (particularly, but not only, by non-Scots) and not in the texts themselves.

The project to translate Delisle's play began simply enough when, in 1998, Bill Findlay and I received an invitation to translate a play by a Quebec woman playwright for Stellar Quines. Twenty years earlier, when Bill had asked me if there was a Quebec play we might try in Scots, I had chosen unhesitatingly Michel Tremblay's ground-breaking *Les Belles-soeurs* ('The Guid Sisters' in our translation). I was even more impetuous in deciding on the work for Stellar Quines as I knew my chosen play only by reputation. In March 2000 I wrote about the germ of the idea in an article in *The Scotsman* where I describe walking past the Théâtre du Nouveau Monde in Montreal one wintry evening in 1981 and seeing on the marquee a title in vernacular French with the word 'reel' in it (Bowman, 2000). At the time, however, Bill and I were still waiting – with little expectation of success – for something to happen with 'The Guid Sisters'. We had finished our translation of Tremblay's play in 1980, but it received no attention until 1987 when it was 'discovered' by Professor Ian Lockerbie of Stirling University and given a professional reading directed by Tom McGrath at the Edinburgh Fringe Festival in August that year. Many years later, however, the play with the intriguing title had remained with me, and, when I read *Un «reel» ben beau, ben triste* in 1998, I found a play that seemed to me to fit the mandate of the commissioning company as described in its publicity material: 'Stellar Quines was formed in 1993 to reflect the energy, experience and perspective of women in Scottish theatre. It is a company to stimulate, support and enable women to take control of their professional lives in theatre by producing work of the very highest quality, in collaboration with men who share their vision'.[6] I wrote a detailed 13-page proposal for Stellar Quines, including a full summary of the action, and the play was accepted for production by the company's board.[7]

The working title for our translation was literal and, like the original, in the vernacular: 'A Gey Braw, Gey Sad Reel'. When we thought it over, however, the title highlighted for us one of the principal challenges of finding a Scots equivalent for Delisle's Abitibi voice. We were certainly fully conscious that this was a world very different from what we had become accustomed to in translating Tremblay. We were uncomfortable with the connotation of the word 'gey' in the context of Delisle's vision. An accurate translation of 'ben', the dialect form of bien (meaning really or very), 'gey' is a word tarnished by its association with the Scottish 'literary' school known as 'the kailyard', which presents an idealised and sentimentalised rural world. Furthermore, one could forgive a potential audience in Scotland for failing to realise that a night out with fiddle music was going to present a cruel, bleak place in the landscape of the human heart. Martial Dassylva, reviewing the 1979 production at the Théâtre du Bois de Coulonge described an audience spellbound and troubled by the closed universe of the play (1979a) 'where the most secret emotions are identified, where the most primitive desires are declared, and where the Quebec family is demytholigised with the brutality of a fist in the face'.[8] In another article he explained further, and not without humour: 'Delisle's play places itself at a great distance from the clichés of the good settler quietly smoking his pipe in the midst of a thick cloud of children and black flies' (1979b: B4).[9] So we dropped the word 'gey' from our title, and eventually 'A Braw, Sad Reel', at the suggestion of Muriel Romanes, became *The Reel of the Hanged Man*, named after '*Le Reel du pendu*', the specific Quebec reel that Delisle features in her play.

Vernacular Music: The Function of the Reel in the Play

This reel – this music of the folk – is the foundation of the play, its essential form as well as its central symbol. Through the reel Delisle transcends language and creates the musical arc, as it were, of her transformation of the Abitibi dream into the hard reality that undermines it, and which is at the centre of the malaise of the family drama acted out in the play. For Abitibi, perhaps more than any other region in Quebec, embodies a failed social dream. As Gilbert David (1979: 116) wrote, 'Jeanne-Mance Delisle's text plunges into the heart of the disillusionment that is Abitibi, in the fifties, at the moment when the sons and daughters of the first settlers felt the effects of the unhealthy fallout of an ideology of the 'promised land ...'[10] I explained this for the audience of *The Reel of the Hanged Man* in a programme note:

> During the Depression, the government granted land in Abitibi to southern Quebecers who wished to try their luck at farming, but within a generation the dream of a new life of prosperity had shattered against the rock of that hard place. For many, the project of resettlement ended in failure even in the first generation. It is these people and their children who are the subject of Delisle's play. (Bowman, 2000)

Delisle begins and ends her play with the vernacular music of the fiddle. In fact, the fiddler is on stage and involved in the performance throughout the play. In a note in the published text, Delisle explains her musical intention:

> The '*Reel du pendu*' ... is the musical theme of the whole play. At the

> beginning of Scene One, [the] rock music [is] inspired by the melodic line of the theme. Throughout the play ... it is essential that the reel, the traditional music of the people, should not lose the character of its origins in society. Other instruments must not drown out the sound of the fiddle; it is that instrument which must dominate. (Delisle, 2000: 105)

Music then is at the heart of the vernacular voice of the play. If language, as Linda Gaboriau has noted (Bowman, 2003: 43), is an additional character in most Quebec plays, then in Delisle's play, there are two such characters: the spoken demotic, a symbol itself of the failure of social relocation that gives Abitibi one of its principal characteristics, and the musical language into which the spoken language is subsumed. Both, of course, have their equivalents in Scotland. Gilbert David in his review notes this conjunction of music and narrative in Delisle's play:

> Poverty, ignorance, and moralism let their discordant voices be heard loud and clear. In the manner of a lament, the acting, which is extremely taut and physical, elongates the gestures, the ... movements, and the silences. In this vertiginous style, the fiddler becomes the principal agent of the action; the player of the *reel* does not only comment on the action like the chorus in a Greek tragedy, he is, in his torn accents, his staccato, his broken sounds, his savage lyricism, a *primary* interpreter, a collective moan lamenting the smallness of a humanity so fallen and defeated. (David, 1979: 117)[11]

This aspect of Delisle's use of vernacular fiddle music is nowhere more important than at the climax of the play in the seventh of eight scenes where there is a kind of ritual dance of death. Delisle explained her conception in an 'Author's Note' at the beginning of the scene:

> *In this scene, the music should follow* Pierrette [who is dancing to rid herself of an unwanted pregnancy] *at the same time as she drives it forward in a violent and wild rhythm. There is something spell-binding and bewitching about the music (conveyed by a complementary improvisation between the actor and the musician). It is music for a primitive sacrificial dance which envelops* Pierrette *in a spiral of madness. Find in the fiddle the accents and rhythms of desperate violence.* (Delisle, 2000: 138)

Not only does the music become the agent of the drama, but the structure itself of Delisle's play is based, as André G. Bourassa has noted, on the musical form of the reel: 'Actually, the entire play is a reel, a work which turns and returns in all its aspects to the same problem, that of impossible love and that of art as the opponent of fate ... one should hear '*Le Reel du pendu*' as a ritual, repetitive, warding off of fate' (Bourassa 1981: 37).[12]

This defiance of fate can be seen in the narrative of the reel that Delisle includes in the play:

> Once upon a time there was this man, a fine gentleman, but he'd done a very bad thing. So bad that he had to be punished for it. [...] The judges sentenced him tae hang fae a rope. (*Making a gesture to show a noose closing around a throat.*) Cric! But before they put his heid in the noose, they asked him if he had a last wish. The bad man up and answered: 'Aye! A fiddle.' Well, the judges burst their sides laughin: 'Ha! Ha! Ha!' But they agreed tae his request and brung him a fiddle; jist as he'd asked for. It was a fiddle jist like yours, wi wan string the same as yours. And do you know what that bad man did? He played a reel. A braw, sad reel – a sort ae jig that naebody had ever heard before. In fact, it was that braw that the judges couldnae bring themselves tae punish him. So he wasnae hanged, and there wasnae the terrible sound ae 'Cric!' Instead, the fine gentleman played his fiddle like billy-oh and the haill crowd danced wi delight! Everybody danced! (Delisle, 2000: 114)

And everybody did dance in the real family upon which Delisle based her play. In fact, there would be no play if Delisle as a young woman had not known this family. *Un «reel» ben beau, ben triste* is very much a quest for understanding on the part of its author into the emotional complexity of an idiosyncratic family she knew when growing up in Abitibi. The story of '*Le Reel du pendu*' serves as a kind of declaration of artistic intention on the part of Delisle, who, positioning herself as an observer, resists hasty or simplistic judgement.

The Play in Quebec

In October 1999, I travelled to Abitibi to meet Jeanne-Mance Delisle and to talk about the play. Born in 1939, she told of an upbringing where she was taught to observe and respect the principles of an austere, strict form of Roman-Catholicism. There was a family, however, who lived a life full of music and laughter, committing with gusto virtually every mortal sin and living a kind of savage freedom. They went to church but just for the social outing. Their wild energy fascinated Delisle (Corrivault, 1979).[13] She said that everything in their life was a pretext for laughter. There seemed to be no morals and no rules; there was a sensual vigour in the freedom they lived. Unlike her own home, theirs was full of music. They sang. Everyone played the fiddle. Even at eight in the morning, there was a record on the gramophone. Delisle also spoke of the violence and constant tension in the house, of great fights between father and son, and exuberance for this kind of behaviour. She discussed at length the man who became Tonio Morin in the play, the father of the family. He had been one of those settlers who came up from the south to the promised land of Abitibi. When the dream went sour, so did the father's life. He became a rebel and rejected everything. He turned towards the love of his daughter in a way that was like going back to the time when he was young with his wife. Delisle spoke of his incestuous feelings as a kind of primitive reflex. In a way, he was going subconsciously as far as he could to achieve his own destruction. Delisle said he went much further than his sexual desire in expressing the anarchy that was his response to what had happened. The family was unable to escape. It was as if they were in a boat in a storm and just had to ride it out. When you are in that kind of situation, you've got to row. However, and this was the crux of Delisle's fascination, if there wasn't any hope, there was a lot of fun.

The play that was made out of this material, of course, is a work of imagination rather than history. The story is simple though the treatment complex. Tonio, in his fifties, and his 48-year-old wife Laurette Morin – she is identified throughout the play not by name but as the Mother – have four children living at home in an isolated part of the country: mentally-retarded Gérald, 20; Pierrette, 18; Simone, 16; and Colette, 15. An older daughter named Réjeanne lives in Amos, the closest town, but does not appear in the play. However, her husband Camille, who is in his thirties, plays an important part in the action; it is he who is speaking to Gérald, also known as Ti-Fou (or Little Crazy One), in the passage quoted above about '*Le Reel du pendu*'.

The play begins with a card game in which Delisle establishes Tonio's desire for his daughter Pierrette. He leaves for town, returning after three days' absence at the beginning of the second scene. Among the purchases he has made is a one-string fiddle, a gift for Gérald. He gives Pierrette a watch, and they flirt. In the ensuing action, Tonio is angered by the mocking behaviour of his wife and daughters and menaces them by brandishing a knife.

In the third scene, Camille arrives, ostensibly on a social visit. He recounts the story of the reel to Gérald. Colette volunteers another, cruder story about a man who leaves his starving family for three days and returns with nothing but a baloney sausage and sanitary napkins. Everyone laughs at her punch line: 'Try makin a sandwich oot ae that' (Delisle, 2000: 115). Various stories, all of which make fun out of the family's miserable condition, end in laughter. Camille, getting serious, suggests that Tonio should be charged with neglect of his familial responsibilities as well as for corrupting Pierrette, but the women are at first unwilling to incriminate him. Camille says he has already notified the police. In the fourth scene Tonio arrives, drunk and singing. Policemen enter, and he is arrested.

In the fifth scene, the Mother tells Gérald the story of Rapunzel, which Pierrette disrupts with her own unromantic version. By the end of the scene, Pierrette's version takes precedence: the princess has drowned herself in the river and the prince has become an overweight alcoholic. Left alone, Camille and Pierrette play silly games that become increasingly erotic. They go off together to a bedroom. The Mother interrupts them and tells Camille to leave. In the sixth scene there is a harrowing confrontation between Tonio and the Mother. At the end, she tells him to leave. He does so quietly. She strikes the door with a knife.

In the seventh scene, Pierrette, who is pregnant by her boyfriend and not, it is important to realise, by her father or her brother-in-law, is terrified about her father's response, should he find out. Pierrette enters into a frenzied dance to try to lose the baby. Gérald, the innocent, enters and is so taken up by the dance that he joins Pierrette, grabbing her by the neck. She falls dead. In the final scene, the Mother, Colette and Simone are sitting around the kitchen table reading sympathy cards. The news from a self-pitying Tonio in prison is that he has cancer. At the very end, the three women remain seated at the table. Simone remembers that they used to have a lot of fun. They wonder if someone might come. The Mother mentions Gérald, who has been institutionalised. Simone says that once there was a girl who said it was permitted to sleep with your father. Colette turns to Simone and asks her if she is crazy. The three women laugh. The reel begins quietly and eventually drowns out the laughter. The music stops. There is only the plucking of one string as the Mother laughs in the darkness.

No summary, of course, can begin to give an accurate sense of a play. In its barest bones, the play may sound like an unsavoury slice of life, a kind of rural kitchen sink drama. Delisle, however, conceived the play unnaturalistically. When I interviewed Delisle in 1999, she expressed reservations about the later productions of the play, in Montreal and in Quebec City. One had been too sensationalist, and the other too realistic. In a way, the text itself is a kind of trap for those who assume that vernacular language inevitably indicates a work of realism. The first production, in Rouyn, Abitibi, was set in an abandoned chapel, the ruin suggesting both the social failure of Abitibi in the 1960s and the injured psyches of the characters. It was as if one had entered a derelict house – to this day the back roads of Abitibi are strewn with such places – the wood stove rusting, a disorder of broken furniture, a damaged aesthetic. Delisle spoke of the actors coming on to the stage to assume the identities of the characters. She did not use the word identity, but rather *sortilège,* a word suggesting phantom, or embodiment. Delisle understood that a realistic production of the play would distort her meaning by reducing and oversimplifying the subject matter. Commentators on the play in Quebec understood this aspect of Delisle's conception. Martine R. Corrivault, reviewing the 1979 production in Quebec City, identified 'an artistic form that does not distort the realism of the subject, but smashes it into a thousand pieces (or subjects)' (Corrivault, 1979).[14] This approach, which one could argue is the essence of theatre, allows for the presentation of the subject from as many perspectives as there are characters. And so the work does not become a polemic about a scandalous subject with emphasis on the condemnation of apprehended immorality, but rather an analysis of the circumstances in which a particular phenomenon, in this case incestuous behaviour, occurs. The real villain of the play is the hypocritical Camille, who represents society's propriety and who goes entirely unpunished by that society. It is important to note that Delisle constructs the character of Tonio so that, despite his incestuous desire, he does not have sex with Pierrette. This displacement of judgement from Tonio to Camille allows for what Michelle Talbot saw as Delisle's masterstroke: 'incest is treated in the first instance not as a scandalous fact deserving of scowls and pointed fingers, but as a sickness of the family, a weakness, a cancer slow in showing its effects ...' (Talbot, 1979: B2).[15] Jacques Larue-Langlois (1979: 8) underlined the importance of the play in Quebec theatre as a whole, identifying the subject of the play as 'a classic of the theatre despite the fact that the author's epic inspiration has nothing in it of Racine'.[16] The approach is anti-sensationalist as Corrivault noted:

> ... the physical desire of the father Tonio for his daughter Pierrette is one of the elements which creates the dramatic action, but one could almost find it secondary ... to the ignorance and violence, the tolerated misery in the lives of the other characters. (...) The real subject of the play is the relationship between the dominator and the dominated. (Corrivault, 1979: A10)[17]

The appeal to Stellar Quines lay in this unpolemical approach of Delisle's: 'The play treats in a complex manner the subject of sexual abuse within the family, a subject as pertinent to a Scottish audience today as it was when Delisle wrote her tragedy'.[18]

Reception of the Translation in Scotland

Given the critical success that Muriel Romanes's production of *The Reel of the Hanged Man* enjoyed in Scotland, the pre-production controversy can now be seen in a perspective that none of us involved in the production felt at the time when there was suddenly the possibility that the work might not be produced. Keith Bruce in *The Herald* summarised what had happened: 'A schism in the performing company led to the departure of one of its founders, a playwright withdrew the rights for the company to perform her current work, and a theatre manager pulled his venue out of the proposed tour' (Bruce, 2000). It is beyond the focus of this paper to rehash the story of the play's 'controversial gestation' (Bruce, 2000) in Scotland, except in terms of the misreading of the text that the controversy implies. A kind of politically-correct censoriousness raised its head in the press, and the result could well have been the silencing of an important text based in inquiry rather than polemic. The problem does not so much lie with the objections of Gerda Stevenson, co-founder of the company, and Janet Paisley, the playwright who withdrew her permission for Stellar Quines to produce her work, but with the way in which the Scottish press distorted and reduced the work of a playwright utterly unknown in the country. The headlines alone tell the story: 'Artists quit as theatre group stages incest play' (*The Scotsman*, 1999); 'This play about incest is morally bankrupt. I'm appalled by it' (*Scottish Daily Mail*, 1999) 'Theatre group insists "incest" play will go on' (*Scottish Daily Express*, 1999); 'Theatre chief explains banning of "incest" play' (*The Press and Journal*, 2000). The most worrying statement about the play was the opinion expressed under the title 'Unnecessary act' on the editorial page of the *Scottish Daily Express* (17 November, 1999): 'Although we have not seen *The Reel* – it has never been performed in Europe – we are ready to accept the views of those acquainted with its lack of moral perspective'. Some of the articles took a more balanced view than the attention-grabbing headlines would indicate. David Taylor of the Scottish Arts Council, for example, was quoted as saying (Harding, 1999), 'This play comes with a strong pedigree. We acknowledge that the subjects covered by the play are sensitive, but believe that theatre in the right hands can help the public to explore and understand difficult issues'.

In the end, thanks to Muriel Romanes's understanding of the play and her unnaturalistic production, *The Reel of the Hanged Man* won through. I described the production in my diary for 29 March 2000:

> The production begins with the entire cast sitting. There are four benches, one on each side of the playing area. The backdrop is a kind of wall of discarded clothes, an abstraction of abandonment. The only furniture is a wooden table and chairs. The performance begins with the primitive rhythm of step dancing, which gradually intensifies in complexity. This leads into the card-playing scene. The music segues into the French 'Bang Bang' and the two girls dance in a back corner. The stage is darkly lit throughout ... And the ending was brilliant as Muriel went back to the beginning, the dancing, and the opening scene with the music taking over, the fiddle tune, the masked fiddler upstage.

At the end of the performance the reel seemed poised to begin again, underscoring the cruel and sad ritual that Delisle had put at the centre of her play. The story may be rooted in Abitibi, Quebec, in the 1950s, but the conception of the action as ritual brings a powerful universality. Delisle's approach had taken vernacular language into a new territory, a sort of ritual epic in the demotic. It is as if one is witnessing an age-old story that is doomed to endless re-enactment. The epigraph that Delisle chose for the play best identifies the exact place where Delisle (2000: 99) situates the work: 'Tragedy situates itself in the intermediary and ambiguous place between ritual and the spontaneous model that this ritual is striving to reproduce (René Girard, *La Violence et le Sacré*)'.

The critics who responded to Muriel Romanes's production showed to what degree Stellar Quines had succeeded in refuting the pre-production controversy. Sue Wilson (2000) in *The Independent* wrote that the play's 'underlying motivation ... in seeking to understand the deepest dynamics of such an appalling yet endemic human dysfunction seems an eminently moral and responsible one'. On 30 April 2000, under the heading 'Theatre *The Reel of the Hanged Man*, MacRoberts Art Centre, Stirling', the anonymous critic in *Scotland on Sunday* described the play as 'a work which demands to be seen as much as the issues it considers demand to be discussed' whilst describing the Morin family as 'almost unimaginably dysfunctional, yet still recognisable in our society'. And in *The Scotsman* Joyce McMillan (2000) saw the play as dealing 'with the subject of incest and abuse in the family not so much by condemning it as by trying to explain it, as a response to powerlessness and emotional repression'. More lyrically, Neil Cooper (2000) said that 'Muriel Romanes's production ... whirls, crashes, burns and bleeds with a blind power of spiritual self-laceration'. In claiming that the play 'addresses something in the Scottish national psyche', Steve Cramer was another critic who saw the relevance of the play for a Scottish audience. He seemed to have his eye on the controversy as well as the play when he wrote, 'It's not the incest itself which Delisle's play is concerned with, this is in no way endorsed, but rather the capacity of our culture to condemn without recourse to analysis' (Cramer, 2000). Cramer recognised the complexity of Delisle's treatment by saying that the work explores '... an emotional landscape which is too fraught with complex causalities to bring us simple solutions, as the play's tragic momentum visits upon one and all' (Cramer, 2000). Cramer's insight implicitly recognises the musical form of the play, as a reel turning back on itself in potentially endless reiteration. Thus, at the end of the play, the three surviving women remain paralysed with no alternative but to imagine a visitor who will start the bitter inescapable ritual all over again.

In some ways the most heartening and deeply understanding review of *The Reel of the Hanged Man* was written by critic John Haswell of *The Shetland Times*. Without overdrawing the parallel, Shetland, as a Scots-speaking territory beyond the Highlands, is perhaps the place in Scotland most like Abitibi and certainly a place far from the perceived center of the culture. *The Reel of the Hanged Man* was given one performance at the Garrison Theatre in Lerwick on 5 April 2000. I quote Haswell's review at length as it describes what those of us involved with the production hoped to achieve:

> *The Reel of the Hanged Man* studied the total dysfunction of one particular family living on the outermost edges of all forms of civilisation. Faced with extreme poverty, an unyielding environment and the effects of finding solace through drink, the father of this family sought to reinforce his status as its natural head through increasingly desperate and morally bankrupt means (neglect, violence, bribery and physical abuse).
>
> The physical relationship between the father and one of his daughters was the most disturbing manifestation of a man at war with himself and with the world around him and it is to the great credit of the play that it attempted to explain rather than universally condemn. The incest was portrayed as a cancer affecting everyone in the family and the destructive nature of such abuse was strongly presented.
>
> This production was both as controlled and as wild as the family that it featured and as emotionally frightening and yet full of life as the step dancing which embraced it. It was not a show just about incest. It was a show about dreams broken by an all-pervading poverty in an unyielding landscape and an emotional and physical isolation. It was brave, bold and thought-provoking. That a Shetland audience had the opportunity to witness such a powerful production ... is something to be applauded. What a shame that there are those who over react to possible controversy. *The Reel of the Hanged Man* with all its rage, its life and its destruction was the very stuff of theatre. (Haswell, 2000: 31)

What began as a play in a regional theatre in Rouyn, Abitibi, Quebec in 1978 had crossed more than an ocean in getting to the Garrison Theatre in Lerwick, Shetland, Scotland in 2000. Its success there, however, in a region regarded within its country as remote as Abitibi is in Quebec, is a confirmation not only of the importance of Jeanne-Mance Delisle's play but testimony to the relevance of vernacular theatre beyond its original culture. Bill and I were particularly pleased that Haswell had entirely neglected to mention that the play he attended was a Scots translation. This critic had received the play directly, noting its 'raw, expletive-ridden language' but hearing it in the *ur*-language of the universal tongue of the people. That was the dream with which Bill Findlay and I began our collaboration together over a quarter of a century ago. We wanted to discover whether Scots language could be the vessel for plays from beyond Scotland. The importance of *The Reel of the Hanged Man* to this work should not be underestimated. We were lucky in Michel Tremblay, but had our success been limited to his work, the point we were trying to make would be less surely proved. Jeanne-Mance Delisle gave us a play with such a thorough-going vernacular quality – its language, its music, and, above all, its form situated between ritual and the demotic – that Scotland, reluctant as it was, found another playwright that it had never had.

Author's note
Page references were not always available for reviews and articles in theatre archives.

Notes
1. Muriel Romanes, the artistic director of Stellar Quines, with Maggie Kinloch as director, presented a staged reading of *The Skelfs* at the Traverse Theatre on 2 November 2005, an evening of celebration of the contribution to Scottish theatre of Bill Findlay, who died on 15 May 2005 at the age of fifty-seven.
2. Michelle Talbot, in '*Un reel ben beau ... un réel de maux!*' (Talbot, 1979: B2), describes this difference. She sees in Delisle's play a style 'without exhilarating and lyrical transpositions as in Tremblay and without unbelievable endings ...' (this is my translation of: '... *sans véritables transpositions exaltantes et lyriques à la Tremblay, sans incroyables finales*').
3. The full quotation (my own translation) is as follows:
   Jeanne-Mance Delisle of Abitibi ... has a unique voice, an aptness as poetic as it is dramatic. Tremblay has cast a shadow over such writing and one believes that Quebec theatre is realistic, urban, proletarian, and rooted in misery when in these texts, sometimes superior to his, one finds a nobility of character, a grandeur, an erotisation of the soul which relegates the plays of Tremblay to a simplification of the world, to a substitute for tragedy.
   L'Abitibienne Jeanne-Mance Delisle ... a une voix unique, une justesse poétique autant que dramatique. Tremblay a jeté de l'ombre sur ces écritures-là et l'on croit que le théâtre québécois est un théâtre réaliste, urbain, prolétaire, misérable, quand dans ces textes parfois supérieurs aux siens on trouve une noblesse de caractère, une grandeur, une érotisation de l'âme qui relègue la dramaturgie de Tremblay à une simplification du monde, à un succédané du tragique. (Lévesque, 1999: 53)
4. A4, etc. are page numbers in Canadian newspapers where each section is designated by letter: A4 is page 4 in Section A.
5. Reviewing *The Guid Sisters* in the production that the Tron Theatre, Glasgow, brought to Montreal's Centaur Theatre in October 1992, Lévesque described *Les Belles-soeurs* as 'the tragicomedy which is the wellspring of modern Quebec theatre' (my translation of: '... *cette tragédie bouffe qui est à la source du théâtre québécois moderne*' '*D'Écosse, une grande production des* Belles-soeurs'.
6. Quoted with the permission of Stellar Quines.
7. In October 1998 I held a one-month translation residency funded by the European Commission Ariane Programme at the British Centre for Literary Translation at the University of East Anglia, Norwich. It was in Norwich that I completed the first (literal) draft of the script.
8. My translation of:
   Tous ceux qui ont participé à la reprise de la pièce de Jeanne-Mance Delisle ... se sont dits à la fois envoûtés et profondément troublés ... car peu de spectateurs échapperont à la fascination de cet univers clos, à la densité où les sentiments les plus secrets sont nommés, les désirs les plus primaires sont avoués et la famille québécoise démythifiée. Avec la brutalité d'un coup de poing en pleine face. (Dassylva, 1979)
9. My translation of:
   '*La pièce de Jeanne-Mance Delisle ... se situe à mille lieux des clichés sur le bon colonisateur fumant tranquillement sa pipe au milieu d'une nuée d'enfants et de mouches noires.*' (Dassylva, 1979: B4)

10. My translation of:
   Le texte de Jeanne-Mance Délisle [sic] plonge au cœur de le désillusion abitibienne, dans les années cinquante, alors que fils et filles des premiers colons se ressentent des retombées malsaines d'une idéologie de la terre promise.
11. My translation of:
   La pauvreté, l'ignorance, le puritanisme laissent entendre fortement leurs voix discordantes. À la manière d'un lamento, le jeu extrêmement physique et tendu étire les gestes, les mouvements concentriques et les silences. Dans ce registre du vertige, le violoneux pourrait bien être l'actant principal; le joueur de reel ne fait pas que commenter l'action, comme le chœur dans la tragédie grecque, il est, dans ses accents déchirés, ses hocquets [sic], ses sons brisés, son lyrisme sauvage, un interprète primaire, une plainte collective exacerbant la trivialité d'une humanité déchue, défaite. (David, 1979: 117)
12. My translation of:
   '*En réalité, toute la pièce est un reel, une œuvre qui tourne et retourne sous toutes ses faces un même problème, celui de l'amour impossible et celui de l'art comme anti-destin. (...) ... il faut entendre «Le Reel du Pendu» à la façon d'une rituelle, répétitive, pour conjurer le destin'.* (Bourassa, 1981: 37)
13. See Martine Corrivault (1979: D3), '*La tragédie en chaise berçante: le beau reel triste de Jeanne-Mance Delisle'*. Delisle is quoted as saying '*J'étais littéralement fascinée par cette famille-là qui vivait avec une intensité, une force incroyables. Il régnait dans la maison une telle sensualité, une telle énergie, ils étaient si beaux et pleins de santé que j'en étais renversée'*.
14. My translation of: '*...une forme artistique qui ne dénature pas le réalisme du sujet, mais le fait éclater en mille sujets.*' The French is capable of a pun of which English is not.
15. My translation of:
   Mais la carte maîtresse de Jeanne-Mance Deslisle [sic] *est d'avoir traité de l'inceste, non pas, au premier degré, comme un fait scandaleux à pointer du doigt en grimaçant, mais comme une maladie de famille, une tare, un cancer lent à aboutir.*' (Talbot, 1979: B2)
16. My translation of: '*L'auteur ... s'attaque ici à un classique de la dramaturgie, l'inceste. Malgré que son souffle épique n'ait rien de proprement racinien ....*
17. My translation of:
   ... le désir physique du père, Tonio, pour sa fille Pierrette, est un des éléments qui s'ajoute à l'action dramatique, mais on pourrait presque le trouver secondaire ... d'ignorance et de violence, de misère tolérée dans la vie des êtres. (...) Le vrai sujet de la pièce est ... les relations dominants-dominés ... .
18. Unpublished publicity material of Stellar Quines. Quoted with permission.

References

Bourassa, A.G. (1981) Le temps d'un reel. *Lettres québécoises* 22 (Summer), 37–8.
Bowman, M. (2000) The Reel of the Hanged Man: Historical background. Performance programme. Stellar Quines.
Bowman, M. (2000) On the edge of civilization, no one can hear you scream. *The Scotsman*, 24 March.
Bowman, M. (2003) *Michel Tremblay in Scots: Celebration and Rehabilitation. Performing National Identities: International Perspectives on Contemporary Canadian Theatre* (pp. 38–50). Vancouver: Talonbooks.
Brown, D. (1999) Quebec play causes Scottish drama. *National Post*, 17 November, B4.
Bruce, K. (2000) Fussing and feuding over family values. *The Herald*, 30 March.
Cooper, N. (2000) Theatre: The Reel of the Hanged Man, Traverse Theatre, Edinburgh. *The Herald*, 30 March.

Corrivault, M. (1979a) Vraiment la tragédie en chaise berçante. *Le Soleil*, 23 July, A10.
Corrivault, M. (1979) La tragédie en chaise berçante : Le beau reel triste de Jeanne-Mance Delisle. *Le Soleil*, 21 July, D3.
Cramer, S, (2000) Quebecois Theatre: The Reel of the Hanged Man. *The List*, 13–27 April.
Dassylva, M. (1979a) D'Abitibi, une histoire ben belle et ben triste. *La Presse*, 28 July, B1.
Dassylva, M. (1979b) Des images pour hanter vos nuits et vos veilles. *La Presse*, 28 July, B3.
David, G. (1979) Un reel ben beau, ben triste. *Cahiers de Théâtre Jeu* 12, 116–7.
Delisle, J.M. (2000) The Reel of the Hanged Man (M. Bowman and B. Findlay, trans.). *Edinburgh Review*, 99–143.
Fisher, M. (1992) The House Among the Stars. *The Guardian*, 29 October.
Harding, C. (1999) This play about incest is morally bankrupt: I'm appalled by it. *Scottish Daily Mail*, 17 November.
Haswell, J. (2000) Powerful, bold and thought-provoking. *Shetland Times*, 14 April, p. 31.
Larue-Langlois, J. (1979) Un texte riche dans un théâtre d'été. *Le Devoir*, 31 July, p. 8.
Levesque, R. (1992) Les Belles-soeurs. *Le Devoir*, 2 October, A4.
Lévesque, R. (1999) Le petit pays où Gauvreau est mort. *Ici*, 23–30 December.
Linklater, J. (1992) Intimate words. *The Herald*, 26 October.
McMillan, J. (2000) Searing light on a family's dark secret. *The Scotsman*, 31 March.
Talbot, M. (1979) Un reel ben beau ... un réel de maux! *Dimanche-matin*, 29 July, B2.
Wilson, S. (2000) Theatre: The Reel of the Hanged Man. *The Independent*, 5 April.

Chapter 3

Speaking the World: Drama in Scots Translation

JOHN CORBETT

Introduction

In *The Translation Zone*, a survey of the field of comparative literature, Emily Apter devotes a chapter to the 'New Scotologists', Irvine Welsh, Ian Banks, Duncan McLean and James Kelman (Apter, 2006: 149–59). This chapter, entitled 'The Language of Damaged Experience', links the non-standard urban argot of Welsh and company to the conditions of class oppression and internal colonialism suffered by the main characters in novels by these writers:

> [who] use accent to situate readers directly in the mental basin of urban regional consciousness. Typically, how the narrators see the world is filtered through how the narrators speak the world, that is, through orally inflected interior monologue. (Apter, 2006: 153)

While acknowledging the power of scatological urban Scots to calibrate the reader's worldview with those of junkies, schemies and dossers, Apter nevertheless implicitly condemns the language to the role of 'the subaltern carrier of cognition's soma' (Apter 2006: 150). This chapter seeks to redress the balance by exploring the uses of Scots in European plays translated over the second half of the 20th century.[1] I shall argue that the characterisation of Scots as 'the language of damaged experience', while undoubtedly true of an estimable sector of Scottish literature, is also reductive when the canon as a whole is considered – and it is particularly reductive if applied to the considerable body of European drama translated into Scots.

Crude Thinking, Crude Language?

Apter prefaces her discussion of the 'New Scotologists' with citations from Benjamin and Adorno, which, since they form the theoretical basis of her discussion, are worth revisiting. In a discussion of *The Threepenny Opera*, Benjamin characterised 'crude thinking' thus:

> Created by the masses, according to Benjamin, crude thinking is epito-

mised by proverbs such as: 'There's no smoke without fire' or 'You can't make an omelette without breaking eggs'. These lead-weight utterances belong to the 'household of dialectical thinking', because they enable action; indeed 'thought must be crude in order to come into its own in action'. For Benjamin, the raw, prole commonplace typical of 'crude thought' operates as the engine of Brechtian satire, which pivots on the expressions that 'lay bare the fellow citizen' peeling back life's 'legal drapery' to the point where 'human content ... emerges naked.' (Apter, 2006: 150, citing Benjamin, 1973: 81)

The 'raw, prole commonplace' is clearly appropriate to satires such as *The Threepenny Opera*, in which bourgeois pretensions are burlesqued by the language and behaviour of the lower orders. This function of the non-standard idiom is evident in another of Brecht's plays, *Mr Puntila and His Man, Matti*, translated into the urban demotic by Peter Arnott:

> PUNTILA: Ye want tae ken something? There are fermers roon here wha'd pochle the breid fae their workers' bairns, they would. Would ye credit it? Me? Ah'd feed ma hinds oan venison, Ah wad, gin it was but practical, I mean, how come no? Wir aw Jock Tamson's bairns, hint we?
>
> MATTI: Aye, sure. (STM: 273)[2]

The drunken, temporary and therefore insincere *bonhomie* of Puntila the landowner is undermined by his clichéd assertion, 'Wir aw Jock Tamson's bairns' (that is, we are all part of one common humanity). Matti, the manservant, expresses his scepticism with a sardonic 'double positive'. The exchange is characterised by the kind of stock phrases that Benjamin identifies as marking 'crude thinking' and as such it bears out the common use of pantomimic Scots to parody middle class pretensions.

Apter then draws on Adorno to further her case for Scots as the vehicle of damaged experience:

> To play off workers' dialects against the written language is reactionary. Leisure, even pride and arrogance, have given the language of the upper classes a certain independence and self-discipline. [...] The language of the subjected, on the other hand, domination alone has stamped, so robbing them further of the justice promised by the unmutilated, autonomous word to all those free enough to pronounce it without rancour. Proletarian language is dictated by hunger. [...] Being forbidden to love it, they maim the body of language, and so repeat in impotent strength the disfigurement inflicted on them. Even the best qualities of the North Berlin or Cockney dialects, the ready repartee, the mother wit, are marred by the need, in order to endure desperate situations, without despair, to mock themselves along with

the enemy, and so to acknowledge the way of the world. (Adorno, 1974: 102; cited in Apter, 2006: 151)

Obviously, since Adorno wrote these words, attitudes to non-standard varieties of language have undergone a considerable change. Today, Adorno's vivid characterisation of 'worker's dialects' suggests an internalisation, no matter how reluctant, of some part of the mythology of the oppressor, namely that among the freedoms granted to the privileged is the right to express 'unmutilated, autonomous words'. And while some characteristics of proletarian language are given credit ('the ready repartee, the mother wit') even these are tainted by their association with the mockery that guards against despair. It is now impossible to think of language existing discretely as an 'autonomous, unmutilated' system somewhere apart from the communities, bourgeois and proletarian, that speak and write it. Even so, while Adorno's words might be redolent of the unreconstructed linguistic prejudices of his times, their continuing force is evident in Apter's appropriation of them to portray the work of the 'New Scotologists'. Ironically, it is in drama translation into Scots that the views epitomised by Adorno and revived by Apter find their strongest challenge.

Reactionary or Resisting?

Adorno's branding of literature in the 'worker's dialect' as 'reactionary' is based on the false assumption that non-standard dialects are essentially inferior to standard dialects. Even the description of the standard variety as a *dialect* will still strike some as semantically dissonant: for some, like Adorno, there is still an opposition between inferior dialect and pure language. However, several decades of sociolinguistic theory have challenged this dichotomy, arguing instead that the standard variety of any language is based on a functional written dialect, developed to ease the life of civil servants, and whose influence begins to extend to the spoken mode of the bourgeois classes (cf Crowley, 1989). So-called 'dialects' such as Black English Vernacular or Scots serve the purposes of their speech communities in as effective a way as the standard variety serves its writers and speakers. Speech communities also change in character: Adorno's evocation of the proletariat of the hungry 1930s is less applicable to the working classes of the late 20th century. Even so, attitudes are often slow to change, and the ambivalence of the Scots tongue is evident in much Scottish literature: the medium and the communities it represents can still signify impotence and damaged experience, as Apter demonstrates, but its range of significations is broader than this.

Certainly, those dramatist-translators who chose to write in Scots from the 1940s onwards were not conscious reactionaries; they came, like Brecht, from the political left or they supported the nationalist cause. Some took their cue from the poet and controversialist, 'Hugh MacDiarmid' (Christopher Murray Greive), and combined socialism and nationalism, sometimes in idiosyncratic ways (cf Findlay, 1998, 2004). Before the 1940s the lack of a professional Scottish theatre was an issue of some concern amongst the Scottish intelligentsia, as can be seen in the following excerpt from an article by Murray McClymont in the magazine *Modern Scot*:

> I know of only one theatre in Scotland, the English theatre, which has been established here for over two hundred years and is the true explanation of our dramatic poverty. Scotland has no national drama because she has failed to provide her writers with a national medium for the release of Scottish genius in terms of drama. There is no Scottish theatre: there are merely obstructionists who delay its coming by asserting its existence without proof. (Winter, 1930; reprinted in McCulloch, 2004: 137)

In the decades that followed, Robert Kemp was one of the founders of a revived Scottish drama tradition, and an integral part of this revival were his translations of Molière into Broad Scots (cf. Findlay, 2003). As I have argued elsewhere (Corbett, 1999, 2007), translation into Scots has been a consistent thread running through Scottish literature since the 15th century. The significations of translations into Scots are varied and indeed function as a litmus test of the political and social climate of the times in which they appear.

The Language of the Maister

Robert Kemp began his career in the semi-professional Gateway Theatre of the 1940s, helping shepherd it into a fully professional organisation in the 1950s. Inspired by visits of French theatre companies to Edinburgh in the early years of the Festival, Kemp translated Molière's *L'Ecole des femmes* as *Let Wives Tak Tent* for a Gateway Theatre production in February 1948. This play successfully transferred to the Citizens' Theatre in Glasgow, and has enjoyed regular professional revivals, the most recent being in 2001. Kemp followed its success with further translations, including *L'Avare* (*The Laird o'Grippy*), and inspired other dramatist-translators, from Victor Carin and Hector MacMillan down to Liz Lochhead, to follow in his footsteps with a constant flow of translations, of both Molière and his theatrical kindred spirit, Goldoni. The remarkable and abiding surge of interest in 'MacMolière' in late 20th and early 21st century Scotland has been charted by Peacock (1993, 2004).

The success of Molière and Goldoni in Scots translation is significant in several ways. First, the period flavour to the setting is usually retained, although Liz Lochhead's versions of *Tartuffe* and *Le Misanthrope* (as *Misery*

Guts) update Molière to early and late 20th century Scotland respectively. The usual period setting of Scots versions of Molière and Goldoni is 18th century Scotland, the last century in which it might truly be said that both master and servant spoke Broad Scots. In the 18th century there was a gradual language shift amongst the Scots middle classes that led to the emergence of a middle class 'Scottish English' form of speech (see Jones, 1995). This shift is vividly dramatised in Robert Louis Stevenson's *Weir of Hermiston* (1896) which, set in the 18th century, has at its core the generational conflict between the Broad-Scots-speaking auld laird, based on hanging judge Lord Braxfield, and his genteelly-spoken son, Archie. The 18th century, then, was a point when Broad Scots did not necessarily signify 'damaged experience' or 'workers' dialect', although as the century progressed the bourgeoisie progressively began to stigmatise Scots as 'vulgar', leading in time to the language attitudes displayed by Adorno and Benjamin.

For dramatist-translators, setting a play in period, or even appropriating a period text for translation, gives them licence to recreate the conditions of a Scotland in which Broad Scots is spoken by all social classes, from maisters both foolish and wise, to servants both silly and shrewd. The period plays, of course, were viewed by audiences through a filter of 20th century sensibilities and prejudices about the language, and so they were cued into expectations that a Scots-speaking bourgeois would be a buffoon. In Molière, of course, this invariably proves to be the case.

Recreating an 18th century setting, or even alluding to it, as Lochhead does in *Tartuffe*, also allows playwrights to appropriate some of the literary Scots of the vernacular revival, the flowering of poetry in the vernacular instigated by such poets as Allan Ramsay and Robert Fergusson, and climaxing with Robert Burns. Robert Kemp's stage Scots is a blend of his own north-eastern Scots and the Ayrshire idioms he knew from his reading of Burns. This is evident in this exchange from *Lat Wives Tak Tent*, in which the minor Laird, Oliphant, is telling his friend Gilchrist of his plans to marry a girl he has reared from childhood in conditions of innocence and simplicity:

> GILCHRIST: This dings aa!
>
> OLIPHANT: You'll be spieran, 'Why this unco lang story?' My friend, it's to let you understand the precautions I've taen, and the end o it is that I invite you to sup wi her this very nicht, as you are my trusty fiere. I wad like you to tak a look at her, Maister Gilchrist, and see if I'm to be blamed for my choice. (STM: 7)

Kemp's Scots was influenced by the 'Lallans' movement in poetry in the earlier half of the century, a movement that sanctioned the appropriation of Scottish terms from different places and times to recreate the full range of registers of a national language. Here the spelling 'aa' (rather than, 'aw') suggests a rural, north-eastern Scots pronunciation, while the archaic 'my trusty fiere' is a straight lift from Ayrshireman Burns' 'Auld Lang Syne'. However, Kemp felt that the demands of writing a 'Classical' Scots that would be comprehensible to a modern audience demanded that he moderate the density of his stage medium, and the blend of contemporary speech, Burnsian literary Scots, and English was both popular and influential. A similar blend is evident in the Scots translations of Kemp's protégé, Victor Carin, who, like Kemp, grew up in the north-east of Scotland. In Carin's 1965 version of Goldoni, it is a prosperous merchant, Pittendree, now resident in Edinburgh, who speaks with a Scots that has strong north-eastern inflections, especially in the 'aa' pronunciation again, and in the presence of regional words like 'loon' (young man):

> PITTENDREE: There's young chiels tae, mind ye, the party's na aa auld deils lik masel. A maun gie ye a rare joke about Jockie's. Ae nicht, Tammy Collie an' his second auldest son, Robert, a muckle loon no a year abune saxteen, had a fecht ower ane o Jockie's maids. But she was speirt for aaready, sae they focht in vain. Weel, they baith got that fu', an' Jockie had them bedded, an', guid sakes, they waukened up wi' sair heids an' bad tempers, for Jockie had pitten tham baith i' the same bed, an' a muckle soo pig atween them. *(He laughs.)*
>
> SARAH: Sae ye hae merry times in Embro? (STM: 181–182)

As translations of Molière tumbled from the pen of Scottish dramatists, the spoken idiom on which the stage Scots is based changed from rural to urban. This change is evident in Hector MacMillan's version of *The Hypochondriak* (1987). MacMillan grew up, not in rural Aberdeenshire, but in the East End of Glasgow, and his original plays, *The Sash* and *The Rising*, explore sectarianism and politics in that city. The Scots of MacMillan's Molière adaptations is now much closer to the 'worker's dialect' of Adorno, but the conventions of translation allow it to be put into the mouth of merchants like Argan, the hypochondriac, and lawyers like Bonnefoy:

> BONNEFOY: Yir guid-lady did ootline yir intentions, sir, and the provision ye'd mak for her. Ah'm here tae advise ye, sir, that there's absolutely naethin ye can lea her in onie wull.
>
> ARGAN: Naethin! Hoo can that be?
>
> BONNEFOY: Because o whit we cry Customary Law. Gin we were in a district that operatit Statutory Law, 'twad be a different story; but here in the city, under Customary Law, it's just no possible.
>
> ARGAN: Ah cannae mak a wull for ma wife? (STM: 231)

Another Glasgow dramatist and translator, Liz Lochhead, recuperates Kemp's eclectic approach to his stage Scots, but again, like MacMillan, from an urban rather than a rural base. In her introduction to *Tartuffe* (1985), she delights in the polyphonicity of her stage idiom:

> Actually, it's a totally invented and, I hope, theatrical Scots, full of anachronisms, demotic speech form various eras and areas; it's proverbial, slangy, couthy, clichéd, catch-phrasey and vulgar; it's based on Byron, Burns, Stanley Holloway, Ogden Nash and George Formby, as well as on the sharp tongue of my granny; it's deliberately varied in register – most of the characters, except Dorinne, are at least bi-lingual and consequently more or less 'two-faced'. (LL: introduction)[3]

Yet it is to Burnsian Scots that Lochhead specifically appeals in order to set the tone for her portrayal of religious hypocrisy. When Tartuffe is at prayer, his language shifts largely towards the English of the King James Authorised Version, yet the rhymes and rhythm echo a paradigm of Scottish religious humbug, as portrayed in Burns' 'Holy Willie's Prayer', a poem whose cadences are familiar from the countless Burns Suppers held at home and abroad around the 25th January every year:

> TARTUFFE: May merciful heaven grant to thee and thine,
> Health, wealth and grace baith temporal and divine.
> God's humblest servant, ask, and ask in all sincerity,
> May he crown you all your days wi' bountiful prosperity. (LL: III: iii)

If the use of various gradations of Broad Scots to portray the language of the powerful in drama translations acts as a counter-example to its use to signify 'damaged proletarian experience,' as Apter contends, yet it might still be argued that such 'crude language' serves the satirical ends that Benjamin describes. Molière and Goldoni satirise human foibles, and it can certainly be stated that, for today's audiences, the use of Broad Scots in the mouths of lairds, merchants, lawyers and ministers of the church is a linguistic means of 'laying bare' their common humanity to the point where 'human content ... emerges naked' (see above; Apter, 2006: 150, citing Benjamin, 1983: 81). In other words, no matter what sociolinguists assert about the equal validity of all kinds of language varieties, playwrights and audiences communicate via popular myths and prejudices about which forms of language are affected or natural, pure or inferior. By depending on these myths for their dramatic effects, authors and audiences sustain and reinforce them.

The Hybridity of Speech and Writing

In her discussion of Adorno, Apter focuses on part of his argument that she finds 'really strange':

> If the written language codifies the estrangement of classes [*due Entfremdung der Klassen*], redress cannot lie in regression to the spoken,

but only in the consistent exercise of strictest linguistic objectivity. Only a speaking that transcends writing by absorbing it, can deliver human speech from the lie that it is already human. (Apter, 2006: 151, citing Adorno, 1974: 102)

Apter comments on this passage:

> Though on one level Adorno seems to be fingering working-class dialect as a resource of *ressentiment* capable of turning against the master from within his own house, on another level he seems bent on militating in favor of the 'literarification' of all human speech, such that, purged of barbarism, it realises historical objectivity, and thus feeds itself no longer on the junk food of infelicitous grammar. (Apter, 2006)

Apter goes on to link this passage again to Benjamin, seeing Adorno's call for the 'deliverance of human speech from the lie that it is already human' as analogous to Benjamin's assertion that 'crude language' shows humanity in its naked rawness. From this standpoint, Apter embarks on her analysis of the signification of non-standard speech in the fiction of Welsh, Kelman and McLean):

> Welsh's Scottish vernacular is not so much a transposition of accent and slang, but a subcultural *Sprache* that has the effect of wounding Standard English with the slings and arrows of warped speech, at least for a Brit or Anglophone reader outside of Scotland. Though some critics may argue that this warping effect is simply a matter of 'eye dialect' – the use of non-standard spelling to identify colloquial pronunciation – I would venture that Welsh's orthography contains a multigrained political aesthetic, a postcolonial politics of class. (Apter, 2006: 155–6)

Again, my anxiety about this reading is not that it is necessarily untrue with respect to the authors that Apter discusses, but that it is unduly constrictive when the use of Scots in literature is considered more generally; moreover, it raises issues that it neglects to resolve. Adorno rightly distinguishes between speech and writing – two modes of discourse that have separate conventions and whose influence one on another is continuously negotiated. When in the 18th century, middle-class Scots adopted the norms of English in their speech, they appealed to the grammar and vocabulary of the written standard, norms increasingly regulated and disseminated by mass education. Fiction and poetry that adopt 'eye-dialect' move the pendulum back towards the norms of speech, seeking to recreate in writing the conditions of the spoken word. Those 20th century political and linguistic nationalists who wished to create in 'Lallans' a national language for a modern Scotland were as scathing about regional infelicities as Adorno is about 'mutilated' or 'maimed' language, and sought to 'purge it of barbarism' by forging a literary medium (cf Milton, 1995/6). The assertive literariness of Lallans is seen in the opening verse of Sydney Goodsir Smith's 'Epistle to John Guthrie', who had complained that Lallans was artificial:

> We've come intil a gey queer time
> Wham scrievin Scots is near a crime,
> 'There's no one speaks like that', they fleer,
> – But wha the deil spoke like King Lear?

As we have seen, dramatists bent on extending Broad Scots into the literary domain, that is, devising 'a speaking that transcends writing by absorbing it', face a peculiar challenge. From Kemp to Lochhead, the dramatist translators' strategy was to found their stage medium on colloquial speech, whether rural or urban, and then enrich it from literary sources (Burns and the vernacular revivalists) or from more general popular culture (Lochhead's George Formby to Ogden Nash, referred to above). The written Scots of the vernacular revivalists itself owed much to the oral tradition of ballad and song, and therefore does not represent a dramatic move from speech to writing. Neither does the appropriation of the language of popular poets and performers such as Nash and Formby. For this reason, 'Hugh MacDiarmid' preferred the 16th century poet, or 'makar', William Dunbar to Robert Burns as a model for new writing in Scots – Dunbar commanded a range of written styles, from courtly celebration to rustic satire, that seemed to owe little debt to what we know of the speech of his time. 'MacDiarmid' wished to demonstrate that a written Broad Scots was viable.

A scholar, political activist, poet and dramatist translator who owed much to the inspiration of 'Hugh MacDiarmid' was Douglas Young, a Classics professor at St Andrews University. Young translated two plays by Aristophanes in the late 1950s and early 1960s, *The Puddocks* (The Frogs) and *The Burdies*. Young was as unapologetic as Goodsir Smith about the alleged 'artificiality' of the Broad Scots he used in his poetry (cf. Young, 1946); however, he did make concessions when it came to presenting his Scots on stage, as he notes in his own introduction to *The Burdies*:

> This printed version is designed primarily for those reading at leisure and has been equipped with a glossary for the convenience of English and American and other readers not wholly familiar with the Scots language. It is, at this writing, not known how far the producers will cut the play or alter the phrasing of this text. Some cutting and some alteration there certainly should be for the most effective production before a modern general audience. (STM: 50)

Even so, Young's Scots is more experimental than that of the 'MacMolières' and their ilk: both high-born and low-born characters dispute in a dense Broad Scots that is clearly asserting itself as a rich, 'unmaimed', 'unmutilated' medium of dramatic discourse. The hero, Sir Wylie Bodie (Peisthetairos), is not the spectacularly flawed Scots-speaking bourgeois whose pretensions and conceits will be stripped bare; instead he is a crafty negotiator whose skills will be rewarded by marriage to the goddess, Basileia. A flavour of Young's 'literate' Scots can be seen in the following exchange between Peisthetairos and a Herald from the kingdom of the birds:

> HER: Sir Wylie Bodie, happiest and wycest,
> and famousest, and ... wycest, and ... maist sleekit ...
> thrice happy ... och, help me oot, sir!
>
> PE: What's this?
>
> HER: Wi this here gowden croun, first prize for wisdom
> Ye're crounit and honourit by the United Nations.
>
> PE: *(Takan the croun)* Be thankit. Why dae the Nations honour me sae?
>
> HER: O, you that foondit the famed etherial city,
> ye kenna hou muckle honour ye win frae mortals,
> hou monie lovers are grienan for this country.
> For afore ye ever grundit this city here,
> the hale o mankind was daft on Spartan fashions.
> Lang-haired and hungert, clorty, juist like Socrates,
> they cairried crummocks. Nou they hae turned aboot;
> they're burdie-daft. And wi the pleisur o't
> they imitate us burds in aa they dae. (STM: 109)

Apter's (2006) analysis of Scots as a 'subcultural *Sprache* that has the effect of wounding Standard English with the slings and arrows of warped speech' clearly has to be modified in the light of this kind of Broad Scots. In Adorno's terms, Young's stage Lallans is non-standard speech arguably purged of barbarism by the fire of literariness. Ideologically, this stage medium is conditioned by nationalist aspirations rather than class warfare. It neither wounds nor feeds on Standard English but seeks to function as a full alternative to it, a national *Sprache* on its own terms. Less immediately accessible – and consequently less successful as a vehicle for Broad Scots on the stage, rather than the page – Young's experiments of the 1950s and 1960s might have remained a dead end in the use of literary Scots in translation were it not for the intervention of another great experimentalist, Edwin Morgan.

Better known as a poet and translator into English and Scots, Morgan turned to stage adaptations in the 1990s, during a period when Scotland,

Wales and Northern Ireland were pressuring successfully for increased political autonomy, resulting in the establishment of devolved assemblies, and, in Scotland, a new Parliament in 1997. It is surely more than a coincidence that in this climate of renewed national self-assertion came two translations, of Rostand and Racine, that again extended the possibilities for using Scots on the stage. Morgan's version of *Cyrano de Bergerac* (1992) nevertheless can still be fitted into a postcolonial paradigm: Cyrano, the Gascon outsider falls in love with Roxanne, the Parisian representative of the centre; he is ashamed of his physical appearance and so woos her with the excessive language she desires through an intermediary, Christian, who dies in battle. He then conceals his love for her until he too is attacked and dies, but not before revealing his passion to her directly. The plot, with its themes of the outsider's self-loathing, erasure and exploitation (the state exploits his courage and prowess in battle; Christian usurps his skills to woo Roxanne; Roxanne exploits him erotically if unknowingly) accords neatly with the tropes of postcolonial criticism. Yet Morgan in his introduction to the play identifies its language as based specifically upon Glaswegian, and the text itself confirms that Morgan's 'Glaswegian', like Young's 'Lallans', is extended beyond the constraints of transcribed speech into the domain of the literary. After all, no Glaswegian chef ever spoke like Morgan's Ragueneau:

> RAGUENEAU: Leave me, ma Muse, in case yer charming eyes
> Should go all bloodshot in thae pungent fires!
> – Ye've made a balls a the crack in thae roon cobs:
> Caesura, hauf-wey, hemistichs equal, bob's
> Yer uncle. – You, pit a roof on this crust-castle…
> – And you, at that endless spit, a touch a class'll
> Alternate cheapo chicks and burstin bubblyjocks,
> Just as, my son, auld Malherbe amazed folks
> Wae alternatin lang and shoart verse-lines.
> Turn yer roast stanzas in sic skeely designs! (EM1: 39–40)[4]

Yet if Cyrano is a hero, whose hero is he? Does he represent marginalised Scotland in the face of English imperialism or, more likely, marginalised Glasgow in the face of a re-empowered Scottish state? The relationship between regional and national literature has often been blurred in post-Union Scotland, and there is an ambivalence here, further complicated by Morgan's subsequent elevation from official 'Poet of Glasgow' to 'Scotland's Makar'. Still, if we read *Cyrano de Bergerac* as a specifically Glaswegian play, then the politics of class that Apter discusses re-enter the fray, and we are given a further option for 'purging the barbarism' of perhaps Scotland's most derided *patois* by celebrating its potential for literary expression, from flyting to lyricism.

Perhaps a more audacious experiment than *Cyrano de Bergerac*, Morgan's version of Racine's *Phèdre* (*Phaedra*) adopts a 'literary' version of the language of Welsh's *Trainspotting* as a vehicle for a Broad Scots version of the canonical French retelling of a classical tragedy. The titular character, Phaedra, is again an outsider, but her tragedy is triggered not by the exploitation of the state or its representatives, but by her uncontrollable yet forbidden passion:

> PHAEDRA: Ah wahnt nae truck wi bein a king's mither!
> It's no the thing! Mak me a spectacle?
> Is thon the wey ye're goanny ease ma hert?
> Raither hide me! Ah'm a spectacle awready.
> Ma radge imaginins huv skailed the cloaset.
> Ah've sayed things naebdy hiz the richt tae say. (EM2: 39)[5]

As I argue elsewhere (Corbett, 2006), along with Liz Lochhead's versions of *Medea* (2000) and *Thebans* (2004), *Phaedra* marks a post-devolutionary return to neo-classical drama in Scots, and resists a simple postcolonial reading. In these recent translations, modern urban Scotland takes centre stage and dramatises its troubles and tragedies in language that has its roots in 'workers' dialect' but is neither crude nor parasitical on some 'objective' standard.

Conclusions

This chapter has revolved around shifting perceptions of non-standard language as a literary medium, and in particular as a vehicle for the translation of the classic repertoire of European drama. There are many other plays that could have been mentioned even amongst this group (a list is given in Corbett & Findlay 2005: 331–5). The examples chosen are sufficient to question the use made by Apter of Benjamin and Adorno, by suggesting that an uncritical acceptance of non-standard varieties as mutilated dialects, at once parasitic upon and offensive to the standard, serves post-colonial readings of some modern Scottish fiction, but is not equally applicable to other literary genres.

There are of course fundamental differences between fiction and drama. Part of the legitimate thrill of the fiction that Apter discusses is allowing its language to calibrate the mind-style of a social outsider with your own: as long as the spell of reading endures, you inhabit the skin of a junkie, dosser or other social outsider. At worst the reader takes on the role of voyeur, temporarily in thrall to someone else's addictions, fantasies, pleasures and miseries, before setting the book down and returning to his or her normality. At best, the reader takes a critical stance, transmuting vicarious experience into political evaluation and even, perhaps, social action.

Drama of course lacks the intimacy of this kind of fiction; the audience always observes rather than inhabits the characters on display. And yet the language used in drama can trigger powerful feelings of identification, as Neil Gunn observed in 1938, when he too contemplated the apparently receding mirage of a Scottish national theatre, and contrasted the situation at home with that in Ireland:

> In Dublin, Irish national life was so strong that it created a drama out of itself. It had not to appeal to patrons by promising foreign plays and ballet and opera. It did not say: Endow us so that we may give you artistic satisfactions. It said: We will show you your own life translated into drama, and make you sit up, and look at it, and realise it as you have never done before. [..] I have seen most of the great Abbey plays in the Abbey, and remember vividly still the shock I got when, at my first visit many years ago, I heard the Irish voices in the *Shadow of a Gunman* coming over the footlights into the darkened auditorium. I had forgotten, if I had ever known, that contemporary drama could act on one like this. (Gunn, 1938; reprinted in McCulloch, 2004: 145–6)

Having your own language mirrored to you by actors onstage can lead to a profound relationship of identity; even if, as in the case of Gunn, it is not 'your' language that is actually being presented. Non-standard accents and dialects on stage invite communal identification and ownership, while fiction might offer the reader a 'subcultural *Sprache*', for leisurely contemplation and analytical dissection.

In his essay, Gunn goes on to question whether Scotland in the late 1930s can provide the stuff of a national drama, a question that was proposed anew as the National Theatre of Scotland finally launched its inaugural programme in 2006. However, the past 70 years of professional theatre in Scotland have shown that an exciting national drama is possible, and, sitting proudly alongside indigenous plays of European reputation, are European plays rendered into a vibrant Broad Scots.

Notes

1. The chapter is influenced greatly by the experience of co-editing the anthology *Serving Twa Maisters: Five Classic Plays in Scots Translation* (Glasgow: Association for Scottish Literary Studies, 2005) with the late Bill Findlay, the scholar, translator and dramatist to whom the present volume is dedicated. From this anthology are taken quotations from Robert Kemp's version of *Lat Wives Tak Tent* (Molière), Douglas Young's version of *The Burdies* (Aristophanes), Victor Carin's version of *The Servant o' Twa Maisters* (Goldoni), Hector MacMillan's version of *The Hypochondriak* (Molière) and Peter Arnott's version of *Mr Puntila and his Man, Matti* (Brecht). Extracts from these plays are referenced as STM with the page number. Other play excerpts are from Liz Lochhead's *Tartuffe: A Translation into Scots from the Original by Molière* (Glasgow: Third Eye Centre/Polygon, 1985), referenced as LL plus act and scene numbers; and Edwin Morgan's

translations of Emond Rostand's *Cyrano de Bergerac* (Manchester: Carcanet, 1992), referenced as EM1 plus page number; and from Jean Racine's *Phaedra* (Manchester: Carcanet, 200), referenced as EM2 plus page number.
2. Findlay's translation, see Note 1 above.
3. Liz Lochhead's translation, see Note 1.
4. Edwin Morgan's translation, see Note 1.
5. Edwin Morgan's translation, see Note 1.

References

Adorno, T. (1974) *Minima Moralia* (E.F.N. Jephcott, trans.). London: Verso.

Apter, E. (2006) *The Translation Zone: A New Comparative Literature*. Princeton: Princeton University Press.

Benjamin, W. (1973) *Understanding Brecht* [*Versuche über Brecht*] (A. Bostock, trans.). London: New Left Books.

Corbett, J. (1999) *Written in the Language of the Scottish Nation: A History of Literary Translation into Scots*. Clevedon: Multilingual Matters.

Corbett, J. (2006) Nae mair pussyfootin: Ah'm aff, Theramenes: Demotic neoclassical drama in contemporary Scotland. In J. McGonigal and K. Stirling (eds) *Ethically Speaking: Voice and Values in Modern Scottish Writing* (pp. 1–20). Amsterdam: Rodopi.

Corbett, J. (2007) A double realm: Scottish literary translation in the 21st Century. In B. Schoene (ed.) *The Edinburgh Companion to 21st Century Scottish Literature* (pp. 336–344). Edinburgh: Edinburgh University Press.

Corbett, J. and B. Findlay (eds) (2005) *Serving Twa Maisters: Five Classic Plays in Scots Translation*. Glasgow: Association for Scottish Literary Studies.

Crowley, T. (1989) *The Politics of Discourse: The Standard Language Question in British Cultural Debates*. London: Macmillan.

Findlay, B. (ed.) (1998) *A History of Scottish Theatre*. Edinburgh: Polygon.

Findlay, B. (2003) The founding of a modern tradition: Robert Kemp's Scots translations of Molière at the Gateway. In I. Brown (ed.) *Journey's Beginning: The Gateway Theatre Building and Company, 1884–1965*. Bristol: Intellect.

Findlay, B. (ed.) (2004) *Frae Ither Tongues: Essays on Modern Translations into Scots*. Clevedon: Multilingual Matters.

Jones, C. (1995) *A Language Suppressed: The Pronunciation of the Scots Language in the 18th Century*. Edinburgh: John Donald.

McCulloch, M.P. (2004) *Modernism and Nationalism: Literature and Society in Scotland 1918–1939*. Glasgow: Association for Scottish Literary Studies.

Milton, C. (1995/6) Shibboleths o the Scots: Hugh MacDiarmid and Jamieson's Etymological Dictionary of the Scottish Language. *Scottish Language* 14/15, 1–14.

Peacock, N. (1993) *Molière in Scotland: 1945–1990*. Glasgow: University of Glasgow French and German Publications.

Peacock, N. (2004) Robert Kemp's translations of Molière. In B. Findlay (ed.) *Frae Ither Tongues: Essays on Modern Translations into Scots* (pp. 87–105). Clevedon: Multilingual Matters.

Young, D. (1946) *'Plastic Scots' and the Scottish Literary Tradition*. Glasgow: William McLellan.

Chapter 4
Staging Italian Theatre: A Resistant Approach

STEFANIA TAVIANO

Introduction

An analysis of key British productions of modern Italian theatre testifies to the cultural and linguistic transformations affecting foreign plays when they are translated from one language into another; it also illustrates the peculiarities of theatre translation into English. While acculturation is an inherent aspect of the translation of theatre texts, there are specific ways in which foreign plays are appropriated by British theatre companies, due to cultural and theatrical constraints peculiar to this society.

This chapter looks at contemporary strategies adopted in staging foreign plays in the UK by taking into account the role of theatre audiences and the function of theatre in affecting and determining social practices. After briefly analysing a predominant British approach to foreign theatre, a number of recent productions of Italian plays, which seem to indicate a tendency towards an alternative strategy in stagings of foreign theatre in the UK, are examined. These include the 2002 joint production of *The Odyssey* by the Italian theatre group Stalker Teatro and the Glasgow-based Working Party, together with some key productions of plays by Luigi Pirandello, Edoardo De Filippo, Dario Fo and Franca Rame. These productions have been chosen for their political content, in some cases, but mainly for their provocative form and function in that they challenge common British stage traditions, such as the tendency to focus on the cultural identity of foreign plays, as well as dominant acting styles. The use of non-standard languages and the commitment of theatre collectives to physical acting will be shown to constitute central elements of a *resistant* approach that distinguishes itself for its challenging interpretations of foreign theatre.

Most British productions of Fo and Rame's plays, reveal, to different degrees, the main aspects of a predominant approach to political theatre which aims at appropriating foreign plays by focusing on their entertainment value and their cultural identity while undermining their political function. The success of the 2003 West End staging of *Accidental Death of an Anarchist* at the Donmar Warehouse Theatre, for example, was achieved thanks to a specific strategy, including the choice of the well-known Simon Nye, both as the author of the play's new translation and as the actor playing the part of the protagonist. Nye's excellent performance of farcical sketches and stereotypical figures, which were not included in the original text, made British audiences laugh but, at the same time, forget the political message of the play, aimed at revealing police brutality and corruption. This staging, together with many others, indicates the tendency to a comic reading of Italian theatre, which is the result of a compromise between the political function of the source text and its assimilation into the British theatrical system, aimed at ensuring the success of stage productions. In other words, Fo and Rame have been, and continue to be, the best known and most performed Italian playwrights in the UK thanks to the commercialisation of their plays, which makes them easy to stage and above all funny, hilarious Italian satire (see Taviano, 2005).

Nevertheless, it is important to acknowledge that a different approach to foreign theatre is now starting to emerge from a number of productions. I have defined such an approach *resistant*, according to a notion of postmodern performance, which, rather than transgressing the limits imposed by society, is *resistant* within the dominant culture. In other words, postmodernist artists and their art cannot be separated from the context in which they belong, but at the same time they can subvert predominant forms of representation. This definition of a resistant approach is based on Philip Auslander's (1992) view of transgressive and resistant politics applied to postmodern American performance. Similarly, a *resistant* approach to foreign playwrights subverts strategies centred on the 'exotic' nature of foreign plays by focusing instead on their political role in stimulating and provoking theatre audiences. The opportunity for British audiences to (re)discover foreign theatre might reside precisely in *resistant* stagings, as in the case of the 2002 joint production of *The Odyssey*. This was a project funded by the Scottish Arts Council, and, despite the fact that the play was staged in a traditional theatre, challenged traditional notions of performance through an active involvement of the local community and the audience by extending its impact beyond the performance itself through workshops, as well as proposing innovative ways to use the Tramway theatre as a performative space.

The Odyssey was part of a month-long season of theatre and literary events in Glasgow between October and November 2002. The show was described in the programme as follows:

> Turin's Stalker Teatro fuses a 25-year history of site specific performance and visual arts to re-create this thrilling epic in Glasgow. In this UK premiere, co-produced by The Working Party, Stalker collaborates with installation artists and participants from communities throughout Glasgow to bring the poetry of *The Odyssey* alive in English and Italian.

Audiences were invited to 'enter the World of the Hero', 'to become the Hero' and 'to embark on Homer's classic voyage of discovery.' This was a truly interactive performance; as audience members when entering the theatre were metaphorically and literally taken through Odysseus's voyage. An actor with a blanket covering his/her shoulders would welcome us, give us a bag full of stones and show the way to our seats by taking us through a dark path with a torch and reciting lines from *The Odyssey*, with the sound of the sea in the background.

The programme provided a journey guide with the breakdown of the eight scenes as follows:

> *Scene 1*, Telemachus; *Scene 2*, At the Court of Alcinous; *Scene 3*, Journey across the Seas; *Scene 4*, The Land of the Lotus Eaters; *Scene 5*, On the Enchanted Island of Circe; *Scene 6*, Hades; *Scene 7*, Homecoming and Slaughter; *Scene 8*, Banquet of Reconciliation.

Each scene took place in a different area of the theatre and represented a different stage in the voyage of Odysseus and the audience. The Lotus Eaters Scene, for example, consisted of a display of local artists's interpretation of Homer's voyage and of the Lotus Eaters chapter in James Joyce's *Ulysses*. The scene included: the artist Vrnda Daktor sitting in front of a mirror while drawing herself surrounded by discarded drawings to symbolise the artist in search of truth and inspiration; a cyclical action performed by Michella Dunne and Gillian Lees working with large blocks of lard and fruit, materials resonant of the Lotus Eaters' experience (in the artists' view) since, when they are exposed to time and human contact, their state is altered. The audience was invited to take an active role by deciding the order in which to observe each piece and the amount of time spent watching each of them. Spectators were also able to interact with the soundscape of the scene through two sound beams that were part of *The Dream of the Sea*, a multi-tracked musical piece. Throughout the performance two narrators, one speaking in English and the other in Italian, marked crucial points in the development of the story, contributing to the rhythm of the performance. The nature of the performance led to an interesting use of the Tramway Theatre, taking advantage of back stage spaces and corridors never used for performances, and above all it encouraged the audience to take an active role throughout the evening. In the concluding scene, that of the reconciliation banquet, audience members were asked to put on a large table the flat stones kept in the bags they were given at the entrance, thus creating an interesting mosaic. They were also given fruit and vegetables to put on top of each stone. As a result, a visually fascinating banquet table was laid, framed by hundreds of glasses of wine that were offered by the actors to the audience as the conclusion to the performance.

The Glasgow co-production of *The Odyssey* was a community theatre performance whose political efficacy was maintained in translation. The co-production, in fact, was the result of four weeks of collaboration between Stalker Teatro, The Working Party, local visual artists and members of the local community who had never performed before. Moreover, it ended with a one-day workshop where artists from the two cities exchanged ideas and experiences. *The Odyssey*, together with the workshop and other related events, aimed at strengthening the artistic collaboration between Turin and Glasgow. While *The Odyssey* would not be classified as political according to traditional notions of political theatre, its political meaning and efficacy were testified by the audience response and above all by the local artists and participants' response. The latter shared their enthusiasm for *The Odyssey* as an opportunity to discover their voice, their creativity and to challenge their role within society.

It is interesting to note that another performance with significant political implications took place in Glasgow 12 years earlier. This was *Glasgow All Lit Up!*, part of the community programme in Glasgow as European City of Culture. For 18 months Welfare actors trained local artists in lantern making using Japanese techniques, and the local artists worked with 250 community organisations from Strathclyde. As a result, on 6 October 1990 there was a parade of 10,000 people carrying about 8000 lanterns across the city. The gathering ended with the Welfare State performance followed by a fireworks display. As Paul Kershaw argues, the semiotics of the lanterns, that is the politics of representation at work in the parade, expressed a plurality of voices signifying the cultural diversity of the city, as well as producing a sense of solidarity and collective belonging. The performance also dealt with state politics. While the police had decided to keep the city centre open to car traffic, in reality the procession dominated the city, and the traffic came to a standstill. Since as a non-violent political demonstration the lantern procession transgressed the decision of the local government, in Kershaw's (1996: 149) view, it 'opened up, metaphorically and literally, a new space for politically democratic action'.

Similarly, *The Odyssey*, as part of a one-month season, created a space for effective political action in its innovative use of the Tramway Theatre by offering an opportunity for a challenging theatrical and artistic exchange between Scottish and Italian cultures, and by encouraging the active involvement of local artists and common citizens in both the production and reception of the performance. Like *Glasgow All Lit Up!*, the plurality of visual artists contributing to the performance guaranteed the expression of Glasgow's cultural diversity. It also created a sense of solidarity between professional artists and common citizens with no previous artistic experience. Most importantly, all this was achieved through the co-production of an Italian community performance.

It is not by chance that such challenging productions took place in

Glasgow. Scotland has a long history of staging foreign theatre that makes it a very fruitful and stimulating context for politically effective performances. The Glasgow Citizens Theatre is renowned for staging foreign playwrights such as Molière, Carlo Goldoni and Dario Fo, to name a few. Moreover, because of the role of its language, Scotland offers fascinating examples of the transposition of plays from one regional context to another. Martin Bowman and Bill Findlay collaborated for a number of years on the translation of Michel Tremblay's works from Montreal French, Joual, into Scots. In Bowman's view, Quebec and Scotland are compatible in many cultural and social aspects, and Scots functions as a valid medium to translate the idiom of the Montreal working class, and vice versa – in 1998 Bowman and Findlay also adapted Irvine Welsh's *Trainspotting* into Joual (Bowman, 1998). In their approach to the source text, Bowman and Findlay tend, whenever possible, to avoid the introduction of target cultural material as a replacement for foreign cultural references. Their work, among other things, testifies to the current tendency to use Scots as the language in which to translate foreign plays, as opposed to English (see also Corbett in this volume).

The Scottish approach to the translation of foreign plays indicates that the use of non-standard languages, such as regional varieties and dialects, might represent a vital element of productions that challenge British images of foreign theatre. Jatinder Verma's productions of Molière's *Tartuffe* for the Royal National Theatre in 1990 and *Le Bourgeois Gentilhomme* for Tara Arts in 1994, based on his own translations, represent a fascinating example. They are the product of what Verma defines as Binglish theatre, 'a contemporary theatre praxis featuring Asian or black casts, produced by independent Asian or black theatre companies' that challenges dominant practices of the English stage (Verma, 1996: 194). Verma is the artistic director of Tara Arts, an independent company created in 1977, that searches for a distinctive theatrical form, based on classical Indian aesthetics and on 'a rejection of the dominant convention of the modern English stage: the spoken word' (Verma, 1996: 199). Through Binglish productions British audiences are confronted with varieties of what Verma calls 'langues' – intended as language and theatre praxis – such as Caribbean, Punjabi, Urdu, Nigerian and Somali. Verma uses varieties of English in his productions to contest the ownership of texts such as *King Lear*. The fact that Binglish productions draw upon non-European traditions of music, movement and imagery is precisely what distinguishes them. As Verma emphasises, Binglish productions are seen as provocative and stimulating by critics and audiences because they 'negotiate a foreign-ness' (Verma, 1996: 200). His productions of Molière were 'exercises in tradaptation', a term he borrows from Robert Lepage (Verma, 1994) referring to annexing old texts to new cultural contexts. By having Indian performers acting in his productions of Molière, Verma challenged British common notions of 'authenticity' in stagings of French theatre.

Similarly, the adoption of English working-class regional idioms, such as Liverpudlian in the case of Peter Tinniswood's adaptation of Eduardo De Filippo's *Napoli Milionaria* in 1991, helped to convey the social status of De Filippo's characters. The play, set in war-time Naples, tells the story of a family kept together and fed by a mother who sells black-market goods. Her husband, Gennaro, who disapproves of his wife's illegal business, is captured by the Germans and by the time he comes back in 1944 his family is destroyed. His wife, who has continued to be a racketeer, has a relationship with another man and his son has turned into a thief (Billington, 2000).

The production received public acclaim, and the show was sold out for months. Michael Billington praised Tinniswood's choice of Liverpool and its language:

> The most radical aspect of Peter Tinniswood's new version is to employ Liverpool speech rhythms. The result gives the show a working-class authenticity and spares us the delight of listening to British actors sounding like a convention of ice-cream vendors. (Billington, 1991)

Billington pointed to two advantages of the Anglicisation of *Napoli Milionaria*. First of all, Liverpool speech rhythms help to convey the social status of De Filippo's characters. The use of an English working-class regional idiom recreates the connection between the language of the characters and their class identity present in the source text. Secondly, it avoids the use of fake Italian accents which, associated with Italian-style gesticulation, has caricaturing effects. In other words, Tinniswood's adaptation contributed to making the social and human issues dealt with in the play resonate with local audiences. In this way *Napoli Milionaria* became a coherent theatre text that spoke to target spectators on an emotional level, rather than being a spectacle of Italianness. This is confirmed by Billington's appraisal of 'the broad-based humanity of a play that shows how ordinary people are all but destroyed by the economic imperatives of war' (Billington, 1991).

All the above productions reflect a translation practice that aims at toning down the cultural identity of foreign plays and at making their *mises en scène* relevant to target audiences for reasons other than their cultural connotations. This strategy, which became more common in British stagings of Pirandello and De Filippo in the 1990s, indicates a different phase and tendency in the process of integration of the otherness of foreign plays into the target system. Peter Hall's production of De Filippo's *Filumena*, translated by the dramatist Timberlake Wertenbaker, and Nicholas Wright's version of Pirandello's *Naked*, staged at the Almeida Theatre in 1998, constitute two further examples of British stagings of Italian plays that focused on evoking their validity as theatre texts within a coherent theatrical structure (De Filippo, 1998; Pirandello, 1998).

Wertenbaker chose to translate the Neapolitan dialect of the source text in plain English, without adopting any particular regional connotations, as she explained in an interview with *Corriere della Sera*, but to convey the dialect inflections of the Neapolitan dialect through the rhythm of the dialogue (De Carolis, 1998). The long speeches of the source text, often organised in a crescendo of repetitive statements, are replaced by concise dialogues and punchy phrases in the style of contemporary British stage prose. In John Gross's view, Wertenbaker's new translation of the play was one of the aspects that made Hall's staging successful (Gross, 1998). Critics were unanimous in praising Judy Dench and Michael Pennington's performance and spectators gave them standing ovations. The following remark by John Stokes's indicates that De Filippo was no longer perceived as an exotic Italian playwright, but one accessible to European audiences: 'Children are children – it is this creed – banal, heartbreaking – that makes Filumena both as Neapolitan as a painted effigy and, at the same time, broadly European' (Stokes, 1998). This means that Hall's production of *Filumena* struck a cord with English audiences. The unique bond between parents and their children, instead of being perceived as a specifically Italian phenomenon, became relevant to local receivers of De Filippo's text.

Similarly, according to Charles Spencer, it was 'the passion and the anguish' of Pirandello's theatre that the Almeida production of *Naked* 'powerfully captured' (Spencer, 1998). Spencer also described the show as an 'intense, atmospheric experience that will trouble the memory'. The positive response that both the above productions received seems to suggest that British audiences and critics are becoming more receptive to challenging stagings of foreign plays.

I have been involved in a theatre project that aimed to make the human and social significance of Italian plays resonate with Anglophone audiences. This was the British première of Spiro Scimone's play, *Nunzio*, during the International Playwriting Festival at the Croydon Theatre in London, in October 1999. The play is set in a one-bedroom flat, and the protagonists are two Sicilians who have emigrated to the North of Italy. Nunzio is seriously ill because of the fumes he breathes at work, Pino is a killer and travels all over the world. The flat is a claustrophobic environment where both characters hide from the surrounding world. The outside world is constantly threatening through phone calls, cars passing by the flat and mysterious envelopes pushed under the door. In this environment Nunzio and Pino develop a co-dependent relationship: they care for each other, but often get close to fighting, in the way that Estragon and Vladimir do in *Waiting for Godot*. In the isolation of the kitchen, they begin to discover each other: Pino realises how serious Nunzio's illness is and tries to protect him;

Nunzio, in his naiveté, dreams about travelling to Brazil, like his friend. Both the claustrophobic setting and the repetitive nature of the dialogue remind us of Harold Pinter's theatre, particularly *The Dumb Waiter*.

Jennifer Varney and I, as translators of the play, decided to set *Nunzio* in Glasgow and to translate it into Scottish English to convey the cultural and linguistic distance between standard Italian and the Sicilian of the source text, which was written in the dialect spoken in Messina, my hometown (Scimone, 1999). The decision to translate into Scottish English automatically excluded the adoption of a stage Italian accent, or any other aspect of the stage representation of Italians, such as excessive gesticulation. The nature of the relationship between the two characters, their inability to communicate with each other on a very basic human level as a result of their difficulty in expressing themselves through words, were aspects of the play that we tried to bring out in this production because they can speak to a British, or any other audience. The play was well received and, most important of all, audiences seemed to relate to central issues such as the characters' isolation and inability to communicate, rather than their Italianness. Although the above production does not have the same political resonance as *The Odyssey*, it nevertheless subverts common British stage traditions that tend to focus on the cultural identity of foreign plays.

Returning to Fo and Rame, in December 2005 the world première of a new play, *Mother Courage, Cindy Sheehan's Real and Imaginary Diary*, translated by Tom Behan, was staged at Pimlico School, in Central London, starring Frances de La Tour. It was directed by Michael Kustow and promoted by Stop the War Coalition at the time when Cindy Sheehan, mother of Casey, a 24-year-old US soldier who was killed in Iraq on April 4 2004, took her anti-war campaign to Britain. The performance was part of a peace conference that promoted global peace demonstrations to take place on 18 March 2006. It is a monologue, based on newspaper articles and above all letters written by Sheehan to George W. Bush and to Barbara Bush. More precisely, as indicated in the press release by Stop the War Coalition:

> Her efforts to get an explanation from President Bush about the death of her and other mother's sons led her to pitch camp outside the presidential ranch throughout August this year. The persistence and growing anger of this woman who was nicknamed 'Peace Mom' made her the focus of a nationwide movement against the war, which goes from strength to strength.

Mother Courage, a straightforward, colloquial monologue of a common, anonymous mother, is extremely powerful in voicing the anger and protest of thousands and thousands of US citizens who, like Cindy Sheehan, personally rebel against the war in Iraq and do not hesitate to condemn Bush and his government as criminals and killers. The immediacy of her words, combined with details of the events following her protest, have the effect of what the poet Buskaar calls 'turning stones' in his ballad dedicated to Cindy Sheehan, as explained in the play:

> These stones are out in the Nevada desert, at the edge of the Great Prairies. They're round and almost hollow inside, apart from a small stone, which is round as well, but that acts like a shuttlecock. When the wind starts blowing the stones start turning, and inside them the smaller stone moves faster and increases the whole momentum. If you slightly push one of these stones you'll hear a strange sound come out, which makes a noise like somebody who's talking but who makes no sense. That's why these stones are also called the 'talking stones' or the 'singing stones'. [...] Cindy's story is like the old Indian tale about the singing stone, blown by the wind, it's forced to spin around out on the prairie. But its movement drags other stones along with it, and they all rub up against each other, creating sparks that set fire to the whole prairie.

As in the case of various plays by Fo and Rame, this monologue is the product of specific political events narrated and brought to life on stage to encourage everyday people in their struggle against injustice. This is confirmed by Sheehan's comments: 'I hope the play can be used as an anti-war tool, to put a human face on this war, to show Casey had a life, was a person' (quoted in Higgins, 2005). To this end, after publishing a first draft on Jacopo Fo's website (www.alcatraz.it; accessed 10.06), Fo and Rame's provided the final script, as requested by many, together with the English version (www.alcatraznews.com), accompanied by the following appeal to make the text known in the English-speaking world by sending it to US and British citizens: *'Lanciamo a tutti un appello affinché questo testo possa viaggiare nei paesi anglofoni e arrivi al maggior numero possibile di statunitensi e inglesi'* ('We launch an appeal to everybody in the hope that this text can be staged in English-speaking countries and reach as many US and British citizens as possible'). As indicated on the web, plans are afoot to contact Michael Moore for a version of the play to be produced in the United States.

There are numerous plays by Fo and Rame, which have never been translated into English and are unknown in Anglophone countries for various reasons, particularly because of their documentary or didactic structure, which makes them difficult to transpose to foreign countries. The world resonance of *Mother Courage*, the fact that, rather than being based on the Italian social or political context, refers to the war in Iraq, having therefore a significance for the whole international community, facilitates Behan's commitment to the translation and staging of unknown theatre texts by Fo and Rame. Moreover, the staging of this, together with other plays, particularly within politically-relevant contexts, as in the case of the peace conference promoted by Stop the War Coalition, makes it even more valuable since it can further contribute to reinforcing a *resistant* approach, which allows us to rediscover the political function of Fo and Rame's plays. Last but not least, given that *Mother Courage* is not set in Italy, nor has Italian characters, its cultural origins become irrelevant when it is put on stage, hence the monologue is safe from the above-mentioned British approach that focused on the cultural connotations of Fo and Rame's theatre.

The adoption of non-standard 'langues', as shown by Tinniswood's adaptation, appropriate acting techniques, an innovative use of theatrical spaces, as in the case of *The Odyssey*, and, I would add, the translations of playwrights unknown to English-speaking countries are some of the ways through which it is possible to infuse new life into foreign theatre in the UK. My personal experience as a translator and, above all, current practices of translation and postmodern theatre, seem to confirm that British stagings of foreign plays are taking innovative and exciting directions. It is therefore vital that theatre scholars and professionals document and discuss the productions that adhere to such translation strategies, in order to better understand if and how theatre translation practices affect our interaction with other cultures.

References

Auslander, P. (1992) *Presence and Resistance: Postmodernism and Cultural Politics in Contemporary American Performance*. Ann Arbor: The University of Michigan Press.
Billington, M. (1991) Family at war with itself. *Guardian*, 29 June.
Billington, M. (2000) Making a living out of war. *Guardian*, 29 April.
Bowman, M. (1998) Trainspotting in Montreal: From Scots to Joual. Unpublished paper presented at the University of East Anglia.
De Carolis, P. (1998) Judy Dench: Filumena diventa inglese. *Corriere della Sera*, 10 October.
De Filippo, E. (1998) *Filumena* (T. Wertenbaker, trans.). London: Methuen Drama.
Gross, J. (1998) Old but still smashing. *Sunday Telegraph*, 11 October.
Higgins, C. (2005) Dario Fo's new play: Anti-war cry of a Peace Mom. *Guardian*, 12 December.
Kershaw, P. (1996) The politics of performance in a post-modern age. In P. Campbell (ed.) *Analysing Performance* (pp. 133–152). Manchester: Manchester University Press.
Pirandello, L. (1998) *Naked* (N. Wright, trans.). London: Nick Hern Books.
Scimone, S. (1999) *Nunzio* (S. Taviano and J. Varney, trans.). London: Arcadia Publishers and Agents.
Spencer, C. (1998) Binoche bares her soul in a play of passion. *Daily Telegraph*, 19 February.
Stokes, J. (1998) Priceless tears. *Arts*, 23 October.
Taviano, S. (2005) *Staging Dario Fo and Franca Ram: Anglo-American Approaches to Political Theatre*. Aldershot: Ashgate.
Verma, J. (1994) An interview with Lepage. *Guardian*, 5 October.
Verma J. (1996) The challenge of Binglish: Analyzing multi-cultural productions. In P. Campbell (ed.) *Analysing Performance* (pp. 193–202). Manchester: Manchester University Press.

Chapter 5
The Style of Translation: Dialogue with the Author

JOSEPH FARRELL

Introduction

Translation theory as an academic discipline has flourished in recent years and indeed has taken on a life of its own, independent of the activities of translators, although no more so than literary criticism from the creative work of writers. It may have in the 20th century assumed a more systematic form, but it is not as new a branch of intellectual activity as its more ardent proponents believe, if only for the reason that no one can ever undertake translation without being puzzled, baffled, intrigued and occasionally morally concerned about, on the one hand, the importance and necessity of translation, and, on the other, about the limits, difficulties, frustrations and temptations of the enterprise. In consequence, there is a corpus of intriguing thought from other times, often in the form of scattered reflections, occasional remarks in prefaces or casual thoughts in letters rather than in the form of systematic treatises, which can enrich, and widen the scope of, the thinking of those who dedicate themselves either to translation or to theorising on the nature of translation.

If many of these occasional sayings from the past, like the lengthy treatises from the present, concern the difficulties of rendering the substance and essence of meaning, a significant number address the problems of rendering *style*, a question that has not assumed due prominence among contemporary theorists. '*Numquam verbum pro verbo*', wrote Cicero, the first of the advocates of a translation free enough to respect the spirit of an original passage, or piece of oratory, but accurate enough to respect style, in his case the 'Attic style' of rhetoric he admired in the Athenian orators' (Weissbort & Eysteinsson, 2006: 21). Other ages, especially the Age of Enlightenment with its belief in rules in individual genres and in universal standards of taste, were concerned with canons of appreciation, and were convinced of their own right to intervene to correct the carelessness or ignorance of writers from earlier times who had not heeded these rules. There are two points that make these *obiter dicta* of interest to translators or theorists today. Firstly, in their egoistic struggle with the writer they set out to render how in another language the practice of 18th-century operatives impacts on, and clashes with, contemporary notions of the 'invisibility' of the translator. Secondly, Enlightenment translators were concerned, implicitly or explicitly, with questions of pure stylistics. Even if the precepts advocated are judged unsatisfactory, the questions raised are worthy of attention from modern theorists, who are frequently more concerned with barriers to understanding created by divergences between cultures.

Respect for Style

Alexander Pope, in his introduction to his English version of the *Iliad*, expatiated on the need to respect not only substance but also style, noting the poem's 'graceful and dignified simplicity as well as (its) bold and sordid one,' and concluding that, since Homer was closer in spirit to Biblical writing, 'his style must of course bear a greater resemblance to the sacred books than that of any other writer' (Pope, 1996: 13). A similar concern with style is shown by the Italian poet and translator, the *abate* Melchiorre Cesarotti (1730–1808), remembered now as translator of Ossian.[1] Cesarotti did not speak English, but it was he who produced, from the French, the edition of Ossian that Napoleon read and re-read and carried with him on his campaigns. It was Cesarotti who was, more than any other single individual, responsible for the Ossian craze that swept continental Europe, and led to Ossian influencing, and being quoted admiringly by, such writers as Goethe and Ugo Foscolo. Cesarotti had not visited Scotland but that did not prevent him from including a few lines of wild Romantic speculation about the country in his introductory remarks, the *Ragionamento preliminare attorno ai caledoni* (Preliminary Considerations on the Caledonians). Once these have been set aside, the preface is stimulating for Cesarotti's views on the totality of tasks facing the translator. Like Pope, Cesarotti focused on questions relating to taste and style, and it is in this context that his queries and perplexities have an enduring relevance and can be used to deepen contemporary theorising.

Cesarotti's approach was dictated by Enlightenment notions of rationality and order, as were those of James Macpherson[2] (1971), who was Cesarotti's source and the man who first published and gave shape to the Ossian cycle, drawing it from different Gaelic narrative pieces but claiming it, falsely, as an original 'epic'. What are the aspirations and limits, asked Cesarotti, that a translator must set himself in his endeavours to render concepts as elusive as the spirit of a work of poetry? He stated that his intention had been not so much to render the letter of the original as to *rischiarare, rammorbidire, rettificare e talora di abbellire* the work of the person he believed to be Ossian. These verbs can be translated, with no violence to Cesarotti's views, as 'to illuminate, to soften, to rectify and at times to embellish.' It is clear that there is much here that could be debated. Macpherson, again motivated by the same Enlightenment scepticism as Cesarotti, had intervened in the original Gaelic poetry to eliminate all reference to the supernatural or to fairy folklore, in the belief that his readers would be put off by the notion that spirits or gnomes had once wandered the hills and valleys. The *abate* Cesarotti still found Macpherson's prose-poetry, at least in the French version he had before him, too coarse and rough for the tastes of the salons and academies that were his ideal audience, so he modified its harshness, decided to render it in verse and to make the style conform to contemporary, neo-classical standards. The good *abate* was candid about his procedures, and he added another, more enigmatic, verb to his list. Such were his love, respect and admiration for the poem that his ambition was *gareggiar con esso* (literally to 'struggle with it'). This verb does not have the weak contemporary sense of puzzling over problems, of tussling with the vocabulary or of having doubts over various interpretations. Rather, it has the more robust sense of seeing the original as an adversary, as an opponent against whom the translator is required to pit his wits, gladiator to gladiator. It is in the act of *gareggiare* that the translator can permit himself what must otherwise seem like the arrogance of believing that he is entitled to *rettificare o abbellire* a work written in accordance with dated canons that are not those of his own day. The translator, in this perspective, is the reverse of the humble, invisible servant of the source text. He is like a botanist who abrogates to himself the right to uproot plants, or words, sentiments, ideas and cultural concepts and plant them in a different soil, climate, temperature and culture. He will also question himself in public over the ethics of this operation, precisely because he recognises that he is engaged in a dialogue – which may well be the equivalent modern term which best conveys the deep sense of *gareggiare* – with the author.

As a preliminary and for purposes of clarity, I would like to add that I have no sympathy with the view that the mere fact of transposing a work across cultures gives the translator the right, always and inevitably, to the status of 'second creator.' The novelist, playwright or poet is 'onlie begetter' and as such is responsible for the whole range of creativity required to produce an imaginative work of fiction. It is the writer who chooses the narrative voice, who establishes the scale of values underlying the fiction, who elaborates its elusive vision, who determines the pace of action, the unfolding of revelations, the maintenance or relief of suspense, the direction of the plot, the vivacity of individual scenes and encounters, the tone of dialogue, the felt life of the emotions depicted, the depth of characterisation, the rhythm of the prose, the quality of the descriptive passages, the credibility of the created complex and indeed all the multiple factors that constitute creativity. The translator works only on the language, but it has to be stated that this is a task concerning not only individual words or passages, as has been known since Cicero, but also the delicate entity known as style. *'Le style, c'est l'homme'*, La Rochefoucauld famously wrote, so what are the possibilities of being true to the man by maintaining style in translation? Eighteenth-century translators had the merit of being aware of the complexity and validity of this problem.

The Translator in Dialogue

These dialogues between translator and author are more frequent today when the demand for the translation of contemporary texts is greater than at any time in previous history. The authors of the great classic translations in English – Sir Thomas Urquhart of Rabelais, John Florio of Montaigne, Dryden of Virgil, Pope of Homer or even Scott-Moncrieff of Proust – were engaged in dialogues with dictionaries. But translators of literary work by living authors will often find it natural, if not essential, to seek advice and clarification from the authors of the original work. At times, translators may receive novels chapter by chapter, play scripts scene by scene or early drafts of film scripts with requests not only for translation but also for reaction. At one level, this interaction can produce material for amusing anecdotes. The novelist Hugh McIlvanney, after writing a novel set in Glasgow, tells of receiving a request from his Japanese translator for an explanation of what 'Partick Thistle' was. The puzzled Japanese assumed from the context that it was some arcane rite, while it is in fact a football team that plays in the west of the city. Conversely, the late William Weaver, the distinguished translator of Umberto Eco and Italo Calvino, tells of a discussion with an Italian author who insisted that the expression *i morti* should be translated, not as 'the dead' as Weaver had written, but as 'the deads'. The Italian argued, with impeccable logic but faulty semantics, that the corpses in question were more than one. When engaged in fruitful debate, the translator takes on the position not only of cultural mediator between source and target culture, but also that of participant in creative dialogue with the author. This status does, however, give birth to new dilemmas.

Some of these were examined recently by André Aciman in his trenchant critique of the recent retranslation of Proust's Recherche:

> Should English resolve the ambiguities that were conveniently overlooked or left intentionally opaque in the original French? One might be tempted to say 'yes' but 'no' is the correct answer. An author says what he says in the very way he says it not necessarily because he is after the utmost clarity, or, for some mysterious reason, not unrelated to what we call the creative process, because he wishes to see so far and no further, to see one thing without highlighting all of its ancillary, shadow meanings, but because the words he has selected in the order

that he selected them allow him to suggest things he does not wish to say or know how to come right out and say. (Aciman, 2005: 74)

If the writer chooses to leave certain matters unsaid, it may be because he does not know, not because he elects not to tell. What is left unstated has the same claim to the translator's respect as what is asserted or declaimed. There is a temptation to interpret, and at times a need to interpret among various competing meanings, but the translator has no right to impose where the original is ambiguous. Translation never confers the right to rewrite, nor to invent style.

The reflections of Alistair Reid, himself a poet and writer as well as translator of Pablo Neruda and J.L. Borges, are illuminating both on the nature of the writer–translator dialogue and on the dilemmas related to transferring style. In a poem significantly entitled What Gets Lost/*Lo Que Si Pierde*, Reid writes:

I keep translating *traduzco continuamente*
Entre palabras words *que no son las mias*
Into other words which are mine *de palabras a mis palabras*
Y finalmente de quien es el texto
Who do words belong to?
Del escritor e del traductor writer, translator
O de los idiomas or to language itself? (Reid, 1994: 221)

The Voice of the Writer

Words may belong to language, but the voice belongs to the artist. There are different motives for undertaking a translation, of which a passion for the work in hand is not the least, but that passion will, of necessity, include a love for the writer's voice. 'There is a vast body of translation in which in which the enlightened disclosure of admiration is primary – a kind of substantive embodiment *of praise*', wrote Ben Belitt (1978: 32), another distinguished translator of South American poetry. One of the paradoxes of the discussion of the value of a translation is that it can be carried out only by those who have no need for a translation in the first place. The fundamental question, whether a translation will serve those with scant knowledge of the original, can be answered only by such cognoscenti, but should be among the concerns of the translator. Is it enough to produce a translation that reads well in English, but which, while it does not mistranslate or mislead in any significant way, is more of a parallel text than a rendering of the style in which the original narrative voice expresses itself? Proust, Joyce and Pirandello may be taken as supreme examples of a trait common to the vast majority of the writers of modernity who have achieved classic, or canonical, status: the prose they employ is more than a vehicle or conveyance but has the flow and lilt of poetry. Joyce and Pirandello produced volumes of poetry, while Proust arrived at his own style after familiarising himself, and writing about, the style of John Ruskin, the essayist who, unlike his contemporaries Macaulay and Carlyle, was an exponent of the belletristic style.

Of no contemporary Italian writer is this more true than of Vincenzo Consolo (1933–), on whom I would now like to focus to examine questions of style in translation. Consolo, author of just a few highly wrought and elaborately worked novels, is a Sicilian who recognises himself as belonging to a Sicilian tradition that sees Luigi Pirandello, Giovanni Verga, Luigi Capuana and Federico De Roberto as its 19th-century founding fathers, and Vitaliano Brancati and Leonardo Sciascia as its prime exponents in the 20th century. It is not possible here to summarise Consolo's own poetics, except to say that he combines a radicalism of socio-political outlook with a polemically expressed contempt for the language of the contemporary 'mass-media' novel. Partly for this reason, Consolo has striven to achieve a poetic style, fit for an art novel and shorn of all taint of contamination by the debased, commercialised plainness of media-speak. As he said in an interview published in French:

> *Nous sommes assiégés par la communication totale. Je crois que la façon pour retrouver un espace littéraire nouveau c'est de rapprocher la prose de la narration de la forme poétique, je dis forme et non pas substance, lui conférer une certaine dignité poétique, de la rendre moins consommable. Tout en étant laïque je dis qu'il faudrait déplacer la prose vers une aura plus sacrée et moins commerciale.*[3] (Cederman, 1993: 472)

Consolo's subjects are taken from the past or present history of Sicily, but he distrusts 'narrative' as thoroughly as did Paul Valéry, and his novels are a conscious, even self-conscious, mosaic whose stones send back echoes of other writers and references to works of art. His radicalism extends to the language he uses: not Sicilian dialect but an elaborate idiom that allows for no distinction between standard Italian and local Sicilian terminology. This lexis is not a venture into antiquarian purity, but an attempt to dispute the authority of centres of political power and linguistic acceptability, and to assert the dignity of the language used by people in places far removed from media, political, industrial, financial or linguistic authority. The result is a style, conventionally described as 'Baroque,' which can be in turns as hard as flint and as delicate as a blossom and which has been forged according to Consolo's own aesthetic canons. The objection is often made that there is a clash between his radical idealism in politics and an allegedly élitist complexity of style which means that his novels are accessible only to a learned minority. Consolo rebuts this, insisting that his aesthetics and linguistics move in tandem with his politics, in the sense that as writer he reasserts the dignity of peasant speech, while his characters assert their claim for dignity as human beings. Consolo's language has also been called 'Joycean,' and while it is true that he admires James Joyce, the comparison is misleading. Joyce cheerfully coined and created words that had never previously belonged to any lexis, but Consolo employs only terms that have some basis in historical use, even if they have not been accepted into national use.

There is, in other words, a convergence between linguistic and political radicalism in Consolo's writing, but his style presents difficulties for the mainland Italian, as well as for the translator. I would like to discuss these problems in relation to one of Consolo's novels, *Il sorriso dell'ignoto marinaio* (*The Smile of the Unknown Mariner*).[4] The title, in illustration of the points made above, is the name given to a well-known painting by the early Renaissance master, Antonello da Messina, which is now in the Sicilian city of Cefalù in a collection once the property of Baron Mandralisca, the protagonist of the novel. Some writers with little interest in translations of their work hand it over to the translator in the spirit of a motorist ignorant of mechanics taking his car into a garage for repair. However, in the case of this novelist, collaboration with the author is indispensable, and generously given. One small example might suffice to illustrate the difficulties with vocabulary. In a descriptive passage (Consolo, 1976: 119), the word *iracò* occurred. From the context, it was plainly some kind of plant, but no dictionary, either Italian or Sicilian, could indicate which one, and it was not known to other Sicilians I consulted. Consolo explained that it was a flower of the genus magnolia, now almost extinct, which he had once seen growing wild in the province of Trapani in eastern Sicily. The word itself was in use in the village of Màcari, whose population numbered perhaps 200, few of whom were likely to be readers of Consolo's works. There was no reason to believe the word had any wider circulation inside Sicily, and it was certainly not used on the far side of the Straits of Messina. Consolo had been enchanted by the word, not because of its rarity, but because of its sound, its cadence, its poetic quality. It enhanced the flow and rhythm of his own prose-poetry in the passage in question, and so he incorporated it. Meaning itself was not secondary, but his readers' awareness of that meaning was. The sentence flowed like a wave, breaking over individual words, whose potency came not from their sense or even their associations, but from their impact as part of a passage that sparkled. In spite of the unflinching questioning that underpins his fiction, Consolo creates delicate sound systems, which are not necessarily onomatopoeic. At the same time, he draws word pictures by references to known works of art: he uses, for example, the titles of Goya's series of etchings, *Desastres de la guerra*, to illustrate the devastation of the town of Alcàra li Fusi after the riots. He uses the brush as much as the pen, but since he does not identify the paintings in question, the translator has to avoid the temptation to reveal more than the writer chooses to.

The Use of Dialect

The question was how to convey in English the impact created by a distinctive style. Problems relating to words such as *iracò* can be taken as part of a wider discussion about the use of dialect, which is a recurring problem with Italian texts. The Renaissance playwright Ruzante, the 18th-century Venetian playwright Carlo Goldoni, many generations of Neapolitan writers as well as contemporary figures such as Dario Fo and Pier Paolo Pasolini all employ dialect. Some use it instinctively as the native, natural language used in the place where they were writing; others use it for deliberate effects. Several writers have asked that some equivalent dialect be found for translations of their work, but dialects have a different function and status in Italy from what they enjoy in other countries. Standard Italian only latterly achieved the primacy of place in Italy that the national language had long enjoyed in other European countries. It is acceptable to perform or write all over Italy in Neapolitan or Venetian, but to imagine that, for example, Scots or Irish could command comparable prestige in all English-speaking countries is a mistake. This is not to question the worth of doing translations into Scots, Irish or whatever for performance or publication in those countries, as Bill Findlay (to whose memory this volume is dedicated) did so splendidly with his Scots translations of the Quebecois-dialect works of Michel Tremblay, but we need to establish parameters for its use.

Yet if dialect is rejected, the task of transposition of all that is called style in Consolo, and others, is made daunting to the point of being virtually impossible. Is standard English capable of capturing the manifold nuances of meaning, the variety of social implications implied by vocabulary, the hierarchy of rank implied by choice of idiom, the synergy of word and position? Consolo's gilded prose also questions the nature of language, pointing to its role not a system of communication but as cypher of power. In his novel, Consolo aims to give voice to those who never had a voice – the peasantry – but the Baron who sides with them is aware that, precisely because of his position as an aristocrat, he can only ever speak for them, never as they speak. Consolo's style is totally idiosyncratic and is at one with his civic conscience. Cesarotti's decision to *rischiarare, rammorbidire, rettificare e talora di abbellire*, to recast in an idiom judged more acceptable is not an option for a modern translator, for whom the aim is to reproduce and not rewrite. Let us return to the passage that included the word *iracò*. The rebels who had risen against the old landowner class, and in favour of Garibaldi and the new Liberal order, had been put down brutally by the liberating army they thought they were supporting. While awaiting execution, they were imprisoned in a grim castle, which Consolo describes, casting the description as part of an appeal for clemency by Baron Mandralisca to a colleague in arms in the Risorgimento struggle, now promoted to the position of prosecutor. Mandralisca quotes Plautus, then continues:

> *E Virgilio ... Ma che dico? Di echi parlavamo. Ci tornavano indietro gonfiati anche le voci nostre, i bisbigli, i fiati, l'asma di Matafú, i risolini del Granza, i passi. Prendemmo a camminare in giro declinando. Sul pavimento a ciottoli impetrato ricoverti da scivoloso musco e da licheni, tra le pareti e la volta del cunicolo levigate a malta, jisso, a tratti come spalmate di madreperla pesta, pasta de vetro, vernice d'India o lacca, lustre,come porcellane della Cina, porpora in sulle labbra, sfumante in dentro verso il rosa e il latte, a tratti gonfie e scalcinate per penetrazioni d'acqua, che dalla volta gocciola a cannolicchi càlcichi, deturpate da muffe brune e verdi, fiori di salnitro e capelvenere a cascate dealle crepe: luogo di delizie origine, rifugio di frescura pel principe e la corte lungo i tre giorni infocati di scirocco, come le cascatelle della Zisa, i laghi e i ruscelli a Maredolce, i giardini intricati di bergamotti e palme, le spalle a stelle di jasmino, trombette di datura e ricci d'iracò, le cube e le cubale dei califfi musulmani, o come le fantasie contorte d'acque sonanti e di verzure, di pietre e di conchiglie dell'architetto Ligorio Pirro pel Cardinale D'Este.* (Consolo, 1976: 118–9)

[And Virgil ... but where was I? We were talking about the echoes. Our voices, whispers, breathing, Matafu's asthmatic wheeze, Granza Maniforti's sniggers, our footsteps, inflated beyond recognition, pursued us as we began to descend, following the circular path. We made our way down on cobblestones covered with layers of slippery moss and lichen, between tunnel walls and ceiling smoothed and shining with mortar or gesso, in some places seemingly coated with mother-of-pearl, crushed glass, Indian red paint or lacquer, with purple edgings shading into milk-white and pink tints in the inner sections, and all as bright as Chinese porcelain; in others, bulging and peeling with water dripping from the vaults to form calcified razor clams, tarnished by brown and green mildew or by saltpetre and maidenhair fern tumbling from the numerous cracks. A place of prime delights, a refuge of refreshment for the prince and the court during the three days of scorching scirocco, like the flowing waters of the Zisa, the lakes and streams of Maredolce, the gardens planted with bergamots and palm trees, the espaliers with jasmine stars, datura trumpets and magnolia curls, the kiosks and cubical pavilions of the Muslim caliphs; or like the wayward fantasies of gurgling waters and lush greenery, the riot of stones and shells devised by the architect Ligorio Pirro for Cardinal D'Este. (Farrell, 1994: 105–6)]

Consolo stretches syntax beyond the point of tolerance. The cardinal sin in any translation of a prose-poetic style such as Consolo's is to lose the melody, the music, the cadences, the rhythm, or alternatively the dryness, the anger, the despair. The central aim must be to release the energy, to hint at that underlying magic that defies analysis and to avoid flattening a style that has the quality of song. The distaff side of that aim is to ensure that phoney lyricism must not be written into the asperity of a style designed to convey brutality, inhumanity and savagery. The translator's obligations must include regard for style. Not to allow the distinctive voice to be heard is to accept failure.

Notes

1. Ossian (1807–1810). All references are to this edition.
2. For a wider treatment of Macpherson, and refutation of notions that his *Ossian* was a vulgar fraud, see F. Stafford (1988) and H. Gaskill (ed.) (1991).
3. 'We are besieged by total communication. I believe that the way to rediscover a new literary space is to bring narrative prose closer to poetic form, and I mean form and not substance, to give it a certain poetic dignity, to make it less consumable. While I am non-religious, it is my belief that it is important to endow prose with a more sacred, less commercial aura.' (author's own translation)
4. I must crave indulgence if I base this part of the article on my experiences in translating this novel. The quotations I provide are offered not as proof of success in meeting the stylistic challenges discussed here, but as an empirical example of the difficulty.

References

Aciman, A. (2005a) Proust's way? *New York Review of Books*, 1 December, pp. 62–5.
Aciman, A. (2005b) Far from Proust's way. *New York Review of Books*, 15 December, pp. 74-5.
Belitt, B. (1978) *Adam's Dream: A Preface to Translation*. New York: Grove Press.
Cederna, C.M. (1993) Entretien avec Vincenzo Consolo. *Critique* XLIV, part 553/4.
Consolo V. (1976) *Il sorriso dell'ignoto marinaio*. Turin: Einaudi.
Farrell, J. (trans.) (1994) *The Smile of the Unknown Mariner*. Manchester: Carcanet.
Gaskill. H. (ed.) (1991) *Ossian Revisited*. Edinburgh: Edinburgh University Press.
MacPherson, J. (1971) *The Poems of Ossian*. Introduced by J. MacQueen. Edinburgh: James Thin.
Ossian, (1807–10) *Poesie di Ossian antico poeta celtico tradotte da Melchiorre Cesarotti* (4 volumes). Florence: Molini, Landi e Comp.
Pope, A. (1996) Preface to *The Iliad of Homer*. London: Penguin Books.
Reid, A. (1994) *An Alistair Reid Reader: Selected Prose and Poetry*. Hanover, NH: University Press of New England.
Stafford, F. (1988) *The Sublime Savage*. Edinburgh: Edinburgh University Press.
Weissbort, D. and Eysteinsson, A. (eds) (2006) *Translation: Theory and Practice*. Oxford: Oxford University Press.

Chapter 6
Chekhov in the Theatre: The Role of the Translator in New Versions

HELEN RAPPAPORT

Introduction

Over the last 30 or more years, the English stage has provided fertile ground for a burgeoning theatrical phenomenon: the new version or adaptation of a foreign-language play by a contemporary playwright. Undoubtedly one of the most popular foreign playwrights with British audiences is Anton Chekhov. Theatregoers never tire of him, even now, almost 100 years after his death and seem always ready to accommodate yet another new production of what is, in essence, a very slim opus. Much of this is probably down to the fact that he shares with Shakespeare that rare quality of being what David Hare (2001: 5) called 'the ultimate universalist'; he is able to convey life in all its layered complexities and, in so doing, seem relevant to every age, every generation.

Since the autumn of 2001 there have been several major Chekhov revivals in London alone – *Platonov* at the Almeida, *Ivanov* at the National Theatre, *Uncle Vanya* at the Donmar Warehouse and *Three Sisters*, the West End production of which, starring the film actress Kristin Scott Thomas, was closely followed by yet another new version at the National Theatre in August 2003. This is not to mention other regional Chekhov productions in 2003, such as the Oxford Stage Company's tour of *The Cherry Orchard* and Peter Stein's production of *The Seagull* at the Edinburgh Festival (the latter using, to the surprise of many critics, Constance Garnett's 1920s translation) which ran concurrently with a *Seagull* production at Chichester, in yet another new version, this one by Phyllis Nagy. And in the spring of 2006 there was yet another *Seagull*: the National Theatre staged a new version by Martin Crimp.

In an interview in 2002, prior to the opening at the National Theatre of his own mammoth 'Russian' trilogy, *The Coast of Utopia*, dramatist Tom Stoppard observed that everyone wants to write a Chekhov play. Failing this, if playwrights cannot write one, then many aspire to at least adapt one. Indeed, one might say it is now the theatrical norm for any playwrights worth their salt sooner or later to offer their own take, not just on one of the four great plays, but even on those that Chekhov considered failures. The fashion, of course, is not confined solely to Chekhov, but has long since spread to other major European playwrights, whose work is similarly being revisited. In many ways, one might argue that this is a very good development: that the advent of new versions of the work of obscure or long-forgotten European playwrights is extremely valuable – for it brings to the attention of the theatre-going public a range of foreign-language plays that they might otherwise never see.

John Arden was one of the first to set the trend way back in 1963 with his version of Goethe's *Götz von Berlichingen* as *Ironhand*. Christopher Hampton, a fine adaptor of Chekhov, has, since the 1970s, become well known also for his new versions of Molière and Ibsen and for resurrecting the work of the forgotten Austrian playwright Ödön von Horváth. Yet even his own long-standing version of the latter's *Tales from the Vienna Woods* has now been superseded by a new version for the National by a new kid on the block, the up-and-coming Scottish playwright, David Harrower.

Like Hampton, Tom Stoppard similarly reinvented the work of *Mittel Europeans*, such as the Austrian Johann Nestroy and the Hungarian Ferenc Molnár. Peter Tinniswood has tackled the Italian of Eduardo de Filippo; Lee Hall and Ranjit Bolt have reworked Brecht and Goldoni; Frank McGuinness, as well as working on new versions of Chekhov, has adapted Ibsen and Brecht; and Nick Wright, another playwright-adaptor who with *Three Sisters* at the National in August 2003 had his first Chekhov, has given us new versions of Wedekind's *Lulu*, as well as works by Pirandello and Ibsen. Even the novelist Anthony Burgess turned his hand to new versions of old theatrical classics – Rostand's *Cyrano de Bergerac* and an inventive English version of Griboedov's *Woe from Wit* under the title *Chatsky*. For an interesting overview of such versions, but one which fails, sadly, to discuss the role of the literal translator at all, see Rosenthal (2001). Another veteran playwright adaptor of both Chekov and Ibsen is Pam Gems who, in the spring of 2003 provided the newly refurbished Almeida Theatre in London with a new version: *The Lady from the Sea*. In all cases, however, I use the word 'version' advisedly. Because that is not, of course, what the press announcements say. Almost without exception, when trumpeting the arrival of a new version of a foreign play, they will talk of the playwright-adaptor's 'new translation'.

The Advent of a New Theatrical Genre

The vogue for new versions of foreign plays can be traced back to the innovative work of London's Royal Court Theatre in the late 1960s, at a time when the British subsidised theatre first began receiving funding from the Arts Council to enable the commissioning of new work. Prior to that, the commercial theatre had adhered to the traditional 'bums-on-seats' policy with regard to foreign-language works, rarely staging anything more than the occasional Chekhov or Ibsen play, and usually as a star vehicle for big-name actors. From the 1930s to the early 1960s, revivals of the four late great Chekhov plays, in standard, off-the-shelf translations, had been the preserve of that great British triumvirate John Gielgud, Laurence Olivier and Michael Redgrave. Gielgud was actor/director of *The Seagull* in 1936, *Three Sisters* in 1937, and *The Cherry Orchard* in 1961; Olivier staged *Uncle Vanya* during the 1944–5 season at the Old Vic and toured with *Three Sisters* in 1967, and Redgrave appeared in a memorable Chichester Festival/Old Vic production of *Uncle Vanya* in 1962.

A change in direction, and in casting, came with the revival in 1960 of Chekhov's huge, rambling early play *Platonov* at the Royal Court, starring Rex Harrison, an actor largely known for his film roles. Five years later, *Ivanov*, starring Gielgud, had its first major London revival (although it had been seen at the much smaller Arts Theatre in 1950 starring Michael Hordern) and transferred to Broadway a year later. The Gielgud version was one of the first of what would be a new wave of adaptations, the text being accredited to Gielgud, 'from a translation by Ariadne Nicolaeff'. In 1967 new ground was again broken with an adaptation of *Three Sisters* by the then highly fashionable Edward Bond, 'assisted from the original Russian' as the title page states, 'by Richard Cottrell', director of the Cambridge Arts Theatre and himself a Russian-speaker (Bond, 1967). This was also the first Chekhov production to cast a non-actor and pop star – Marianne Faithfull – in a lead role.

From here on, a distinct shift in new Chekhov productions began, with the move from actor-vehicle to playwright-vehicle becoming more and more the fashion. The old guard of reverential literary translators such as Constance Garnett, Elisaveta Fen and David Magarshack would be rapidly superseded by a new generation of non-Russian-speaking playwrights working from literal translations, whose major preoccupation would be the accessibility of new 'acting versions' of Chekhov's texts. The primary argument in favour of this new approach, as well as in the rejection of the old, more academic texts, was that academic practitioners were deemed unable to translate for stage performance because they lacked the essential knowledge of stagecraft and the experience of working with actors.

Bond's *Three Sisters* was rapidly followed, at the Royal Court in 1970, by Christopher Hampton's version of *Uncle Vanya*, from a translation by Nina Froude. After this, there was something of a hiatus until 1977, when a new benchmark for Chekhov adaptation was set, with Trevor Griffiths's Marxist take on *The Cherry Orchard*. This opened the floodgates to many more new versions of Chekhov plays by British and Irish playwrights, including Pam Gems, Michael Frayn, Peter Gill, Tom Stoppard, Brian Friel, David Hare,

David Lan, Frank McGuinness, Thomas Kilroy, Ann Jellicoe, Howard Barker, Mustafa Matura and, most recently, David Harrower and Martin Crimp. And this is not to mention those translating and adapting Chekhov in the USA, such as David Mamet, Paul Schmidt, Langford Wilson, Jean-Claude van Itallie and George Calderon, as well as the arrival of cinematic regionalisations, if not transpositions to another country altogether, with *Uncle Vanya* alone being reworked in film versions set in New York by David Mamet in *Vanya on 42nd Street* (1994), in Wales by Anthony Hopkins in *August* (1996), and even in the Australian outback, in Michael Blakemore's *Country Life* (1994).

The Role of the Literal Translator

My own, somewhat unexpected, entry into theatre translation came in 1977 as literal translator of *The Cherry Orchard* for Trevor Griffiths's version at Nottingham Playhouse. It was something I fell into quite by accident. At the time, I was working intermittently as an actress, having studied Russian at Leeds University. A call to an audition at Granada Television for a TV series *Bill Brand*, written by Griffiths, had led to a meeting with him and a conversation about my passion for things Russian. I got a small part in the series but, more important, weeks later, Trevor Griffiths, who lived half a mile away from me in Leeds, rang me up and asked if I'd be interested in doing a literal translation of *The Cherry Orchard* for him. It proved to be the first of twelve translations of Russian plays that I have worked on, including revisits to both *The Cherry Orchard* and *Three Sisters*, albeit many years apart.

Having worked closely with the director, when I was asked to translate the play again for a National Theatre production, in a version by David Lan, in 2000, my first thought was that there was little more linguistically that I could usefully add. On reflection, it occurred to me that maybe the accumulated wisdom of another 15 years' acquaintance with Russian might make a difference. And I was right, for, as soon as I started working on the text, I was surprised at how many new things I found, particularly when prompted by the analytical minds and detailed questioning of David Lan and director Katie Mitchell. Mitchell, of all the playwrights and directors I have worked with, has an extraordinary, some might say worrying – I'd say noble – concern with textual analysis and getting at the truth. It takes even the most jaded translator of what seems an over-familiar text down new and untrodden paths.

People often talk about the concept of the 'actor's director'; Katie Mitchell is probably the translator's director *par excellence*. She places an enormous trust – as well as huge expectation – in the role that the literal translator can play in the creation of a new version of a Chekhov text. In my own work with her on three Chekhov plays, she has been generous in according me much more than the title of 'literal translator', a somewhat belittling tag that many translators who do the work reject. If only the theatre managements would stop insisting on using it!

Whenever I have worked with Katie Mitchell, she has always credited me as dramaturg cum Russian consultant and draws exhaustively on my specialist knowledge of things Russian, not just during the preparation of the text but also throughout rehearsals. Some directors and even playwrights can, in my experience, have a somewhat cavalier attitude to the literal translation. For them, the translator's role ends as soon as the text is delivered, often with virtually no questions or feedback being sent to the translator thereafter. In so doing, they can be completely blind if not insensitive to the useful role that the translator can play, not just during the ensuing translation/adaptation process, but also beyond that, in discussion with the actors.

A few directors, such as Mitchell, have grasped the crucial role that the translator can play as the all-essential conduit between the original-language text and the actors who perform it. My first experience of working with her in 1998 on *Uncle Vanya* opened up a whole new world of what one might call 'forensic' translation. We spent many happy but intense hours together, and later with David Lan, on a detailed analysis of the text and what we came to call its crucial 'buzz words'. Katie Mitchell's many questions prompted me to draw up copious contextual notes, not just on the language, but also on the historical, literary and social background to the play – notes that she, David and the actors found invaluable in rehearsal and which, to my own gratification, prompted discussion that afforded all of us moments of profound insight. More important, from a linguistic point of view, a more in-depth analysis of the nuances of meaning of Russian words, idioms and phrases led in many cases to the preservation in the final version of the original *literal* meaning of the text.

Trevor Griffiths had astutely picked up on this back in 1977 when, to cite a very simple example, rather than go for the until-then-accepted translation of the endearing Russian word *ogurchik* ('my little cucumber') as 'my little peach' – on the grounds that English audiences would find this peculiar – he opted to preserve the original. More recently, a critic reviewing Mitchell's production of *Uncle Vanya* commented on David Lan's rendering of Constance Garnett's original translation of '25 wasted years' of the Russian *'dvadtsat' pyat' let perelivaet is pustogo v porozhnee'* as '25 years pouring water from one empty bucket into another' as being inspirational. But in fact, the metaphor was Chekhov's ('25 years pouring from one empty thing into an emptier one'), and the playwright's final version of this was directly facilitated by the literal translation.

In my experience, good playwrights and directors of new versions are often delighted by the wit, quirkiness and natural charm of the original Russian, qualities to which as non-Russian speakers they had previously been oblivious, thanks to decades of over-papering by translators of the original, vibrant Russian idioms with lacklustre English equivalents. Such playwrights and directors are usually also receptive to the translator's defence of the integrity of the original text, even if they do not ultimately take on board their objections to what seem rather-too-free renderings of it. But whilst dedicated theatregoers might be able to recognise liberties being taken with a long-familiar classic play, they will not be aware to what extent a new version of an obscure or forgotten foreign playwright is the exaggeration or even invention of the adaptor.

The playwright approaching a new version of a foreign-language play is bedevilled by many conflicts, not the least of which are maintaining a degree of linguistic loyalty to the original text and honouring the original playwright's intentions, whilst making the text accessible to the actors. But, more important, they must constantly resist the injection into the script of their own personal bias and linguistic tics. Writing in the *Sunday Times* about his own production for the Oxford Stage Company of a new version of *The Cherry Orchard* by Sam Adamson, Dominic Dromgoole (2003: 22) argued that 'you have to bring yourself, and your own time and your own language, halfway towards [the original]. And you have to make sure you don't impose any pattern, social or political or aesthetic, on an independent life that only wants to stay free'.

In an illuminating introduction to his new version of *The Seagull*, commissioned by Peter Hall for the Old Vic in 1997, Tom Stoppard touched upon the difficulties of adaptation, and of grappling with what he called the 'ledger principle' of adaptation–the need to scrupulously account for every linguistic nuance, word by word, line by line (Stoppard, 1997: vi). Arguing that the main purpose of the playwright's craft in this instance is to serve the actors, he stressed that ultimately the playwright had to work 'for the event', that is the performance, at the risk of sacrificing elements of linguistic authenticity. His aim had been, he explained, to 'liberate' the text 'without taking undue liberties' (1997: vi). In similar vein, in the introduction to his 1977 version of *The Cherry Orchard,* Trevor Griffiths made the point that his primary objective had also been 'to prepare a version of the play for *performance*'; it was 'not, finally, the *literary* tradition' that he intended to act upon, 'but the theatrical' (Griffiths, 1978: v).

A particularly complex challenge is presented by Chekhov's *Platonov* – 'six hours of sometimes repetitive and ludicrously overwritten speechifying', as David Hare described it, that he, in the process of adapting, nevertheless found full of 'thrilling sunbursts of youthful anger and romanticism' (Hare, 2001). Hare's was the second most recent reworking of Chekhov's deeply problematic play, which had previously been adapted in a new version, *Wild Honey,* by Michael Frayn in 1984. Frayn, who is the only Chekhov adaptor who is also a Russian-speaker, openly admitted that, for his version, he had cut out many sub plots and minor characters and reorganised the chronological sequence; he even went so far as to change the suicide at the end. David Hare, for whom I provided the literal translation for the 2001 production, was more rigorous in retaining Chekhov's original structure and plan, his objective being to 'recoin and rebalance' the play, as he put it, by 'clearing away massive amounts of repetition and indulgence' rather than implementing a more drastic reworking. In so doing he hoped that his new English version would still reveal to the audience a young, unrestrained Chekhov who 'lets his own passion, emotional confusion and political despair show uncensored and unmediated' (Hare, 2001).

Surprisingly perhaps, it is often not the freer linguistic versions of Chekhov's original Russian text that provoke objections in the translator; indeed, some of the best versions I have worked on are those that capture the *spirit and atmosphere*, the 'dramatic core' as fellow translator David Johnston has put it, of the original whilst being fairly free. It is the *truth* of Chekhov that matters, and where adaptation becomes dangerous and erroneous is where assumptions are made about Chekhov's personal point of view, and where the historical or social context is distorted to the point of no longer being 'Russian'.

Trevor Griffiths' version of *The Cherry Orchard* was a bold attempt at unshackling the play from the deadening English theatrical tradition of nostalgia, the hallmark of which Jonathan Miller once described as the 'Keats Grove, genteel, well-mannered' style of acting. Griffiths's intention was clear: to do away with the tired old standard approach that had set Chekhov productions in stone in the British theatre – what he called 'the fine regretful weeping of the privileged fallen on hard times'. For 50 years Chekhov had, Griffiths (1978: v) argued, been 'the almost exclusive property of theatrical class secretaries for whom the plays have been plangent and sorrowing evocations of an "ordered" past no longer with "us", its passing greatly to be mourned'.

Eschewing what he called the 'sentimental morality' of such all-too-familiar versions, Griffiths cut to the jugular in his own version by refashioning the student Trofimov in his own image, as a clear-headed Marxist, with overt, revolutionary intentions, who lambastes the tsarist oppression of the poor by famously describing the urban masses as living in 'shit'. The original Russian word is, of course, typically Chekhovian in its neutrality. Trofimov, talking of the overcrowding in urban tenements, says– and this is as literal as I can make it – 'everywhere bedbugs, a (bad) smell, damp, moral uncleanliness'. In Elisaveta Fen's (1954: 364) version for Penguin, this is translated as 'bedbugs, bad smells, damp and immorality everywhere'. In Griffiths' version, we leap to 'bedbugs, shit, leaking roofs, moral degradation'. It may only be a single word, but it's a word that expresses *Griffiths's rage* rather than *Chekhov's point of view*. Its ring is as hollow, as also, in the production was the Marxist-cum-black-power salute given by Trofimov at the end of another pedagogic speech in Act 2. This new and more dynamic Trofimov certainly lent an edgy, political dimension to Griffiths' version of the play, but one can't help agreeing with critic Michael Billington, that for all its power, Griffiths's text was offering us a 'cunningly editorialised version' of the original (Billington, 1984: 15).

The danger, as Billington so rightly observed, was that whilst the Griffiths *Cherry Orchard* was a highly intelligent and playable translation, it perhaps offered rather too much hindsight in its more overt suggestions of political change in the air. Griffiths's view, however, was that by strengthening the roles of the 'new men' (that is Trofimov and Lopakhin) and moving the emphasis away from Ranevskaya, he had 'shifted the forces of the play and re-ordered its inherent balances' (Griffiths, 1978: vi). Such an interpretation, based on a reading of *The Cherry Orchard* as demonstrating Chekhov's faith in progress, is in fact a very Soviet one. And it is one that kept Soviet academics occupied for many years, as they struggled to offer up communist readings of an unrepentantly apolitical playwright. Throughout the 73 years of Soviet rule, productions in Russia strived to overcome the obstacle of what Chekhov himself called his 'indifferentism' (Frayn, 1996: xvii) and present his plays as the clarion call of revolution. But this is to deny one of the fundamentals of Chekhov's art: his insistence that the author must be an *impartial witness* – nothing more (Frayn, 1996: xx).

The 2002 production by Sam Mendes at the Donmar Warehouse of Brian Friel's version of *Uncle Vanya* presented a particularly vexed problem for me, as Russian consultant. In places it was utterly inspired in its distillation of the spirit of the original and in some of its more imaginative reworkings of idiom. But it was also very free with the original text, and, more troublingly, in places it totally ignored historical accuracy. I wondered, when I opened the programme on the first night and saw its title page cheekily announce that I was about to see '*Uncle Vanya* by Brian Friel, a version of the play by Chekhov', whether I was the only person to be more than a little taken aback by Friel's chutzpah. *Guardian* critic Michael Billington's review of the production, which he praised for its 'visual clarity and emotional charity' was quickly tempered by the observation that the production was nevertheless 'more a Friel-isation than a faithful realisation' (Billington, 2002: 20). And indeed, as one reads through the text, despite being impressed with Friel's undoubted flair as adaptor-playwright, his use of artistic licence results in a wholesale reworking of Telegin's character.

What also alarmed me was to find in Act 4, where Vanya and Sonya sit down to itemise their expenditure on staple Russian commodities such as lenten oil and buckwheat flour, that Friel's version had transformed this into a discussion about the purchase of barbed wire and fencing posts. In 19th-century, rural Russia? It was as though the Voinitsky estate had suddenly been picked up by a whirlwind and plopped down in the American Midwest. It is utterly absurd to talk of land being fenced off with barbed wire and posts in the black earth region of 19th-century Russia. Vanya does not manage a cattle ranch; and in any case, he is far too impoverished to be able to afford expensive barbed wire, imported from the USA, or luxuries such as ready-made fencing posts. Such a cavalier reworking of the original text was anachronistic at best and ill-informed at worst.

New Versions: Whose Work is it Anyway?

In the event, despite the objections I raised to this as well as several other points, director Sam Mendes decided to stay with the fencing posts and barbed wire. The production, although it wasn't quite Chekhov, was heaped with praise, although Billington was not the only critic to raise doubts about the very free hand Friel had taken with the original. Billington has in fact been monitoring new versions since the early 1980s with some interest and was one of the first critics to express his apprehensions about the rise of the 'star dramatist' who saw it as his function to leave his or her 'unmistakable signature' (Billington, 1984) all over the work of a foreign playwright that they were adapting. This new trend, has of course been working very much against *literary* translators, who constantly have to battle for theatre managements to stage their own translations of plays without the intervention of a big-name playwright. But all these new versions, as they get freer, distance us ever more from the original. No one now would want to go back to the kind of reverential but stilted scholarly translations of Chekhov first produced by Constance Garnett or Elisaveta Fen, but in the rush to reinterpret Chekhov's – or any other foreign playwright's work – in new and exciting ways – are we perhaps losing sight, line by line, year by year, of the true spirit of the original plays? As Brian Logan (2003) recently observed: 'The cult ... seems as skewed against faithful translation as the academics' monopoly was against drama. ... Audiences ... are being insulated from the original'. So, when a new production of a Chekhov play by Brian Friel, or Christopher Hampton or Tom Stoppard is announced, whose work are audiences really paying to see – the original playwright's or that of his adaptor? And are we rapidly coming to the point where new versions are commissioned just for the sake of it, when there are often more than enough good translations or versions already in existence? With so many new versions of foreign-language plays now appearing in the British theatre, critics, understandably enough, have become increasingly lazy, by blurring the margins between the original playwright, the mediator-translator and the playwright-adaptor. To talk of so and so's 'new translation' has now become an accepted shorthand among critics for what is in fact 'so and so's adaptation of a literal translation of the play by X'. Whilst it is one thing to marginalise the translator, is it right that the dead playwright who wrote the original should be marginalised too?

The Disappearing Translator

Looking through old press cuttings, programmes and published play texts, it is possible to chart the appearance, disappearance and all too occasional re-emergence of the name of the literal translator in press reviews and theatre programmes. The only conclusion one comes to is that the practice is an entirely arbitrary one, dependent on the goodwill of the particular theatre, director and playwright involved in each production. After 25 years and 12 translations, it is hard for me not to feel cynical and discouraged about the position of the much-underrated literal translator. It still galls me to open the paper, as I did in July 2002 on the opening of *Ivanov* at the National, for which I provided the translation, to read leading *Times* theatre critic Benedict Nightingale state (2002: 14): 'Who is translating Katie Mitchell's revival of Chekhov's early *Ivanov*, now in preview at the National? Why, David Harrower, the Scots author of *Knives and Hens'*. Harrower knows not a word of Russian. And whilst one might forgive theatregoers for being oblivious to the contribution translators make, why is it that the British critics so steadfastly refuse to acknowledge them? It has been my own sobering experience that, whilst critics might occasionally stop and question the occasional linguistic liberty taken with the text in new versions, when they *do* find some turn of phrase particularly arresting it never seems to enter their heads that the translator might have played some part in helping the author of the new version arrive at this.

We have now arrived at a point where the vast majority of critics view translation as being synonymous with adaptation, so much so that Benedict Nightingale, writing in the summer of 2002 about the Chekhov productions then running, talked of playwrights working on foreign texts 'with the aid of cribs' (Nightingale, 2002: 14), a less-than-generous attitude to the work of the literal translator. Of course, the irony is that Nightingale has a valid point. All the playwrights I have worked with have certainly admitted to drafting their versions from my literal translation, in consultation with up to half a dozen other published translations. Of our contemporary playwrights, only Russian-speaker Michael Frayn can translate without resort to a literal version. And he has very strong views: 'Translating's hard enough if you can understand the original. Trying to do it from someone else's literal translation would be like performing brain surgery wearing thick gloves'.

Such considerations have prompted David Lan to observe that translations of plays are 'like forgeries. All the time they're made', he argued, 'there's a chance they'll persuade their audience that they're the genuine article' (Lan, 1998: vii). Back in 1984 Billington had talked similarly of this trend as 'the parasitic practice of pseudo-translation in which a dramatist second-guesses what the original said.' He appealed for theatregoers to 'put more faith in the linguist-translator and a bit less in the name-dramatist' (Billington, 1984: 15). The RSC's 2003 staging of Ibsen's *Brand*, in a translation by the highly respected translator Michael Meyer, marks a renewal of interest in the work of the dedicated professional translator rather than the fashionable playwright.

The Deceptive Simplicity of Chekhov

Few playwrights have had to sustain such persistent and repeated assaults on their work as Anton Chekhov. But in the end, of course, no matter how many texts playwright-adaptors have at their disposal to draw on, Chekhov will always elude them. It is easy to be beguiled by his deceptively uncluttered and simple language; to seek ideology where it is not to be found; to intellectualise where the original is spare and elliptical and the language neutral. What Michael Frayn (1996) has described as Chekhov's 'transparency' might seem a gift to the modern adaptor, but it can also be his undoing. For in Chekhov's subtlety and his scrupulous objectivity lies his greatness; to mess with these fundamental qualities quickly distorts, and shifts the very delicate balances that preserve the equilibrium of his beautifully measured plays.

Benedict Nightingale (2002: 14) has described Chekhov's gift as being the ability to write about ordinary human lives 'with a sort of epic intimacy'. And perhaps this is why he will continue to defy any definitive translation. As Stoppard (1997: v) observed, in apologising for offering the world yet another version of *The Seagull*, 'You can't have too many English *Seagulls*: at the intersection of all of them, the Russian one will be forever elusive'.

References

Billington, M. (1984) Villains of the piece. *Guardian*, 9 November.
Billington, M. (2002) Uncle Vanya: Sam Mendes excels with Chekhov. *Guardian*, 19 September.
Bond, E. (1967) Anton Chekhov: Three Sisters. A new version by Edward Bond. Assisted from the original Russian by Richard Cottrell. Royal Court programme and script.
Dromgoole, D. (2003) Trapped by translation. *Sunday Times*, 25 May.
Fen, E. (trans.) (1954) *Anton Chekhov: Plays*. London: Penguin.
Frayn, M. (1996) *Anton Chekhov: Plays*. London: Methuen.

Griffiths, T. (trans.) (1978) *Anton Chekov: The Cherry Orchard. A New English Version by Trevor Griffiths from a Translation by Helen Rappaport.* London: Pluto,
Hare, D. (2001) Chekhov's wild, wild youth. *Observer,* 2 September.
Lan, D. (1998) *Anton Chekhov: Uncle Vanya. A New Version by David Lan from a Literal Translation by Helen Rappaport.* London: Methuen.
Logan, B. (2003) Whose play is it anyway? *Guardian,* 12 March.
Nightingale, B. (2002) Pieces of his action. *The Times,* 9 September.
Rosenthal, D. (2001) Pardon my French. *The Times,* 2 October.
Stoppard, T. (1997) *Anton Chekhov: The Seagull. A New Version by Tom Stoppard.* London: Faber and Faber.

Chapter 7
The Cultural Engagements of Stage Translation: Federico García Lorca in Performance

DAVID JOHNSTON

Introduction

Since 1986 the plays of García Lorca have been performed in English with increasing regularity.[1] But while Lorca's work, or some of it at least, has effectively entered the British and American theatrical canon, there is still a sense that Lorca on stage can be problematic, that underlying all that human passion and stage energy there linger, respectively, the parallel difficulties of a residual cultural opacity and an embarrassing level of melodrama in performance. A number of theatre practitioners have spoken of such difficulties – indeed, Lorca himself had already referred to what he viewed as the untranslatable essence of his theatre (see, for example, Clifford, 1996).[2] Central to the author's perception of his own untranslatability was undoubtedly his awareness that the dramatic actions and stage language of his plays are vivified – that is, made real in terms of audience experience – through what Chomsky would describe as an encyclopaedia of extralinguistic reference, in the case of Lorca one of unusual intensity and coherence – 'a grammar of images', in Stephen Spender's phrase (see Binding, 1985: 51). Routinely, of course, this grammar, this encyclopaedia, is reduced on stage to the simple adjectival appeal of an Andalusian tourist guide, as directors maraud into the idiom and style of flamenco in order to plunder there something of the exotic otherness that they perceive at the heart of Lorca's work.[3] In many ways, this constitutes in itself an act of translation, this time into an English-language theatre culture, of a perception, still widespread even in Spain, that there is a folksy element to Lorca, that his work is rooted in and reflects a popular tradition that is somehow timelessly and quintessentially Spanish (see, for instance, Round, 1997).

Any resistance to translation that characterises Lorca's theatre, however, derives more from the way in which he attempts to negotiate his plays into, and then beyond, the horizon of expectations of his audience, than from any simple rootedness in a specific tradition or unchanging culture. Jauss's crucial notion of the 'horizon of expectations' has always seemed to me to mark the point where translation theory coincides with theories of reception (see, especially, Pavis, 1992: 142). The complicity upon which Lorca's plays depend for their impact is carefully crafted by a writer who was also acknowledged as a great director (for example, in José Monleón's Introduction in his 1971 Spanish-language edition of *Bodas de sangre*, he draws upon the testimony of theatre practitioners who worked with Lorca). Lorca's plays invite their audiences to imagine alternatives to the social and moral codes of the day, an act of imaginative collaboration that may be enabled only through the construction of a stage world that shifts across the terrain of the known, the recognisable, into the challenging realm of the unfamiliar or the taboo. His frequently-quoted view of theatre as 'a school for laughter and tears, an open forum where we can put old or misguided moralities to the test and embody in living examples the eternal truths of the human heart' is based on three central but interconnected notions of dramaturgy.[4] First, there is the idea that the theatre can, and should, re-orientate the spectator towards what he considered to be the most precious fulfilment of our being, the instinctual life. Second, theatre has a central role in the debate between traditionalism and the modern then raging in Spain. Lorca was writing at a time when Spain was slowly emerging from the cocoon that was self-imposed in the wake of the disastrous war against the USA in 1898, a time when the paramount axis of national division – the internal colonisation frequently represented in abbreviated form as the 'Two Spains' – was coalescing increasingly around the characteristics of Marxist ideological conflict. Old historical certainties and dominant cultural modes were being increasingly challenged as new ideas swept in from abroad, and throughout his work Lorca implicitly interrogates the meaning of Spanishness, examining how ingrained codes of behaviour and sets of assumptions shape the contours of an imprisoning identity.

The third element of Lorca's dramaturgy – the idea of 'putting to the test'- is the one that connects most completely with performance. For Lorca, performance is a crucible – people often refer to the 'pressure-cooker' or 'hothouse' feel of his theatre, in terms both of the characteristic entrapment of its protagonists and of the emotional complicity that this entrapment is designed to excite in its spectators. In this sense, performance is the key to an impact that derives from emotional response, an impact whose goal is to extend and deepen the spectator's experience of sources of personal and societal repression. Lorca's view of theatre as 'poetry that stands up from the page and becomes human and, in doing so, it talks and it cries and it weeps and it despairs' works within this concept, because it is through such emotionally-charged language that theatre may make what is invisible or repressed in society visible on stage.[5] It is the marked contrast between this poetry and the flintier, hard-edged speeches that speak of self-control and conformism that forms the central axis of the language universe of Lorca's theatre. Only if the translator is able to re-create meaningfully and coherently the system of culture-specific references within the framework of the linguistic tensions that inhabit this universe will he or she be able to re-create in turn the complicity that Lorca sought for his plays in performance. Much attention has been paid to the need to get these culture-specific references 'right', but in the final analysis, if Lorca's plays are to retain their full impact on stage in English, then translators for performance must translate the plays' potential for performance (see for example, Edwards, 1998). For, in the case of García Lorca, that potential is the lynchpin of his thinking as an artist who believed that theatre – and most particularly tragedy – had its own particular contribution to make to social dynamics.

For as Lorca meditated, as all significant playwrights do, upon the nature of audience complicity, he developed through his practice a performance theory, at the heart of which lies the performance of emotion, of what Seamus Heaney called the human 'non-codified'. In similar terms, Paul Valéry, a poet much admired by Lorca, insists on the inescapable commitment of poetry, whose images *'ne parlent jamais que de choses absentes'*, to the negation of our most ingrained codes. This is exactly what Lorca's richly imagistic drama achieves. It disrupts the established discourse of behaviourism with forceful expressions of the intimate self, of the right to be, beyond the imperatives of both Church and group. The real artistic achievement of Lorca's theatre is the speaking of what Marcuse was to call 30 years later a 'non-reified' language, a way of communicating the intimate denied as an absence both deeply felt in the individual life and the defining reality of a public space delimited by the spirit of conservatism and negation (cf. Johnston, 1999).[6] Writing at a time of increasing social and political polarisation, Lorca's theatre becomes a site of cultural resistance to simplistic politics, with its accompanying social weapon of crude opprobrium.

Writing from the Margins

Importantly, Lorca's is a gaze from the margins. As a gay writer, he obliges his audiences to undertake a journey into the recognition and acceptance of alternative or denied expressions of sexuality, both as a taboo area of public life and as a metaphorical way of apprehending the wider frustrations and limitations of the socio-political realm. In his plays, accordingly, Lorca disrupts the linguistic no less than the cultural codes of Spanish, exciting cultural exogamy in his dramatisation of recognisable forms and modes of the hostile otherness that he himself experienced in his life both as an individual and as a cultural figure (cf. Gibson, 1989).[7]

In *Art and Agency: An Anthropological Theory*, Alfred Gell (1998: 97) notes that 'works of art, images, icons and the like have to be treated, in the context of an anthropological theory, as person-like; that is sources of and targets for social agency'. If this observation is to be useful to the translator, it is as confirmation of the recognition that translators are concerned with the context of a piece of writing, its explanatory background, as well as its interior. Translators of plays for performance work depend more on a sense of linguistic anthropology, with its crucial sense of the cultural embeddedness of language, its rootedness in historical process, than on the exegesis of new critical formalism. It is at this point that the performance translator's analysis of the source text (ST) differs most sharply from that of the linguist, who moves inwards into the text, examining its 'interanimation of words' – in Richards' phrase – as the defining feature of an unchanging literary status (for contemporary analyses of Richards's views on translation, see Johnston, 2004: 1–14). But, in theatre, it is important to remember that such interanimation occurs most completely not on the page, but in the air between stage and auditorium. Wolfgang Iser (Budick & Iser, 1996) and (Iser, 2000) describes the 'liminal' intercultural space that is opened up by the act of translation as a pre-requisite of, or framework for, that 'third space' in which the translation may operate as a text. In terms of theatre, both liminal and third spaces are created simultaneously by the dynamics of performance – in other words, the new play still functions (dangerously, subversively) as it might within its own culture. But its status as a translated text (which before the performance begins is highlighted to the audience in posters, publicity material, etc.) brings difference and new possibilities for meaning. It is here that the spectator's imagination is most powerfully engaged. Rather than approaching the text as a product that is internally fixed, the translator has the opportunity to recreate something of the text's original purchase on the imagination, its cultural 'work', its 'utility'.

This idea of utility is of added importance in a performance art such as theatre. Any cultural artefact may be read as an exteriorisation of artistic identity, in Gell's (1998: 250) phrase 'a place where agency "stops" and assumes visible form'. In other words, the particularity, for example, of a theatre text is inseparable from the way in which that text exteriorises, or performs, the artistic project of its author. Indeed, in the case of theatre, this performance already takes place in a space that is itself highly sensitised to the relationship between personhood and agency, a space where performance is defined by the here and now. To put it succinctly, the translator of plays is crucially concerned with enabling a heavily contextualised cultural product to function within another equally heavily contextualised environment. Richard Jacquemond emphasises the importance of the translator's multiple contextual awareness in such an enterprise:

> Translation is not only the intellectual, creative process by which a text written in a given language is transferred into another. Rather, like any

human activity, it takes place in a specific social and historical context that informs and structures it. In the case of translation, the operation becomes doubly complicated since, by definition, two languages and thus two cultures and societies are involved. (Jacquemond, 1992: 139)

In this contemplation of cultural transfer, Gell's parallel between personhood and identity, on the one hand, and performance and culture on the other, can be further developed. Dwight Conquergood's description of culture as an 'unfolding performative invention instead of reified system' emphasises this interplay between the person and broader cultural realities (discussed in Carlson, 1996: 190–4). Human patterns of activity, and the values underpinning them, are reinforced or challenged when the self is performed to the other within a known context. This is the essential praxis of culture. Performance – in particular, the performance of theatre – implies, in the words of Marvin Carlson, 'a self-consciousness about doing and re-doing on the part of both performers and spectators' (1996: especially, 195–9). Lorca's conviction that theatre is a crucible for cultural self-examination where we reflect upon and define ourselves, where we imagine alternatives and test their potential truths through performance, works wholly within this concept of cultural utility. Accordingly, Lorca's theatre functions as a performative consciousness that reflects and challenges specific historical relations. In other words, it is an act of performance whose primary function is the exploration of self and other, of the world as experienced and of possibilities alternate to that experience. If the translator chooses to ignore the cultural utility implicit in that act, he or she may well produce an acceptable text in English, but in terms of theatre it will be a ventriloquising text: one that is recognisably Lorca, which perhaps enjoys the status accorded to such a text, but that, in the final analysis, will fail to connect intimately – or memorably – with its audience.

The Practice of Theatre

All of this forms what may be termed the intracultural dimension of Lorca's theatre, how it functions – or more exactly, functioned – within its own time and place. The key question here, of course, is the extent to which the translator can – or should – attempt to replicate such cultural utility. After all, we cannot pretend that plays such as *Blood Wedding*, *Yerma* and *The House of Bernarda Alba* have the same impact in performance in Spain today as they did 70 or so years ago. Patterns of activity and the values that underpin them have patently changed, and with them the cultural utility of the plays has also evolved. The cultural utility of the text, the way in which a piece of writing engages with its originating culture, may well develop as culture and society evolve and, in that evolution, texts and artefacts may of course acquire different sets of meanings and significance. Moreover, in the case of theatre, a developing performance tradition gives the play a sense of accumulated richness, one that is closely linked to the fetishising of the author as a name, a 'draw'. In the case of Lorca, this is dangerously true given the vivid circumstances that surround his life and death. It is evidenced in the unusually large number of plays, films and devised pieces that depict or draw upon his life. Of course, Lorca as a cultural brand is much more accepted in the English-language theatrical mainstream than was the case, say, 20 years ago. But his status as a 'dramatist of poetry and passion' is not entirely helpful to any of the practitioners – including translators – who have attempted to make his plays work in English, on page or on stage. Lorca is a writer of dissonances, creating a style that is not only rich with individual and social colour, but that is also expressive of the instinctual vitality and performative energy that will, in his theory of performance, highlight the nature of identity as a site of conflict. Writing provided Lorca with his own liminal space in which he explored both the central tensions between social and personal being, and the darker recesses of the personal. If the stage language does not render precisely these locations and dislocations of identity, the productions may well lurch into self-conscious poeticisation, melodrama or sheer linguistic confusion. These are certainly all charges that have been levelled at performed versions of Lorca's plays. In order to ensure the inter-animation of words and cultural identity within the crucible of the performance space, the translator must undertake a very precise mapping – or through routing – of the relationship between situation, character interaction and individual verbal strategies. Otherwise, as the language of Lorca's plays becomes reified as 'Lorquian', the plays lose their capacity genuinely to move, to provoke and to shock, and the spectator is delivered into a world of remorseless cultural pastiche and ventriloquised passions.

As always occurs with translation, of course, there are a number of strategic choices that translators have to make. Some translators may well choose to work solely at the level of the words, and indeed there are several published translations that are written with all linguistic care but whose impact, in terms of the sort of engagement that great theatre requires, is that of artefacts from a time capsule. It could be argued, of course, that there is a direct parallel here with the way that originals themselves age, that this is the consequence of classic status. But translation can – and arguably should – free itself from this. The act of translating is less about re-affirming the canonical status of the original than with re-animating the play anew. As Willis Barnstone, for example, has noted, 'translation, as with all transcription and reading of texts, creates a difference' (Barnstone, 1993: 18; see also Venuti, 1992: 7). Such difference can be asserted through careful historical attention to the original, not with any textual historicism in mind, but with the goal of re-creating the power of the play in its original performance. The translator's task is analogous to that of the director, in this as in other aspects of their work: to return freshness to the play by negotiating the connections that the play sought to make with its original audience – its cultural utility – into the 'life worlds' of spectators here and now. This is one of the reasons why performance translations date so rapidly, and certainly why they should be discarded without too much heart-searching. They create a connection between the text and the present moment, in the same way that a good performance should do. The act of translation is as vivid and as transitory as the act of performance, because both are concerned with a moving target, the receptive consciousness of an audience of here and now. Once that target is out of range, however, the translation is fit only for the time-capsule (see, for example, Upton: 2000).

The key word above is 'negotiating'. New trends in Shakespearean criticism, for example, confirm that foreign audiences' imaginative collaboration with the performance may be most effectively engaged when the play is located within a cultural interstice that is simultaneously familiar and defamiliarised. In many ways, the infinite Shakespeares that inhabit cultural crossings between, for example, Japanese Manzai and the fast and furious word-games of *Love's Labours Lost* or Southern African politics and the politicking clans of *Julius Caesar*, are an antidote to the globalised classic product distributed from the cultural theme park that is Stratford-upon-Avon. Indeed, it may well be that, as English-speaking audiences' own ability to understand Shakespeare's language continues to erode, the future of vivid and meaningful Shakespeare productions lies within the cultural and post-colonial re-animations of translators abroad – see, for example, the collection of essays from international contributors in *Ilha do desterro* 36, edited by José Roberto O'Shea (1999). A rose by any other name, perhaps, but there is the clearly discernible pragmatics of theatre reception in this. A play realises its potential for meanings, whether authorially intended or not, through the interaction between the fictitious world on stage and the imaginative collaboration of the spectator who lives in the here and now, Unamuno's celebrated and very real 'man of flesh and bone'. This hybrid model of play text, and in particular the liminal space opened up through performance of such a text, permits the new audience to gain access to the assumptions and the secrets that the play shared with its original audience. But the granting of that access must be equally elliptical or else the play courts the risk of didacticism on one hand and stylistic normalisation on the other. A translator for the stage is, in that sense at least, a writer for performance.

Translating Performance

Viewed from this perspective, the translator is centrally concerned at each moment and stage of the process to ensure that the intracultural function of the play is translated, or negotiated, into the receiving culture. Lorca has a cultural predilection for a theatre of ritual and spectacle rather than one of rationally expounded argument. He is closer to Yeats than Ibsen in that sense and, in a very Yeatsian way, his performance translators must find a stage language that speaks both of the passion with which he represents the assumptions and movements of his society, and of the precision that grafts the speech of his characters into the living wood of their culture. This is the through routing, referred to earlier, along which the translator leads individual character strategies to the points where they intersect most powerfully with broader cultural realities. It is only at that moment – when stage language becomes real, when it can be processed by the spectator as naturally-occurring language – that the spectator is provided with a linguistic framework for fully identifying and understanding the deepening and quickening moments of the drama when language moves from the plane of the naturally occurring to that of the stylistically re-arranged. To put it in the most direct way, the template of communicative competence that all native speakers possess must form the basis for whatever dramaturgical remoulding of language takes place in the translation. This is the linguistic underpinning for whatever foreignising, stylistic or idiolectic elements the translator may wish to inject, maintain or re-create. It is a necessary pre-condition which, if not met, may jeopardise the reception of the new text's otherness. This – its cultural voice – now runs the risk of being misunderstood and/or dismissed as mere confusion or, in the specific case of Lorca, as excessively melodramatic. All of the various actions – cultural and linguistic – that vivify Lorca's drama have a singular coherence in the original plays, all contribute to the overall thrust of what the plays are about in performance, all are part of a complicity that is both an aesthetic pre-requisite of performance and a cultural project.

We have already referred to Lorca's systemic patterns of imagery, with their characteristically powerful interplay between animate and inanimate elements drawn, in very large part, from the everyday world of rural Spain. All of this can be treated with the same tactics that translators normally use for culture-specific items, allowing for whatever balance between originating and receiving cultures that is deemed appropriate for the production. But it is important that the translator does not allow Lorca's encyclopaedia of reference to push the process towards a merely linguistic exercise. The aim of Lorca's theatre – arguably, perhaps, of performance in general – is not to foster the growth of knowledge, but to re-frame experience. This means that translation of the culture-specific items of Lorca's original is at least as equally governed by rhetorical and stylistic strategies as by any external referencing.

One much-discussed example, taken from the most frequently performed and translated of Lorca plays, *Bodas de sangre* (*Blood Wedding*), will illustrate this. In the opening scene of the play, the Mother curses '*la navaja, la navaja ...* [...] *y las escopetas y las pistolas y el cuchillo más pequeño, y hasta las azadas y los bieldos de la era*' as items that all represent danger in the world of men (1980: 566). This is translated almost literally in the first Penguin translation of the play: 'Knives, knives [...] And guns and pistols and the smallest little knife – and even hoes and pitchforks' (Graham-Luján & O'Connell, 1961: 33). Ted Hughes (1996: 1) has: 'The knife, the knife! [...] And guns and pistols, even the tiniest little knife, even pitchforks and mattocks'. Brendan Kennelly (1996: 11) widens the curse to 'The knife, the knife. [...] And the curse of God on guns, machine guns, rifles, pistols ... and knives, even the smallest knife... and scythes and pitchforks'. In his 1980 Spanish-language edition of the play, the distinguished Hispanist Herbert Ramsden notes that the farm implements Lorca mentions 'take both their basic meaning and their emotive resonances from a cultural complex different from our own' and puts forward a number of possible translations – 'drag-hoe', 'pick-axe', 'winnowing-fork', 'pitch-fork' – all of which, he argues, will permit English readers (of his published edition) to process the text from within a familiar context (quoted and discussed by Hickey, 1998: 50). Leo Hickey takes an opposing view:

> ... a translator can attempt either to bring the ST to the reader, with all its locutionary, illocutionary and perlocutionary import, wherever the reader may be, or else take the reader, complete with any baggage of cultural or linguistic background that may be attached to such a person, into the world – the linguistic world – of the ST. And I am suggesting that perhaps in the case of these three plays [*Blood Wedding, Yerma, The House of Bernarda Alba*] the tactic of taking the reader into the ST world should be considered. (Hickey, 1998: 50)

But what is going on here in terms of performance? Given the fact that the Mother's invective comes as the first moment of heightened tension in the play (previously we have had only 11 short speeches of deliberate domestic banality) these are clearly key lines, and really have to be viewed from the overarching perspective of the play – its energy, its dominant motifs, and its meanings – as a whole. Moreover, the translator of drama for performance does well to bear in mind that, whatever we might consider to be the indivisible unit of dramatic construction (the individual speech or the individual exchange), it is stamped with purpose. It is a cellular unit that carries within it the shape and force of the play in its entirety. If that cellular structure of dramatic writing is ignored, there is a real risk that the play will lose coherence, on the page and on stage alike, and will be experienced in a piecemeal and de-energised way. So the emotional action of *Blood Wedding* begins, as it will end, with an image of the knife, creating a sense of violence that overhangs the play like a damoclean sword.

'*Navaja*', 'knife', is a continually recurring sign in Lorca's poetry, plays and drawings, taken, as are so many of his motifs and icons, from a reality that is both observed and part of a recognised cultural tradition. The word is invested here with an elemental force that is operative both within the experience of the character herself and within the collective imagination of the audience. If one were translating the force of the word into an Irish situation, then its direct equivalent would be the gun. Knife and gun are both readily intelligible correlatives for a certain type of social and historical violence, both potent agents and harbingers of a destruction whose causes are known to all. In other words, the first mention of the '*navaja*', leading as it does into this list of dangerous weapons and implements, creates a moment of expectation and of recognition; the audience begins to confront the tragedy of a relentless chain of cause and effect that it recognises as being its own trauma. It is this act of complicitous recognition that the Irish poet Brendan Kennelly seeks to re-create by broadening his references to include 'rifles' and 'machine guns'. Indeed, his sense of the parallel between the violent divisions of Irish history and this community that bays for its own blood in Lorca's play, is reinforced by the new lines with which he has his version end. In the closing lines of the play, the Mother's references to 'this blood-haunted place' and her 'dream of peace', with their overtones of the Northern Irish peace process (the play was performed in 1996), bring his version full circle, and re-create a sense of the cultural utility of the Lorca original within Kennelly's own commitment as an Irish writer (Kennelly, 1996).[8] Clearly, however, it would be impossible to translate '*navaja*' as 'gun', and Kennelly is sensitive to the fact that one of the principal strands in the play's grammar of imagery is that of images of cutting, pinning, slicing and piercing. Moreover, while, admittedly, it may speak of a similar macho-style response to historical dislocation, the gun does not have the specifically phallic overtones of the knife, and the sexual connotations of the death of the two men in Act Three would be lost. In this particular case, Kennelly points up connections between Lorca's project, and his own, without allowing the play to be flooded with a spurious Irishness. The spectator's imagination is located precisely where it should be: not in Hickey's Andalusia or in the comfortable familiarity of Ramsden's England, but in the theatre, the liminal space between stage and auditorium, where it belongs.

Having started with the most emotionally loaded motif, the '*navaja*', the Spanish can afford to bring in less elemental items – the '*azadas*' and the '*bieldos de la era*'. Clearly, the issue that the translator requires to negotiate here is whether the specificity of reference should be retained in order, presumably, to mark the difference of the play's setting (and implying, in the process, that this is the sort of thing that goes on in the Spanish countryside), or whether the referents should be strengthened in order to reinforce the energy surrounding the knife. This issue, moreover, cannot be considered in isolation from the cultural play of language that gives Lorca's plays what Kennelly (1996: 11) calls their quality of 'rhythmical and emotional revolution'. Their characteristic linguistic actions – rhythm / repetition, the use of anticipatory poetics, kinetics, kinesics, language that is simultaneously located and dislocated – all need to be considered as an informing aspect of the overall process of cultural negotiation so that the play can be understood without being normalised. Stage language does not simply mean: it does. Indeed, this is surely what 'performability' is all about – giving actors lines that are speakable and that, at the same time, recreate the stylistic marking and cultural significance of the original.[9] Lorca almost certainly chose *'azadas'* from the bewildering array of rural cutting tools at his disposal because of its assonant relationship with the preceding *'hasta las'* and, more crucially, with the word *'navaja'* itself. Moreover, the falling rhythm of *'los bieldos de la era'* allows the actor in question to vary the emotional stress of the phrase so that it ends on a note of apparent helplessness in the face of omnipresent destruction. In terms of sound patterns, therefore, the specificity of these items is expendable. My own solution emphasises the rhythmical nature of the language:

> I hate knives ... [...] Knives, guns ... sickles and scythes ...[10] (Johnston, 1988/2003)

The Truths of Performance

When version-writers, or translators, work as actual practitioners in drama, they engage in processes that are both intra- and interlingual, and intra- and intercultural. These are all processes that move within and across the various languages that, together, constitute the discourse or grammar of performance. And it is by anchoring these processes to the overarching truth, or truths, of the play that, ultimately, the performability of the piece will be secured. These truths (in the sense, of course, of the truths of performance rather than any axiomatic statements) may well connect directly with the experience of our audiences today. Lorca's awareness that women's sexuality is expected to operate within a different set of expectations from that of men, for example, is a prime example of a focus of ongoing relevance.[11] And without doubt Lorca's emphasis on the extended imperatives of individuality were key in asserting the relevance of his work in English at a time when radical Thatcherism was concerned to re-define the individual in terms of aggressive acquisitiveness. Where specific articulations of such overarching elements, however, come across as dated, confused or too embedded within the traditions of the originating culture, then the translator must simply decide how best to serve the overall purpose of this crucial aspect of the text. Such tactical responses may well vary within the ambit of the individual text so that the interests both of preserving cultural specificity and of establishing cultural diversity are served. In a postmodern world, the surface texture of the translation is self-aware, an explicit site for creative tensions and intercultural encounter.

In the heavily-textured theatre of García Lorca, it would be possible to cite numerous examples of such culture-specific negotiations. Indeed, many reviewers and essayists have made it their business to compare working solutions with their own 'perfect understanding' of the meaning of the words in question (the phrase is, of course, Richards's) (Gentzler, 2001: 15; Johnston, 2004: 1–4). Such comparisons are inevitably partial in as far as they ignore the overarching performance context in which the particular image or utterance is embedded. Let us take an example from *La casa de Bernarda Alba* (*The House of Bernarda Alba*). In the climactic scene of the play, the embittered and hugely repressed Martirio confesses her love for the overpowering Pepe el Romano to her wayward sister Adela with the following:

> Yes! Let me say it without hiding my head. Yes! My breast's bitter, bursting like a pomegranate. I love him. (Graham-Luján & O'Connell, 1961: 198)

This act of straight talking bursts the house of Bernarda Alba wide open, leading directly to Adela's rebellion and subsequent suicide. It is a metaphor of expressionist intensity, of a scream forced through silence and denial. In his version of the play (produced at Belfast's Lyric Theatre in 1991), Frank McGuinness opts to change the bursting pomegranate into a sour apple, while at the same time retaining the original setting of rural Spain (unlike the spectacularly unsuccessful version of Charabanc Theatre Company who, in 1993, transferred the action to County Cavan). It could be argued that some of the specifics are lost in the exchange: the red pulpy flesh of the pomegranate, like a bleeding heart, the seeds that spill out (though we need to be careful with this one as the connotative dimension of seeds in English cannot be mapped wholly onto the Spanish). On the other hand, the overtones of sourness that McGuinness brings (pomegranates decay into a sickly sweetness) are, in their own right, a powerful image of the human heart locked away. No matter where we place the translation on the loss/compensation axis, one thing remains clear: McGuinness has chosen to replace an exotic metaphor, arresting in its own way, with one that drives the energy of the scene forward, and which is wholly consonant with the play's central warning: repression leads to explosion. And, in terms of style, the writing is no less overt, no less marked.

In the final analysis, therefore, there is rarely a need to undertake a whole-scale transposition of Lorca's cultural context. If the version-writer elects that option, however, there will be significant implications for the amount of detail that demands to be re-cast in order for the new play to work as a version of the original – it was precisely in this regard that the Charabanc production referred to above fell short (Farrell, 1996: 52–3).[12] More likely, the translator will seek to open windows into the cultural utility of the original and re-create its capacity to engage by identifying the overarching truths of performance – which actors will be searching endlessly for throughout the rehearsal process anyway – and by ensuring that these are both served by, and intimately connected to, each and every one of the cellular units of speech that constitute them. In that sense, the translator writes neither wholly for the stage or the page, but for the air, the liminal space between actor and spectator in which Lorca's plays achieve their full capacity for darkness and danger.

One final example, taken from *Doña Rosita la soltera* (*Doña Rosita, the Spinster*), written in 1935, gives a clear idea of this liminal space where the invisible in society is made visible. In the oppressive Victorian world of a gloomy Granada house, a young woman is withering. On the surface, as Nicholas Round has observed:

> it would be hard to preserve very much of that play, of its tensions, necessities, compulsions – let alone that extraordinary symphony of kitsch cultural references in the second act, which makes such a wonderful comic episode – if you simply replaced those assumptions with the assumptions of present-day Britain, and re-wrote the translation accordingly. (Doggart & Thompson, 1999: 258)[13]

This is undoubtedly the case, but the emotional truth that the actor will probably draw upon to authenticate her performance is that of a woman who has been betrayed, and that core experience will serve the translator in his or her re-creation of that sense of a place where agency has stopped and assumed visible form in the paralysed life of this young woman. The unspoken reality of this particular Genetrix is that she has been condemned, both by her own misreading of her feckless fiancé and by the codes of her society, into a sexless existence, divorced from all pleasure. Lorca frequently used servants to voice the unspoken, and early in the play the Housekeeper recites a daring tongue-twister whose ostensible meaning is that, like nuns, she is on the go from dawn to dusk:

> *Siempre del coro al caño y del caño al coro; del coro al caño y del caño al coro.*[14]
> (Lorca, 1980: 750)

But the latent content it implants in the audience's mind – virtually forces spectators to speak – is the slang word for the female sexual organs. In his version, John Edmunds tries this:

> She never stops: in and out and round about and in my lady's chamber. (Edmunds, 1997: 176)

subsequently adjusting the following dialogue to have her mistress, Rosita's aunt, say reprovingly:

> If you knew what that meant, you wouldn't say it. (Edmunds, 1999: 177)

Unfortunately, what is lost here is the implantation of the bursting word in the audience's mind, so that the spectators become complicitous with the force of desire that is locked away in the play, like a hothouse flower. The meaning has to be deduced rather than exploding into the spectator's consciousness. Moreover, the loss of reference to the world of nuns erodes an important correlative for Rosita's arid existence. Another version attempts to keep the referential elements explicitly alive. '*Coro*' refers to the choir stalls of the church, and '*caño*' to the fountain where the washing is down. The resulting 'from shout to sheet, from sheet to shout' provides a graphic illustration of the limitations of such philological analysis (Graham-Luján & O'Connell, 1965: 134). Not only does it evoke behaviour most unlikely in a nun, but its own bursting word is singularly inappropriate.

It is of course notoriously difficult to write about performance, either actual or intended. Different spectators will inevitably react in very different ways, carrying away with them quite distinct impressions of their experience. Moreover, audiences will vary collectively from place to place. The same production of Shaw's *John Bull's Other Island* will prompt a very different audience reaction in Belfast's Lyric Theatre than, for example, in the Tricycle in London. But the translator, like the director, must have a conscious sense of how a play is intended to work in performance. That clearly does not preclude new perspectives opening up. Even the original writer possesses no unmediated knowledge of what he or she has written, and it is important that the translator does not impose unnecessary closure in the interpretive analysis that precedes the act of translation proper. But to translate a play for performance requires a clear-sighted view of how that play should work on stage. Such a view may be illusory or idealised; or it may fall short of what the play actually achieves, at least for some of its spectators. But translating for the stage means writing towards a play's potential to engage spectators and to charge the air in a theatre.

Notes

1. 1986, the 50th anniversary of Lorca's death, saw the first dropping of estate-held copyright on most of Lorca's output. A subsequent change in international law

has reversed this situation, and the fact that the estate has now adopted a more liberal attitude towards new translations has been instrumental in this latterday assertion of Lorca as a significant dramatist.
2. See, for example, John Clifford (1996) 'Translating the spirit of the play.' A not untypical assessment of the unease – the 'fear of poetry' – that Lorca produces in English theatre circles comes from Paul Hunter, director of Told By An Idiot Theatre Company. He observes, 'I personally think that lots of English theatre practitioners are frightened of Lorca (Gerry Mulgrew is an exception, of course). The fact that you have things like the moon coming on stage – we're not used to that. English actors still want to act in plays where people argue about things like who's left the car door open or something'. Directors' Panel, at the One Hundred Years of Lorca Conference, held at the Newcastle Playhouse in 1998, published in Doggart & Thompson, 1999: 217.
3. See, especially, the transcription of the directors' panel Doggart & Thompson, 1999. The views of Alan Lyddiard, artistic director of Northern Stage, are particularly interesting in this regard (Doggart & Thompson, 1999: 217–9).
4. My translation, from Lorca (Johnston, 1980: 1215).
5. My translation, from an interview given by Lorca barely four months before his assassination. Reproduced in Lorca (Johnston, 1980: 1119). See also M. Thompson's 'Poetry that gets up off the page and becomes human: Poetic coherence and eccentricity in Lorca's theatrem' (Doggart & Thompson, 1999: 67–79). It is also closely linked to Lorca's theory of *'duende'*; see his lecture 'Theory and function of the Duende' in Lorca, 1960: 127–39.
6. This argument is expanded upon in David Johnston (1999: 57–66).
7. Documented extensively throughout the biography of Lorca: *Federico García Lorca: A Life* by I. Gibson (1989). This remains the best biography.
8. This is one among a series of references and additions that combine to give the play a distinctly Irish spin. The additional words referred to are:

    In the very roots of pain / Where death is born / And loves dies / And I am left / With the torn, dirty remnants of a dream, / A dream that I must change, / In this blood-haunted place, / Into a dream of peace. (Kennelly, 1996: 79)
9. This notion is dealt with by a number of theorists. See, for example, House (1997). Hickey (1998: 51) insists, properly, that 'marked should be translated as marked' However, his argument is weakened by his reduction of the issue to the simplified question of 'whether a translation should preserve the markedness of the original or recontextualise it into something unmarked in English'. There are complex issues surrounding performance reception and the hybrid nature of the translated text that need to be borne in mind here.
10. *Blood Wedding* (1988) translated by David Johnston. The version quoted above, however, varies from the published one. This is taken from a script prepared for Bruiser Theatre Company, for an Irish tour, in 2003.
11. This point was made by Arnold Wesker in 1987 in his extended review of Nuria Espert's *The House of Bernarda Alba*, translated as *'Nuria Espert abre las puertas de Londres a Lorca'*. *Insulai* 37, Oct. 1985: 3. In the event, not all critics were convinced. Typical was John Peter, in the times, who also saw the play as 'odd'.
12. See Farrell (1966: 52–3).
13. Translators' Panel in Doggart & Thompson (1999: 258).
14. *Doña Rosita la soltera* (Lorca, 1980: 750).

References

Barnstone, W. (1993) *The Poetics of Translation: History, Theory, Practice.* New Haven: Yale University Press.
Binding, P. (1985) *Lorca: The Gay Imagination.* London: GMP.
Budick, S. and Iser, W. (eds) (1996) *The Translatability of Cultures: Figurations of the Space Between.* Stanford: Stanford University Press.
Carlson, M. (1996) *Performance: A Critical Introduction.* London: Routledge.
Clifford, J. (1996) Translating the spirit of the play. In D. Johnston (ed.) *Stages of Translation* (pp. 263–70). Bath: Absolute Classics.
Doggart, S. and Thompson, M. (eds) (1999) *Fire, Blood and the Alphabet.* Durham: University of Durham Press.
Edmunds, J. (1997) *Lorca, Four Major Plays: Blood Wedding, Yerma, The House of Bernarda Alba, Doòa Rosita the Spinster.* Oxford: Oxford University Press.
Edwards, G. (1998) Translating Lorca for the theatre: Blood Wedding, Yerma and The House of Bernarda Alba. *Donaire* 11, 15–30.
Farrell, J. (1996) Servants of many masters. In D. Johnston (ed.) *Stages of Translation* (pp. 45–55) Bath: Absolute Classics.
Gell, A. (1998) *Art and Agency: An Anthropological Theory.* Oxford: Oxford University Press.
Gentzler, E (2001) *Contemporary Translation Theories.* Clevedon: Multilingual Matters.
Gibson, I. (1989) *Federico García Lorca: A Life.* London: Faber and Faber.
Graham-Luján, J. and O'Connell, R.L. (trans.) (1961) *Lorca: Three Tragedies.* Harmondsworth: Penguin.
Graham-Luján, J. and O'Connell, R.L. (trans.) (1965) *Federico García Lorca: Five Plays.* Harmondsworth: Penguin.
Hickey, L. (1998) Pragmatic comments on translating Lorca. *Donaire*, 11, 47–60.
House, J. (1997) *Translation Quality Assessment: A Model Revisited.* Tübingen: Narr.
Hughes, T. (trans.) (1996) *Blood Wedding.* London: Faber and Faber.
Iser, W. (2000) *The Range of Interpretation.* New York: Columbia University Press.
Jacquemond, R. (1992) Translation and cultural hegemony: The case of French-Arabic Translation. In L. Venuti (ed.) *Rethinking Translation.* London: Routledge.
Johnston, D. (trans.) (1988) *Blood Wedding.* Sevenoaks: Hodder and Stoughton.
Johnston, D. (1999) García Lorca: After New York. In S. Doggart and M. Thompson (eds) *Fire, Blood and the Alphabet* (pp. 57–66). Durham: University of Durham Press.
Johnston, D. (trans.) (2003) *Blood Wedding.* Script prepared for Bruiser Theatre Company for Irish tour.
Johnston, D. (2004) Translation for the stage: Product and process. NUI Maynooth Papers in Spanish and Portuguese. Maynooth: National University of Ireland
Kennelly, B. (trans.) (1996) *Blood Wedding.* Newcastle: Bloodaxe.
Lorca, F.G. (1980) *Obras Completas.* Madrid: Aguilar.
Lorca, F.G. (1960) *Selected Poems* (J.L. Gili, ed.). Harmondsworth: Penguin.
Monleón, J. (1971) *Bodas de sangre.* Madrid: Aymá.
O'Shea, J.R. (ed.) (1999) *Ilha do Desterro* 36. São Paulo: University of São Paulo.
Round, N. (1997) Introduction. In J. Edmunds (trans.) *Four Major Plays* (pp. ix–xxxvii) Oxford: Oxford World Classics.
Pavis, P. (1992) *Theatre at the Crossroads of Culture* (L. Kruge, trans.). London: Routledge.
Upton, C-A. (ed.) (2000) *Moving Target: Theatre Translation and Cultural Relocation.* Manchester: St Jerome.
Venuti, L. (1992) *Rethinking Translation.* London: Routledge.

Chapter 8

To Be or Not To Be (Untranslatable): Strindberg in Swedish and English

GUNILLA ANDERMAN

Introduction

In his *Guardian* review of a recent Peter Hall production of *Miss Julie*, Michael Billington concluded:

> I suspect there are two ways to revivify Strindberg's play. One is to direct it, as Ingmar Bergman did, as a specifically Swedish play in which erotic frenzy is induced by the white heat of a summer night. The other is to rewrite it, as Patrick Marber did, as a modern play about the intersection of sex and class. (Billington, 2006)

Billington's observations may be interpreted as the stark choice between adopting a foreignising or a domesticating approach to the translation of *Miss Julie*. Either you invite the theatre audience to travel abroad, in this case to experience the magic of a Nordic midsummer night, or you 'translate' this culturally-untranslatable event by relocating it to a different place. In *After Miss Julie*, Patrick Marber's version of the play set in the UK, the euphoria of the summer night in Sweden was well matched by the enthusiasm that greeted Labour's post-war election victory in 1945. However, between the two polar-opposite approaches there is a middle way: while some truly untranslatable concepts may defy linguistic transfer, other translation obstacles may be solved, albeit with some effort. Some of these problems are not immediately obvious: in the case of Strindberg they include what has been referred to as 'unreliable narration' (Törnqvist, 1999) which, if not interpreted correctly, runs the risk of adding an element of unwarranted melodrama in translation. A further category of translation problems (to be considered) is concerned with allusions to flora and fauna, the symbolic use of which often has to be left intact and remain foreign and intriguing to theatre audiences.

Linguistic 'Untranslatability'[1]

As in the work of other playwrights, Strindberg's characters speak in their own distinctive voices. In *Miss Julie*, Jean's use of language is often more imaginative than that of the maid and his fiancée, Kristin. It also contains a fair sprinkling of French loanwords which Jean uses with the clear intention of trying to impress Miss Julie. The effect is often comical, a humorous aspect too often lost in translation into English, where many words originally borrowed from French no longer stand out as foreign. When, for instance, Jean talks to Kristin about Miss Julie's *projekt*, the word has an unexpected, out-of-the-ordinary sound in the context in which it is used in Swedish; this is lost in English translation, where 'project' is no longer likely to be perceived as of French origin. At other times, however, Jean's use of language is not dissimilar to that of Kristin's, now revealing their background and lack of education as well as their position as servants, who, in talking about their superiors become overly verbose and polite as if talking to them.

In order to signal the difference in social status between Jean, Kristin and Miss Julie, Strindberg also makes use of the availability in Swedish of several pronouns of address, the Swedish formal versus the informal form of 'you', as well as the third person pronoun 'he'.

Assuring Jean that she does not mind him dancing with Miss Julie, Kristin addresses him in the third person singular, a frequent custom in Sweden at the time between men and women:

> **KRISTIN:** *Inte! – Inte för så lite, det vet han nog; och jag vet min plats också.*
> [No! – Not for so little, he knows (you know) that; and I know my place too.] (Strindberg, 1984: 121)[2]

As Jean is only too happy to tell us, he is not a stranger to foreign lands. Able to speak to Miss Julie in French, she is impressed and asks where he learnt to speak French, now addressing him with '*ni*', the formal pronoun of address:

> (Jean enters dressed in black tails and a black bowler hat.)
>
> **MISS JULIE:** *Très gentil, monsieur Jean! Très gentil!*
>
> **JEAN:** *Vous voulez plaisanter, madame!*
>
> **MISS JULIE:** *Et vous voulez parler français! Var har **ni** lärt det?*
> [And you speak French! Where have **you** learnt that?](Strindberg, 1984: 128: author's emphasis)

Later, when the two return from Jean's bedroom to reappear on stage, Jean, still aware of the social gulf between them, addresses Julie with the formal *ni*. Forcibly reminded of reality, Julie reacts, imploring him to use the informal *du*. But he cannot bring himself to do it:

> **MISS JULIE:** (shy, very feminine) **Ni!** *Säg* **du***!*
> *Mellan oss finns inga skrankor mer! – Säg **du**!*

[Ni (you)! Say du (you)!/There aren't any barriers between us any longer!/Say **du** (you)!]

JEAN: (in obvious agony) *Jag kan inte!*
Det finns skrankor mellan oss ännu, så länge vi vistas i detta hus ...
[I can't!/ There are still barriers between us, as long as we stay in this house ...] (Strindberg, 1984: 150)

The switch in pronominal address as a device to signal shifts in emotion used by Shakespeare before the thou/you distinction was discontinued in English is found not only in other Scandinavian writers of the epoch, such as Ibsen in for example *A Doll's House* and *Hedda Gabler*, but also in plays by Pirandello such as *Six Characters in Search of an Author* and in Russian novelists including Tolstoy in *Anna Karenina* (Lyons, 1980; Anderman, 2005).

Strindberg's writing also shares another feature with Ibsen's dramas that does not lend itself to successful translation into English: the polarity effect. While Miss Julie dreams that she is sitting on the top of a pillar, trying to fall *down*, Jean imagines himself climbing *up* a high tree. This clear-cut either/or aspect of Strindberg's writing is bound to present English audiences with unfamiliar attitudes of extremes. As Michael Meyer has pointed out, there is for instance much in the character of Miss Julie that may be viewed as deeply un-English:

> In the Swedish theatre, as in the German, the unforgivable sin is to under-act. In England, it is to overact; how often have we not seen our best actors, when faced by the peaks of Othello and King Lear, take refuge in gentlemanly underplaying or the evasiveness of theatrical fireworks? It is no coincidence that the only two actors who have fully succeeded in Strindberg in England, Robert Loraine and Wilfrid Lawson, have been actors of most un-English, one might almost say continental vehemence, and consequently difficult to cast in roles of ordinary human dimensions. For a parallel reason there has never yet [...] been an adequate Miss Julie in England. (Meyer, 1966: 70)

These observations seem to imply that potentially melodramatic interpretations of Strindberg's larger-than-life characters are inherent in the parts as written, unrelated to whatever might have been lost or added in translation. Following the London opening of the 2000 production of *Miss Julie*, critics responded to Jean's confessions to Miss Julie – that he had been in love with her from an early age – with a measure of incredulity. It is difficult to believe, it was argued, that this could have been the case. However, the point that appears to have been missed here is that we are not supposed to know whether Jean is lying or telling the truth. Strindberg intended us to be left in doubt as to the veracity of Jean's declaration of his childhood love for his mistress; his lines at this point constitute so-called 'unreliable narration'. In the words of Törnqvist:

> A narrator [...] is unreliable when s/he consciously or unconsciously provides incorrect information (active unreliability) or when s/he is withholding important information (passive unreliability). Although the word 'unreliability' carries negative overtones, it should be noticed that a character may well be unreliable for good reasons. (Törnqvist, 1999: 62)

'Unreliable narration' is found in several of Strindberg's plays, an obvious example being Laura's behaviour in *The Father*. Having just been informed by the doctor that she must, at all costs, try to avoid arousing her husband's suspicions, Laura promptly sets about sowing the seeds that he may not be the father of their daughter, Bertha. What the audience cannot be sure of, however, is whether this is true or not. Strindberg leaves it for us to work out for ourselves whether Laura is lying:

> We may guess that the Captain's doubt about his fatherhood is a fixed idea, with no basis in reality, but nothing in the play contradicts the opposite interpretation. We grope for the reality of the play in the same way that the Captain himself gropes for the truth among the mists surrounding him. (Brandell, 1971; discussed in Törnqvist, 1999: 78)

Other linguistic evidence signalled by the style of language that Strindberg makes Laura use when she 'sows the seeds' in her husband's mind, corroborates an interpretation that she is trying out her hypothesis to dramatic effect. She now delivers her lines in declamatory style, in a language different from that which she has used immediately before. This shift has been captured in Richard Nelson's translation:

> LAURA: You don't know if you're Bertha's father.
>
> CAPTAIN: I know it.
>
> LAURA: You can't. No one can.
>
> CAPTAIN: You're joking.
>
> LAURA: No. It's only what you taught me yourself. How can you ever know if I've been unfaithful to you?
>
> CAPTAIN: You are capable of many things, just not that. And if you were, you wouldn't be talking about it.
>
> LAURA: What if I was ready to give up everything, to be thrown out, despised, all of it, just for the right in choosing how my child is brought up? What if I was willing to tell the world that Bertha is mine, but not yours? What if – ? (Nelson, 1998: 29)

In Nelson's translation, the colloquial exchange preceding Laura's 'What if –' speculation contrasts with her elevated, somewhat melodramatic choice of vocabulary that follows, the shift in linguistic register providing some doubt about the truth value of her later hypothesising. This is not, however, the case in Peter Watts's translation. To a large extent, the problem is closely linked to Laura's use of the word 'doctrine':

> LAURA: Simply that you don't know that you are Bertha's father.
>
> CAPTAIN: Of course I know!
>
> LAURA: No one can tell, so you certainly can't.
>
> CAPTAIN: Is this a joke?
>
> LAURA: No, I'm simply applying your own **doctrine**. Besides, how do you know that I haven't been unfaithful to you?
>
> CAPTAIN: I can believe a lot about you, but not that. Nor do I believe that you'd talk about it if it were true.
>
> LAURA: Suppose I were ready to put up with anything, to lose my home and my good name, for the sake of keeping my child and bringing her up. Suppose I was telling the truth just now when I said Bertha was my child and not yours.
> Suppose – (Watts, 1958: 43; author's emphasis)

Unlike the translation by Watts, Nelson's translates the Swedish word *lärdomar* (learning, knowledge) as 'It's only what you taught me yourself', which accurately captures Laura's sarcastic reference to her husband's interest in the scientific debate at the time. The Captain is a scientist and part of his mounting frustration is attributable to his failure to receive the books that he needs to further advance his reading in the field of Darwinism and the new discoveries made during the latter part of the 19th century. Later in the play we learn that his suspicions are, in fact, well founded; his keen interest in new thinking and ideas is not shared by the women in his household and, as it turns out, owing to his wife's intervention, the eagerly awaited books have not arrived.

Part of the problem in Watts's translation is linked to the choice of the word 'doctrine' as used by Laura immediately before she starts baiting her husband. In choosing the word 'doctrine', Watts seems to have sought and found a one-word equivalent to the original Swedish word. This decision, however, leads to two problems. First, it creates an impression of Laura as being more educated and widely read than she is in the original. One of the reasons why the Captain wants his daughter to be educated away from the home is his fear that she would otherwise remain ignorant of the new age that was now dawning and would prove susceptible to the superstitions widely held at the time among the less well educated. Second, the use of 'doctrine' immediately preceding the 'Suppose –' hypothesising speech tends to pre-empt the effect of what is to come, which requires a change in linguistic register.

While a Swedish reader of Strindbergian drama containing 'unreliable narration' might be able to sense that a change in language also means a change in mood and feeling, stylistic nuances that serve as indicators of these changes are only too easily lost in translation. To return now to *Miss Julie*, linguistic markers are obviously not the only means that Strindberg uses in order to indicate that Jean's assurances of his childhood feelings for Miss Julie might be fictitious. From other aspects of his behaviour — he freely helps himself to his Lordship's vintage wine for example — we know that his character is not unflawed. On stage, however, language plays as important a part as action. If in translation 'unreliable narration' emerges as ordinary narrative, part of the overall design of the playwright's original work has not been given expression, inevitably resulting in the loss of some of his original intentions.

Jean is, however, not alone in giving us good grounds for suspicion that he might be economical with the truth. In the case of Julie, it has been suggested that 'we never know for sure how much of Julie's personal accounts is make-believe, how much is recollection coloured by the present and how much is reasonably accurate retelling of childhood memories' (Brandell, discussed in Törnqvist, 1999: 78). Unlike Jean who, when he no longer feels the need to impress Julie, openly admits that it was 'just talk', nothing overtly stated in the text tells us that Julie's recollection of her childhood might not tally with the facts. Still, it is not possible to be completely sure that she is telling the truth since earlier on she has been caught lying about her broken-off engagement. When Jean confronts her saying that it was her fiancé who broke off the engagement, Julie is unable to accept the truth and accuses her fiancé as well as Jean, the messenger, of lying – when of course it is Julie herself who is now not entirely truthful. This is corroborated by an earlier exchange between Jean and Kristin where we learn of the events that she witnessed in the stable yard; it was in fact Miss Julie's fiancé who walked off and left her.

What Strindberg is trying to do here is to allow the audience to experience the contradictory signals often experienced in real life. We may have a sense that someone is lying, but not be fully aware of their reasons for doing so. Failing to understand it all at the time, we might recall the incident much later when the reasons prompting the lies are better understood. This means, however, that an actor must be able to convey that 'hollow' sound that often accompanies 'unreliable information', which in turn presupposes an understanding that this is an aspect of the text in the first place. And, the more subtly expressed the signals are in the source language, the more likely it is that they might be missed in translation, resulting in a flattened text bereft of a level present in the original. To quote Strindberg on the subject of dialogue:

> I have avoided the mathematical, symmetrically constructed dialogue of French drama allowing the brain to work irregularly as it does in real life where in a conversation a subject is rarely completed but instead one brain responds to the stimulus received from another. (Josephson, 1965: 130)

In order to signal the cross-currents beneath the level of the spoken word, Strindberg's dialogue is broken up by dashes, dots, question and exclamation marks. Sometimes this is a device used to indicate that a character may say one thing but think something else. When, for instance, Jean and Julie emerge from Jean's room, knowing that they now have to face the music, Jean's characteristically male approach to the problem is to embark upon a plan of action, which includes leaving Sweden and travelling south, to Lake Como. He even goes as far as to consult a timetable for information on the departure times of trains bound for the Continent. Julie, on the other hand, listens absent-mindedly, only concerned to hear Jean tell her that he loves her. Finally she plucks up her courage:

> FRÖKEN JULIE: *Allt det där är bra! Men Jean – du skall ge mig mod – Säg att du älskar mig! Kom och omfamna mig!* (Strindberg, SV, 1984: 149)
> [MISS JULIE: All that is well and good. But Jean – you must give me courage – Tell me that you love me! Come and embrace me!]

Since he often completed his plays within a very short period of time, Strindberg, writing in a frenzy, frequently failed to show consistency in adhering to his own highly idiosyncratic system of punctuation. While the dashes in Miss Julie's pleading with Jean may be suggestive of one interpretation, in other contexts they may serve a different purpose. On yet other occasions, they may be used to indicate simply that a speaker has been interrupted.

Strindberg's use of dots is equally inconsistent. While three dots at the end of a line may indicate a pause in the dialogue as *points suspensifs*, they may also show that a character has been interrupted in the middle of a sentence (Josephson, 1965: 138). When in *The Father* Laura first introduces the idea to the Captain that he might not be Bertha's father, her second 'What if –' speculation is concluded by three dots in the original Swedish. In this and several other exchanges, the three dots indicate the speed of the dialogue, that one of the speakers does not have the time to conclude his/her sentence. The liveliness of Strindbergian dialogue is, however, at times also reinforced by question marks and, above all, exclamation marks, the use of which varies greatly from the way they are likely to be used by an English playwright. At times their function is to serve as a form of stage direction. In *Miss Julie*, this is clear when an exclamation mark concludes a line such as:

> FRÖKEN JULIE: (på knä med knäppta händer) *O, Gud i himmelen gör slut på mitt eländiga liv!* (Strindberg, SV, 1984: 155)
> [MISS JULIE: (*on her knees with clasped hands*) Oh, God in Heaven, put an end to my miserable life!]

Here Strindberg is telling the actress playing the part of Miss Julie that she is far from calm and composed. Yet, on a number of other occasions, he chooses not to use punctuation as acting directives; instead he provides specific information such as '(*Screams*)' or '(*Convulsed*)'. Most bewilderingly, perhaps, are lines that seem to be candidates for calm deliverance, but which nevertheless are followed by exclamation marks. In *Miss Julie,* this happens on more than one occasion when Jean is speaking, as in his description of the loving couples at Lake Como, who often leave the idyllic retreat not long after they arrive. 'They fall out of course! but the rent has to be paid, nevertheless!' There is some evidence here that, when Strindberg unexpectedly inserts an exclamation mark in the middle of a sentence, within the framework of his highly personal system of punctuation, he is showing his own emotional identification with the situation. An example of this intense empathy with the subject under discussion is found in *The Ghost Sonata*. At the time that he wrote the play, Strindberg was experiencing considerable problems in finding domestic help. Conversing in the Hyacinth Room with the Young Lady, the Student comments on the apparent wealth of the household as manifested in the domestic help. He receives an answer interspersed and concluded by exclamation marks:

> FRÖKEN: *Det hjälper inte! om man så har tre!* (Strindberg, SV, 1991: 219)
> [THE YOUNG LADY: It doesn't help! even if one has three!]

Confirming the impression of Strindberg's personal involvement with the problems of getting good domestic service are other references in the play to inadequate support with everyday chores, such as beds having to be remade and maids whose methods of cleaning leave something to be desired.

How then are the vagaries of Strindbergian punctuation dealt with in translation? Michael Meyer settles for the following approach:

> What about punctuation? It is, I think, accepted that a translator may legitimately break up a long sentence into two, or join two into one; but what is one to do with for example, Strindberg's repeated use of exclamation marks and three dots? My own feeling is that a translator must have a free hand to excise both. Exclamation marks used as often as Strindberg uses them give a terrible melodramatic effect; and three dots tend to bring out the worst in any actor – the 'meaningful pause'.

Actors nowadays, and readers too, are used to looking for the hidden implication of a phrase; better that a few should miss such an implication rather than saddle the dialogue with something that is as destructive in its way as repeated italics. (Meyer, 1971: 49)

In contrast to the approach chosen by Michael Meyer, in his more recent translation of *Miss Julie*, Gregory Motton chooses to replicate Strindberg's punctuation without any adjustment to English conventions. Below is the exchange between Jean and Julie as they plan to leave the Count's household in Motton's translation:

JEAN: I'll come with you – but now at once, before it's too late. Now this moment!

MISS JULIE: Get dressed then! (*picks up birdcage*)

JEAN: But no luggage! It would give us away!

MISS JULIE: No nothing! Just what fits into the compartment. (Motton, 2000: 132)

Fauna and Flora in Translation

Strindberg's keen interest in nature and his awareness of fauna and flora inform his novels as well as his dramas. As he was inclined to resort to less of a thematic approach than Ibsen in *The Wild Duck* and Chekhov in *The Seagull*, the transfer of Strindberg's bird symbolism in translation is not without problems. In *Miss Julie*, for example, the symbol of the bird in its cage, brutally killed by Jean, clearly foreshadows Miss Julie's own fate. In some translations this bird is described as a 'siskin', in others as a 'greenfinch'. The reason for this variation in translation is not difficult to find. In Swedish, the name of the bird is *grönsiska*, in a word-for-word translation, 'green siskin'. As no such bird exists in English, translators have been forced to choose between 'green finch', the name of a bigger bird belonging to the finch family, and 'siskin', a smaller bird of the same family, more likely to have been kept in a cage but lacking the reference to the colour green. Although, strictly speaking, 'siskin' would seem a more accurate rendering, referring to the bird as a 'greenfinch' does not detract from Strindberg's intentions in the original. More questionable, however, is the decision to give the bird a male gender. Not only does Miss Julie describe the bird as 'the only living creature that loves me' and we now know Julie's feelings about men, but a reference to the bird as 'he' also makes it difficult for the parallel to be drawn between the two victims:

JEAN: All right, give me the little beast, I'll wring its neck.

MISS JULIE: Don't hurt him will you? Don't – Oh, I can't!

JEAN: Well, I can – let's have it. (Watts, 1958: 111)

Somewhat surprisingly, however, a more recent translation of *Miss Julie* into English chooses to disregard the indications made possible by the gender aspect and refers to the siskin with the neutral pronoun 'it'.

JEAN: Give me the bastard and I'll wring its neck.

MISS JULIE: All right, but don't let it suffer, don't – I can't, no –

JEAN: Give me it – I can do it. (McGuiness, 2000: 51)

While the caged siskin may be seen to represent a woman unable to shake off her chains, predators such as the eagle, the hawk and the falcon stand for masculinity with its associated attributes of power and incisiveness. It is true that at times Strindberg saw himself as a dove, but this was more likely to happen when he felt under pressure and the victim of an evil world. But he would also use the word *Örnen* ('Eagle'), his *nom de plume* during his university days, to refer to himself in the hope perhaps that some of the strength and power of the bird might rub off on him. Strindberg even went as far as using a quill from an imperial eagle for writing and was frequently photographed pen in hand (Brusewitz, 1989: 194–5).

Hardly surprising then that Strindberg lets Jean refer to 'the hawks and the falcons' as the 'rulers' soaring high above while those that they 'rule' have to remain content watching from down below:

JEAN: ... Do you know how the world looks from down there – no, you don't! Like hawks and falcons whose backs you rarely see because most of the time they're soaring up there! (Strindberg, SV, 1984: 156)

In Frank McGuiness's version, both predators remain as in the original:

JEAN: ... Do you know what the world looks like from down here – no, you don't. You're like the hawk and the falcon. They fly so high above you rarely see their backs. (McGuiness, 2000: 23)

In Peter Watts's translation, on the other hand, 'the hawks' remain while 'the falcons' turn into 'eagles':

JEAN: ... You don't know how the world looks from down below, do you? No – of course you don't, any more than hawks and eagles do; and we don't see their backs, because they're nearly always soaring up over our heads. (Watts, 1958: 90)

In Helen Cooper's translation, the two birds appear as one but in the plural form, 'hawks':

JEAN: ... Do you know what the world looks like from down here? No, you don't see. Because you see the world from up there – hovering like great hawks, high above us. What's it like? I've never flown with the hawks. (Cooper, 1992: 15)

A possible reason for the decision to turn the two birds into the same species might have been to reinforce the focus on the hawk image, one to which Strindberg returns later in the play. Upon their return from Jean's bedroom, Jean and Miss Julie have the following, sexually-charged exchange:

> MISS JULIE: And now you've seen the back of the hawk ...
>
> JEAN: Not exactly the back ... (Strindberg, SV, 1984:156)

Helen Cooper solves the problem in the following manner:

> MISS JULIE: So now you've flown with the hawks ...
>
> JEAN: Not exactly *flown*. (Cooper, 1992: 25)

Frank McGuiness prefers to stay close to the original:

> MISS JULIE: Now you've seen the hawk on its back.
>
> JEAN: Not quite on its back. (McGuiness, 2000: 34):

In its use of bird symbolism, *The Ghost Sonata* presents problems of an even greater complexity. When the Mummy is using parrot language, Strindberg alludes to a number of facts familiar to a Swedish but not an English theatre audience.

> MUMIEN: (som en papegoja) *Vackra gojan! Å Jakob ä där? Kurrrrre*! (Törnqvist, 1976: 22–3):
>
> [THE MUMMY: (*Like a parrot.*) Beautiful parrot! And Jaco is there? Currrrr?]

Here the translator is faced with the following problems. The first part of the line would naturally be translated as 'Pretty Polly' were it not for the fact that *goja* is also a colloquial Swedish expression for nonsense used in the context of talking rubbish, which is of course exactly what the Mummy is doing. In addition, Jacob is not only a well- known name for a parrot in Sweden, probably derived from 'jako', the generic name for the kind of parrot most skilled in imitating human language, there is a further dimension to the reference to Jacob. 'Jacob, where are you' is the name of a form of Swedish 'Blind man's bluff' which draws on the biblical image of the blind Isaac feeling his son Jacob dressed as Esau. In *The Ghost Sonata*, the name Jacob is also likely to refer to Jacob Hummel, the father of the Mummy's child, who has abandoned her and for whom she is now looking. The likelihood that this intricate web of references in the original could be transferred into English with any degree of success would undoubtedly seem slim.

In addition to fauna, Strindberg's work also makes frequent references to flora. In northern Europe, after many months of cold and snow, the signs heralding the arrival of spring are eagerly awaited. Among the first signs are the green shoots of the willow tree, used by Strindberg at the very beginning of *Easter* to set the tone for the play:

> ELIS: (*looking round*) The double windows down, the floor scrubbed, and clean curtains! It's really spring again! They've scraped the ice off the street, and down by the river the willows are out. Yes, it's spring ... (Watts, 1958: 124)

In Sweden, as in Chekhov's Russia, intense interest is centred on the birch tree; the reappearance of new green foliage is traditionally linked to the arrival of a warmer, gentler season. Birch trees, sprigs and wreaths interwoven with flowers worn by children on festive occasions during the summer occur repeatedly in the Swedish idylls captured on canvas by Strindberg's friend, the artist Carl Larsson. When towards the end of *The Father*, the Captain, enveloped in a straightjacket, starts reminiscing about spring, it is among the birch trees, representing light, warmth and carefree happiness that the birds and flowers start to appear. It is doubtful, however, that these deeply felt emotions expressed by the Captain in the original survive in John Osborne's English adaptation of the play:

> CAPTAIN: ... When you were so young, Laura, and we would walk in the birch woods together, among the cowslips and thrushes.
> Lovely, so lovely. Just think of it – how pleasing our life was and how it is now. (Osborne, 1989: 49)

Through minimal English adjustment of Strindberg's floral imagery, the reliving of the moment is more succcessfully conveyed in Richard Nelson's version, albeit at the cost of the loss of the birch trees:

> CAPTAIN: Laura, when we were young we took walks in the woods, there were primroses, thrushes – that was good, that was good!

Scandinavian rituals which mark the arrival of summer, peak on Midsummer Eve. This is the time when Miss Julie steps down into the servants' quarters, fatefully meeting with Jean. Had it not been Midsummer Eve, when traditional rules governing social behaviour are suspended, Miss Julie would not have been able to invite Jean to dance, nor could she have trespassed onto servants' territory. In fact it may be argued that, without the rituals and the enchantment of Midsummer Eve, Strindberg's play could not have been written, as Julie's meeting with Jean would never have taken place. To evoke the atmosphere of the night during which the sun never sets, Strindberg's stage directions call for the kitchen stove to be decorated with birch twigs, the glass doors to reflect lilac bushes in blossom in the garden, and for a jar resting on the table to be filled with cut lilac. When Miss Julie reminisces about the Midsummers of her childhood she recalls lilacs and birch trees. The very fact that it is on Midsummer Eve that Julie meets her fate, the night of hopes, wishes and promises, is in itself a sardonic twist impossible to convey in translation. As Julie recalls:

> JULIE: The memories would start. I'd remember when I was a child – the church on Midsummer Day was thick with leaves and branches. Birch twigs and lilacs. (McGuiness, 2000: 49)

As in the case of Miss Julie recalling her childhood, it is not the flowers *per se* that evoke emotions but what they recall and represent. In *A Dream Play,* immediately following the prologue showing Indra's daughter descending to earth, the gilded dome of the castle emerges out of a 'forest of giant hollyhocks – white, pink, crimson, yellow, violet'. This, the very first floral image of hollyhocks as arguably the symbol of apparent bliss and happy idyll, may not be too unfamiliar to an English audience. Nor is the next floral image occurring only shortly afterwards in the scene in Act 1 where the courting Officer is waiting at the stage door for his beloved Victoria. Viewed as the original, central core of the play (Lamm, 1926: 307) this scene often elicits the strongest response from the audience, not surprisingly perhaps, considering the number of times Strindberg must have been waiting outside the theatre for Siri von Essen, his first wife and then, later in life, for Harriet Bosse, his third. Victoria never appears, however, and as the Officer grows older and his hair turns white, the roses in his hand wither and die. But while the symbol of red roses is well known, Strindberg's stage directions also call for another flower. Through a gate in the wall a passageway leads to a bright green opening with a giant, blue monkshood. And as the Officer anxiously awaits the arrival of Victoria, failing to find her among the actors hurriedly leaving through the stage door, Strindberg provides him with the following line:

> THE OFFICER: She must be here soon ... (*turning to the stage door attendant.*) The blue monkshood out there. I've seen it since I was a child ... Is it the same one? ... I remember in a vicarage once when I was seven years old ... there're two doves, blue doves underneath that hood ... but that time a bumble-bee came and crept into the hood ... Got you, I thought and pressed it shut; but the bee stung through it and I cried ... but the vicar's wife came and put some mud on it ... and then we had wild strawberries and milk for supper ... I think it's getting dark already. (Strindberg, SV, 1988: 23)

According to his own specifications, Strindberg's flower is an Aconitum, which might grow to the majestic height of close to six feet and must have seemed a towering presence to a seven-year-old. In the northern part of

Sweden, one variety of this plant, the *Aconitum eptentrionale*, with its lighter blue, purplish flowers is commonly found growing wild in the mountains. Strindberg, however, to judge from the reference to the dark blue colour of the flower, appears to have encountered the *Aconitum napellus* which, if found in the vicinity of a vicarage, is more likely to be the garden variety. Here Strindberg paints a picture of two doves nestling underneath the helmet or hood of the flower, an image of happiness that matches the initial, blissful state of the Officer, waiting for Victoria. But just as Victoria never appears and the Officer loses the love he thought was his, the happiness of the two doves inside the flower comes to a painful end brought about by a stinging bumble-bee. To this may be added that it is unlikely to have escaped the attention of Strindberg, the scientist, that the monkshood is an extremely poisonous plant, containing the alkaloid aconitine. In the case of the Officer as a young boy, however, there is first some soothing comfort available from the vicar's wife in the form of wet mud to cool the sting. And to make sure the episode had a happy ending, the children finished the day with wild strawberries and milk, every Swedish child's wish come true on a warm summer's evening. For the Officer/author on the other hand, life's problems are no longer solved quite as easily and he concludes, 'I think it's getting dark already'.

The extent to which translators of *A Dream Play* have been fully aware of the details involved in this floral image is difficult to ascertain. In Meyer's translation the two doves are first described as being 'on it', then 'under that hood':

> THE OFFICER: Now, she must be here soon. I say! That flower out there, that blue monkshood. I've seen that since I was a child. Is it the same one? I remember in a parsonage, when I was seven – **there are two doves on it, blue doves under that hood – but once a bee came and crept into the hood**. Then I thought: 'Now I have you!', so I **pinched the flower shut;** but the bee stung through it, and I cried. But then the parson's wife came and put wet earth on it – and we had wild strawberries for supper. I think it's getting dark already. (Meyer, 1973: 14; author's emphasis)

In his American version, Evert Sprinchorn has tackled the problem this way:

> THE OFFICER: She's got to come along pretty soon ... Madame – that blue flower out there – that monkshood. I remember it from the time I was a child. Can't be the same one, can it? ... It was at the parsonage, I remember, the minister's house – the garden. I was seven years old ... **Fold back the top petals – the pistil and stamen look like two doves. We used to do that as children ... But this time a bee came – went into**

the flower. 'Got you!' I said. And **I pinched the flower together.** And the bee stung me ... And I cried ... Then the minister's wife came and put mud on my finger ... Later we had strawberries and cream for dessert at supper ... I do believe it's getting dark already. (Sprinchorn, 1986: 662; author's emphasis)

While Meyer has attempted only a slight adjustment, and added the words 'on it', Sprinchorn has clearly felt the need to expand on the original, perhaps not altogether a wise decision.

Strindberg was not a botanist in the strict sense of the word; he was attracted to flora, primarily because of the variety of shapes and configurations which, to his artist's mind, would trigger off a chain of associations. In an essay written during the latter part of 1875 about an unfamiliar flower found on the bank of the river Danube, Strindberg's initial impression was of a violet. However, he also saw features reminiscent of the orchid family with its gracefully-shaped butterfly flowers. Upon his return from his botanical excursion he put the flower in water. Floating on the water's surface, the plant now recalled memories of the leaves of the water lily (Kärnell, 1962: 250–5). What practising botanists saw as significant details for purposes of classification, was of little interest to Strindberg, the artist, for whom the importance lay in similarity in form, shape and colour. The triggering of a chain of associations, set in motion by visual stimuli, is clearly illustrated in *The Ghost Sonata* in the exchange between The Student and the terminally-ill Young Lady in the Hyacinth Room. Here, according to the stage directions, there are 'hyacinths of every colour everywhere', again a clearly intentional choice of flower, as hyacinths at the time of Strindberg had strong associations with funerals. The conversation starts with a mention of hyacinths, which in turn triggers more floral imagery, then expands to include other micro- and macrocosmic images:

THE YOUNG LADY: Now I see – aren't snowflakes also six-pointed like hyacinth lilies?

THE STUDENT: You're right – then snowflakes are falling stars ...

THE YOUNG LADY: And the snowdrop is a snow star ... rising from the snow.

THE STUDENT: And the largest and most beautiful of all the stars in the firmament, the red and gold Sirius is the narcissus, with its red and gold chalice and six white rays.

THE YOUNG LADY: Have you ever seen the shallot in bloom?

THE STUDENT: I certainly have! It too bears its flowers in a ball, a sphere like the globe of heaven, strewn with white stars ...

THE YOUNG LADY: Yes! God, how magnificent! Whose idea was this?

THE STUDENT: Yours!

THE YOUNG LADY: Yours!

THE STUDENT: Ours! – Together we have given birth to something. We are wed ... (Carlson, 1981: 290)

If Strindberg is to remain who he was, his flight of fantasy and rapid associative powers would not withstand adjustment and large-scale adaptations. There are, however, other instances where his work is not 'untranslatable' and where there is good reason for the translator or playwright creating a 'new version' to dig sufficiently deep into the original to ensure that the hidden depth of his genius is properly brought out.

Notes

1. This is a shortened version of a chapter on Strindberg translation in *Europe on Stage: Translation and Theatre* (Anderman, 2005).
2. Unless otherwise indicated translations throughout are my own.

References

Anderman, G. (2005) *Europe on Stage: Translation and Theatre*. London: Oberon Books.
Billington, M. (2006) *The Guardian*, 15 July.
Brandell, G. (1971) *Drama i tre avsnitt*. Stockholm: Wahlström & Widstrand.
Brusewitz, G. (1989) *Guldörnen och duvorna: Fågelmotiv hos Strindberg*. Stockholm: Wahlström Widstrand.
Carlson, H.G. (trans.) (1981) *Strindberg: Five Plays*. Berkeley: University of California Press.
Cooper, H. (trans.) (1992) *Miss Julie*. From a literal translation by Peter Hogg. London: Methuen.
Josephson, L. (1965) *Strindberg's Drama Fröken Julie*. Stockholm: Almqvist & Wiksell.
Kärnell, K-A. (1962) *Strindbergs bildspråk: En studie i prosastil*. Stockholm: Almqvist & Wiksell.
Lamm, M. (1926) *Strindbergs dramer II*. Stockholm: Albert Bonniers Förlag.
Lyons, J. (1980) The pronouns of address in *Anna Karenina*: The stylistics of bilingualism and the impossibility of translation. In S. Greenbaum, G. Leech and J. Svartvik (eds) *Studies in English Linguistics for Randolph Quirk* (pp. 109–122). London: Longman
McGuiness, F. (trans.) (2000) *August Strindberg: Miss Julie, and The Stronger*. From a literal translation by Charlotte Barslund. London: Faber and Faber.
Meyer, M. (1966) Strindberg in England. In C.R. Smedmark (ed.) *Essays on Strindberg* (pp. 65–73). Stockholm: Beckman.
Meyer, M. (1971) On translating plays. *20th Century Studies* (11), 44–51.
Meyer, M. (trans.) (1973) *August Strindberg. A Dream Play: An Interpretation by Ingmar Bergman*. London: Secker and Warburg.
Motton, G. (trans.) (2000) *Strindberg. The Play* (Vol. 1): *The Father, Miss Julie, The Comrades, Creditors*. London: Oberon Books.
Nelson, R. (adapt.) (1998) *August Strindberg: The Father*. London: Oberon Books.
Osborne, J. (adapt.) (1989) *Strindberg's The Father and Ibsen's Hedda Gabler*. London: Faber and Faber.

Sprinchorn, E. (trans.) (1986) *A Dream Play: Selected Plays, August Strindberg*. Minneapolis: University of Minnesota Press.

Strindberg, A. (1984) *Samlade verk, nationalupplaga* [Collected Works, National Edition]. (SV Vol. 2) *Fordringsägare' Fadren, Fröken Julie*. Stockholm: Almquist & Wiksell.

Strindberg, A. (1988) *Samlade verk, nationalupplaga* [Collected Works, National Edition]. (SV Vol. 46) *Ett Drömspel*. Stockholm: Norstedts.

Strindberg, A. (1991) *Samlade verk, nationalupplaga* [Collected Works, National Edition]. (SV Vol. 58) *Kammarspel, Oväder, Brända tomten, Spöksonaten, Pelikanen, Svarta handsken*. Stockholm: Almquist & Wiksell.

Törnqvist, E. (1976) Att översätta Strindberg Spöksonaten på engleska. *Svensk litteraturtidskrift* 39 (2), 3–31.

Törnqvist, E. (1999) Unreliable narration in Strindbergian drama. *Scandinavica* 38 (1), 61–79.

Watts, P. (trans.) (1958) *Three Plays. August Strindberg: The Father, Miss Julie, Easter*. London: Penguin Books.

Chapter 9
Mind the Gap: Translating the 'Untranslatable'

MARGARET JULL COSTA

Introduction

A cloud of negativity tends to hover over the subject of translation. People say sourly that something 'reads like a translation' or else dredge up Robert Frost's dictum that 'poetry is what gets lost in translation'. A copy editor even said to me once that my translation had almost convinced her that it might be worth reading translations. We translators are a paradoxically much-reviled and much-ignored bunch, and the idea of the existence of 'cultural concepts' that obstinately resist translation can feel like one more stick with which to beat the translator. As a full-time literary translator from Spanish and Portuguese, I suppose I can't afford to believe in the untranslatable. It's my job to translate everything, knowing that there might be some loss, but that there might also be gain, and never giving in to that counsel of despair telling me that a translation is not the real thing, not the same thing, and definitely never a better thing. What I propose to do in this chapter is to discuss how I have dealt with translating the apparently untranslatable cultural 'aura' around:

(1) words – naming the physical world;
(2) phrases – puns, idioms, proverbs;
(3) references – historical, geographical and cultural.

The examples will be drawn from four of my translations: *The Maias* (*Os Maias*) by the great 19th-century novelist Eça de Queiroz; *Seeing* (*Ensaio sobre a lucidez*) by Nobel prize-winner José Saramago; *The Crossing: A Story of East Timor* (*Crónica de uma Travessia: A época do Ai-Dik-Funam*) by the East Timorese writer Luís Cardoso, and *The Book of Disquiet* (*Livro do desassossego*) by the Portuguese modernist poet Fernando Pessoa.

Naming the Physical World

As any bemused tourist will know, food can be very culturally specific, and it can present problems for the translator too. I would like to look at two examples where the writer is using a particular culinary item for its symbolic value within the plot and where finding a precise English equivalent (if such a thing exists) may be less vital than bringing out its symbolic role. There is an episode in *The Maias* in which the love-struck hero, Carlos, goes with a friend to Sintra, the fashionable summer retreat just outside Lisbon, which Byron (1902: 8) memorably described as 'glorious Eden'. Carlos is going to Sintra because he believes that there he will find the woman whom he has seen twice, but never met, and with whom he has nonetheless fallen passionately in love. His friend, Cruges, has been charged by his mother not to return without bringing back a unique Sintra speciality – *queijadas* (tartlets filled with a mixture of sugar, egg, cinnamon and a fresh cheese similar to ricotta). Both men, therefore, are on a mission, and the literary function of Cruges' mission is to act as a bathetic counterpart to that of Carlos. They drive back at the end of the day, with Carlos having failed to encounter his true love, and Cruges having forgotten to buy the cakes. Both woman and cakes are delectable, sought-after consumables and, as we learn later, both can be bought. The chapter ends with Cruges' heartfelt cry: *'Esqueceram-me as queijadas!'* ('I forgot the *queijadas!*') (Jull Costa, 2006: 251).

Any Portuguese reader would know that *queijadas* are a Sintra speciality, but I have decided not to make this explicit at this point in the translation for the following reasons:

- I feel that this is sufficiently clear from the context;
- any British or American reader is going to be familiar with the concept of a special cake or candy that is unique to a particular town, especially a tourist town.

And in a way, how I translate *queijadas* is irrelevant because what matters is the connection the reader is being asked to make between the elusive woman and what prove to be the elusive cakes. That said, a translation has to be found. 'Cheesecakes' conjures up the wrong image, so perhaps 'cheese tartlets' or 'cheese pastries' would be better, and I have, for the moment, opted for the latter (I am still putting the finishing touches to my translation). Leaving the word untranslated and perhaps adding a footnote is, of course, an option (one that I discuss below), but here it would, I feel, draw unnecessary attention to the word. It does not really matter what kind of cakes these are. It does matter that the translation is consistent throughout the novel, however, because these *queijadas*, having once been associated with Maria Eduarda – the woman being pursued – recur later in the novel, either as a gift that has, again, been forgotten or as a gift that comes to nothing. When Ega, Carlos's best friend, first meets Maria Eduarda at Carlos's house, he brings with him a packet of *queijadas*:

*Mas o papel pardo, mal atado, desfez-se; e uma provisão fresca de **queijadas de Sintra** rolou, **esmagando-se**, sobre as flores do tapete.*[1] (Eça de Queiroz, 1888: 473)

However, the brown paper parcel, only loosely tied together, came undone, and a fresh supply of **exquisite Sintra cheese pastries** tumbled out onto the floral rug and promptly **crumbled into nothing**. (Jull Costa, forthcoming)

Here, I have added 'exquisite' in order to underline the deliciousness and specialness of these cakes. I have, in a sense, expanded on *'esmagando-se'* by translating it as 'crumbled into nothing'. However, since *'esmagar'* means not only 'crumble', but also 'crush' and 'exterminate', and since the 'unique' relationship between Maria Eduarda and Carlos is just as fragile as those cheese pastries and will, quite soon, also 'crumble into nothing', this 'expansion' is, I feel, justifiable.

Staying with the culinary world, in Saramago's *Seeing*, it is the turn of biscuits to take on symbolic overtones. The police inspector (the embattled anti-hero of the piece), called in to investigate a supposed conspiracy, is marooned in a rather bleak apartment in which all he has been left to eat for breakfast are some rather old *bolos secos*. These are a kind of thickly textured biscuit, rather like brittle shortbread:

Os bolos pareciam feitos de granito com açucar. Trincava-os com força, reduzia-os a pedaços mais cómodos de mastigar, depois lentamente desfazia-os. (Saramago, 2004: 279):

The biscuits were like sugary granite. He bit into them hard, reduced them to smaller pieces that were easier to chew, then slowly crumbled them up. (Jull Costa, 2006: 260)

As Saramago makes clear here, *bolos secos* grow harder as they grow stale. This, of course, is the opposite of what happens to most biscuits, which, left to their own devices, grow softer. However, as a translation, 'shortbread' is far too Scottish and, as with the *queijadas*, an exact English translation (there isn't one) is less important than what the staleness and inedibility of the *bolos secos* are intended to evoke: the inspector's loneliness, the arid nature of the mission he has been sent on, his dogged adherence to duty (eating the inedible biscuits because they are what have been given to him to eat), as well as the ungenerous, uncaring nature of the regime he is working for. So 'biscuits' or, later, 'stale biscuits' must be relied on to relay all of that.

Another of 'my' authors, the Spanish novelist, Javier Marías, has himself worked as a translator. He says that 'the translator is a privileged reader ... and a privileged writer' (Patterson, 2006). I think he means by this that any good translation inevitably involves a very close reading of a text, which means, as I hope I have illustrated, that any cultural concept must be viewed in the context of the book or story as a whole and translated accordingly. The translator is also 'a privileged writer': if, as a translator, you are lucky enough to work with very fine writers, your own skills as a writer are constantly being challenged and expanded. Indeed, you often have to stretch your own language in order to accommodate the language being translated.

An example: the Portuguese have a word for the area immediately outside a building or house, *testada*. In villages, it was (and may still be) the custom for the women of the house to keep their *testada* swept and clean. In *Seeing*, during a strike by street-cleaners, the women come out to clean up any rubbish themselves:

> ... *e nisto se estava quando, meio-dia exacto era, de todas as casas da cidade saíram mulheres armadas de vassouras, baldes e pás, e, sem uma palavra, começaram a varrer **as testadas** dos prédios em que viviam, desde a porta até ao meio da rua, onde se encontravam com outras mulheres que, do outro lado, para o mesmo fim e com as mesmas armas, haviam descido. **Afirmam os dicionários que a testada é a parte de uma rua ou estrada que fica à frente de um prédio**, e nada há de mais certo, mas também dizem, dizem-no pelo menos alguns, **que varrer a sua testada significa afastar de si alguma responsabilidade ou culpa**. Grande engano o vosso, senhores filólogos e lexicólogos distraídos, varrer a sua testada começou por ser precisamente o que estão a fazer agora estas mulheres da capital, como no passado também o haviam feito, nas aldeias, as suas mães e avós, e não o faziam elas, como o não fazem estas, para afastar de si uma responsabilidade, mas para assumí-la.* (Saramago, 2004: 106)

> ... and then, at midday exactly, while all this was going on, from every house in the city there emerged women armed with brooms, buckets and dustpans, and, without a word, they started sweeping **their own patch of pavement and street**, from the front door as far as the middle of the road, where they encountered other women who had emerged from the houses opposite with exactly the same objective and armed with the same weapons. **Now, the dictionaries state that someone's patch is an area under their jurisdiction or control, in this case, the area outside somebody's house,** and this is quite true, but they also say, or at least some of them do, that **to sweep your own patch means to look after your own interests**. A great mistake on your part, O absent-minded philologists and lexicographers, to sweep your own patch started out meaning precisely what these women in the capital are doing now, just as their mothers and grandmothers before them used to do in their villages, and they, like these women, were not just looking after their own interests, but after the interests of the community as well. (Jull Costa, 2006: 92–3)

Here, the problem for the translator is compounded by the fact that there is also a Portuguese idiom using the term *testada* – *varrer a testada*. This has the literal meaning of 'to sweep the *testada*' and the idiomatic sense of 'to try to slide out of taking responsibility for something'. Faced by two concepts highly specific to Portugal and to Portuguese, I plumped, after much mental wrestling, for 'patch' and invented an English idiom to go with it, feeling that Saramago's comment on the fallibility of dictionaries and lexicographers gave me a certain leeway. After all, the whole passage does tilt at authority and its cut-and-dried ways on behalf of the demotic and the informal. My 'invention' meant that I had both to add to and subtract from the original, as you can see by comparing the sections in bold in the original and in the translation. What matters, I feel, is that I have kept the linguistic playfulness of the Portuguese, and if that has required me to indulge in a little creative infidelity to both the English and the Portuguese languages, then so be it.

Punds, Idioms, Proverbs

Puns, idioms and proverbs are sometimes obligingly easy to translate and sometimes so culturally fixed as to be exceedingly difficult. In the case of Saramago, who loves idiomatic expressions and proverbs, he often compounds the difficulty for the translator by punning on or playing with proverbs, so that, sometimes, the 'normal', 'easy' translation of a proverb has to be rejected in favour of another less obvious version. An example: the police inspector in *Seeing* has returned to the apartment, expecting to meet an ambush. He checks all the rooms and wardrobes, then feels slightly ridiculous when he finds no lurking attackers. In response to the inspector's slight embarrassment, the narrator comments consolingly: *'o seguro morreu de velho'*). The equivalent in English would probably be 'better safe than sorry', but this won't do here, for two reasons. The apartment in which he is staying – a base for police officers working undercover – masquerades as the office of an insurance company, Providential Ltd, and the sentence goes on:

> ... *deve sabê-lo bem esta providencial, s.a. sendo não só de seguros, mas também de resseguros.* (Saramago, 2004: 319)

> ... as providential ltd must well know, since it deals not only with insurance but with reinsurance.[2] (Jull Costa, 2006: 298)

The *'seguro'* in the proverb, meaning more or less 'he who plays safe', is picked up in *'seguros'* and *'resseguros'* – 'insurance' and 'reinsurance'. So the translated proverb has, if possible, to include a reference to 'sure'/'insure'. Also, the inspector, having disobeyed orders, is doomed, and the proverb therefore becomes an ironic comment on his imminent demise, for he has not played safe at all. My solution was, again, to invent: 'slow but sure ensures a ripe old age', which combines all the necessary ingredients and has, I hope, an authentic proverbial ring.

Another example: earlier in the novel, the inspector is bringing to a close an awkward conversation with a suspect in which he has avoided revealing the real reason for his visit: ' ... *veremos se neste caso se confirma o antigo ditado que dizia* **Quem fez a panela fez o testo para ela** ...' (Saramago, 2004: 238)

There did not appear to be a neat English equivalent for this proverb (in bold), although perhaps 'no smoke without fire' would be the closest. However, I opted here for a literal translation: 'She that made the saucepan made the lid' which keeps the pleasing combination of the antiquated, the domestic and the gnomic, and is picked up in the continuing conversation:

> *De panelas se trata então, senhor comissário, perguntou em tom irónico a mulher do médico, De testos, minha senhora, de testos, respondeu o comissário ao mesmo tempo que se retirava, aliviado por a adversária lhe ter fornecido a resposta para uma saída mais ou menos airosa. Tinha uma leve dor de cabeça.* (Saramago, 2004: 238)

> So it's to do with saucepans, then, superintendent, asked the doctor's wife in a wry tone, No, it's to do with lids, madam, lids, replied the superintendent as he withdrew, relieved that his adversary had supplied him with a reasonably nimble exit line. He had a faint headache. (Jull Costa, 2006: 219)

The ludicrous nature of the exchange has thus been preserved.

As with idioms and proverbs, the adjective 'untranslatable' is frequently attached to the word 'pun', and here again it is often impossible for the translator simply to translate what is there. A new and equally appropriate pun has to be invented. In *Seeing*, two elections are held in which the majority of the electorate has returned blank votes – *'votos brancos'*. Now *'branco'* can mean 'blank' and 'white', a fact that sometimes works with the English translator and sometimes against. For example, when a government minister comments that the returning of blank votes could spread like a modern-day black death (*peste negra*), the prime minister corrects him with: 'You mean blank death (*peste branca*), don't you'. The happy fact that 'black' and 'blank' sound similar in English introduces a rather satisfying 'new' pun. However, things grow more complicated when the narrator describes how the word *'branco'* (associated with the election débâcle of blank votes) becomes a taboo word that ordinary citizens take pains to avoid, fearful of being accused of having been part of the supposed 'blank vote conspiracy'. He lists some of the turns of phrase containing the word *'branco'* that people are now careful not to say:

> *De uma folha de papel branco, por exemplo, dizia-se que era **desprovida de cor**, uma toalha que toda a vida tinha sido branca passou a ser cor de leite, a*

neve deixou de ser comparada a um manto branco para tornar-se na maior carga alvacenta dos últimos vinte anos, os estudantes acabaram com aquilo de dizer que estavam em branco, simplesmente confessavam que não sabiam nada da matéria ... (Saramago, 2004: 54)

A blank piece of paper, for example, would be described instead as **virgin, a blank on a form that had all its life been a blank became the space provided, blank looks all became vacant instead,** students stopped saying that their minds had gone blank, and owned up to the fact that they simply knew nothing about the subject ... (Jull Costa, 2006: 43–44)

Here, I had to change two of the examples (compare bold text in original and translation) and a riddle that occurs later in the same paragraph: *'Branco é, galinha o põe'*. The original riddle means literally: 'It's white and a hen lays it'. Since *'votos brancos'* in English are 'blank votes', the word 'white' is of no use to me, and it seems impossible to come up with a riddle that will combine the words 'blank' and 'chicken' or 'hen' and then fit in with what ensues. And so I created my own riddle – 'You can fill me in, draw me and fire me' – and completely rewrote the rest of the passage:

- *mas o caso mais interessante de todos foi o súbito desaparecimento da adivinha com que, durante gerações e gerações, pais, avós, tios e vizinhos supuseram estimular a inteligência e a capacidade dedutiva das criancinhas,* **Branco é, galinha o põe,** *e isto aconteceu porque as pessoas, recusando-se a pronunciar a palavra, se aperceberam de que a pergunta era absolutamente disparatada, uma vez que a galinha, qualquer galinha de qualquer raça, nunca conseguirá, por mais que se esforce, pôr outra coisa que não sejam ovos.* (Saramago, 2004: 54)

    but the most interesting case of all was the sudden disappearance of the riddle with which, for generations and generations, parents, grandparents, aunts, uncles and neighbours had sought to stimulate the intelligence and deductive powers of children, **You can fill me in, draw me and fire me, what am I, and people, reluctant to elicit the word blank from innocent children, justified this by saying that the riddle was far too difficult for those with limited experience of the world.** (Jull Costa, 2006: 44)

So, yes, those puns are, in a sense, untranslatable, but different puns can be created to replace them, as long as they are in keeping with the tone and tenor of the original.

I suppose this and other examples I have given could be construed as 'domestication'. As you are no doubt aware, there are two supposedly opposing camps in translation – the foreignisers and the domesticators – those who feel that some hint of foreignness can and should remain in the translation, and those who believe that a translation should read as if originally written in the target language, in my case, English. I think that most translators probably move between these two camps all the time. Such is the complexity of languages and of cultures, that hard-and-fast rules simply cannot be applied to the art of translation, where one is constantly juggling with linguistic and cultural concepts which may or may not have an equivalent in the target language.

Historical, Geographical and Cultural References

One is, perhaps, on safer ground in the world of cultural, historical and geographical references, since no interpretation is required. Here, though, the problem is how much to explain and how to do it. *Os Maias* was first published in 1888, but is set 13 years or so before that, and refers back to a still earlier period. It is full of references, some of which the author, Eça, explains in the text; others he assumes the reader will understand. For example, the grandfather in the novel was, in his youth, considered a dangerous radical by his overly pious father, and when the grandfather/son apparently recanted and asked to be allowed to travel to England:

> *O pai beijou-o, todo em lágrimas, acedeu a tudo fervorosamente, vendo ali a evidente, a gloriosa intercessão de Nossa Senhora da Soledade! E o mesmo frei Jerónimo da Conceição, seu confessor, declarou este milagre – não inferior ao de Carnaxide.* (Eça de Queiroz, 1888: 14)

> His father kissed him tearfully and gave his fervent consent, seeing in all this the evident, glorious intercession of Our Lady of Solitude! Even his confessor, Father Jerónimo da Conceição, declared this miracle to be in no way inferior to the vision of Our Lady at Carnaxide. (Jull Costa, forthcoming)

I have slightly expanded the original text to explain enough about the reference to make it clear to the modern-day Anglophone reader, giving information about the nature of this miracle. Again, when Eça refers to the *Belfast*, the British ship that carried to safety in England many of the Portuguese liberals fleeing the Miguelista coup in 1828, I have added just a few bits of information to indicate where they sailed from and the nationality of the ship:

> *Ao princípio os emigrados liberais, Palmela e a gente do* Belfast, *ainda o vieram desassossegar e consumir.* (Eça de Queiroz, 1888: 16)

> At first, other liberal emigrés, Palmela and those who sailed from La Coruña in the British ship, the Belfast, came to bother and badger him. (Jull Costa, forthcoming)

I do my best to avoid footnotes. Most publishers of foreign fiction hate them, and I prefer to include information in the text where possible. I have resorted to footnotes in only two translations. The first was in *The Book of Disquiet* (*Livro do desassossego*) by Fernando Pessoa, where I supplied footnotes about some of the Portuguese writers mentioned in the text, and with whom I felt readers might not be familiar. I also explained what the Baixa in Lisbon is – the lower town in Lisbon, where the main shops and offices still are, and where the narrator-diarist, Bernardo Soares, works. I also included a street map. However, when translating the novels of Eça de Queiroz, most of which are also set in Lisbon, I have chosen not to do this, possibly because I feel that plot is more important than place, whereas in the plotless, fragmentary world of *The Book of Disquiet* place is paramount.

The only other book where I felt that footnotes and, indeed, a glossary were indispensable was *The Crossing: A Story of East Timor* by Luis Cardoso (1997), which is full of place names, personal names and terminology that were entirely unfamiliar to me and would be equally unfamiliar to most readers. This was the first time I had translated a book set in a culture and a country about which I know nothing, and it was quite an alarming experience. Despite its long occupation by the Portuguese, East Timor is nothing like Portugal, apart from the education system comprising Jesuit schools and colleges, and the implantation, in its day, of Salazar's fascist youth movement, Mocidade Portuguesa. Fortunately, the author was immensely helpful and patient when fielding my many, many queries. A number of the place names required footnotes because they were not just places, but places of great symbolic meaning to the East Timorese. The Tetum name (Tetum is one of the main national languages in East Timor) for Ramelau which was famous as the highest peak in the Portuguese empire is Tatamailau, which means 'grandfather of mountains' and was adopted by Fretilin (*Frente Revolucionária de Timor-Leste Independente* or Revolutionary Front for an Independent East Timor) as a symbol of the high aspirations of the East Timorese people. As can be seen from the number of parenthetical explanations in that one explanation, there was much to explain! Also Cardoso, writing largely for the East Timorese diaspora, would make oblique references to people and things, which would be transparent to anyone from East Timor, but utterly opaque to anyone not. (The Portuguese edition I worked from also had some footnotes for the benefit of Portuguese readers.) There is a reference in one section to a corral owned by '*uma Corte-Real*', which, apparently, is a common name in the area, and usually denotes some member of local royalty. José Alexandre Gusmão is mentioned as a schoolfellow and failed goalkeeper, but no reference is made to the fact that he is, in fact, Xanana Gusmão, later, the guerrilla leader of the independence movement in East Timor and, subsequently (although not until 2002, five years after the original was published and two years after my translation), its first President. People are commonly referred to, as well, by names that indicate where in East Timor they come from: *dagadá*, someone from the region of Los Palos; *bunak*, someone from the Bobonaro region; *firaku*, someone from the easternmost point of East Timor, etc. The other bit of essential apparatus to be added was a map of East Timor. And there were some things so alien to our culture that only a note would suffice to explain, for example, *rain-fila*. This is a trick that the land plays on intruders to make them lose their way. If this happens, your guide must remove all his clothes, put them on again back to front and then set off once more. The sea plays a similar trick, and this is known as *tassi-fila*. Then there is the whole vocabulary surrounding cockfighting, the chewing of *masca* (betel) and the celebration of *korem-metam* (a party held one year after the death of a relative or loved one). In a way – and this goes against all my instincts as a translator – the book survives and is even, I think, enriched by the inevitable spattering of foreign words and expressions, and the equal spattering of footnotes. In English, it remains what it is, a story from and about East Timor. Here is the penultimate paragraph of the book, where the author's father, who is living with him in Lisbon, has just received permission to go and live in Australia, but dies before he can make the journey:

> *Chegou então a tão desejada carta de chamada proveniente da Austrália. Levei-lhe um dicionário de inglês a seu pedido. Tencionava recuperar a língua que aprendera com o* malae-matam-balanda. *Que a memória tão pródiga em reciclar assuntos não requisitados fora teimosa em devolver-lhe convenientemente as palavras. Irritado, trincava os dentes com raiva, fechava os punhos com que dava murros no ar, exercitando-se na arte de mestre de* silat, *e insultava em mambai. Mas os dias quentes e secos do mês de Junho depressa lhe dificultaram a respiração. Com medo de ficar privado dessa oportunidade única, quis apressar o voo. Achava que tinha uma missão a cumprir na Austrália cobrando uma dívida antiga. Cortou o cabelo rente, fez a barba e vestiu um fato novo. Estava trajado como um cobrador da história. Foi à cidade de Lisboa tirar as fotografias para o passaporte. Duas diferentes, em poses contrárias, como se fossem a frente e o reverso. O ponto da partida e o fim da travessia. No regresso, não conseguiu subir as escadas que o levavam para o primeiro andar. Ficou no rés-do-chão à espera da ambulância. A sirena repetitiva anunciava o sonho desfeito. No quarto do hospital soletrou-me vagamente aos ouvidos os nomes trocados dos combatentes australianos. Delegava em mim a sua tarefa. Quis o destino que se cumprisse o enredo:* mate-bandera-hum. *Um lençol branco, como uma bandeira despida de cores e de símbolos, cobria-lhe o corpo nu e moreno. Pronto para encontrar o caminho do retorno ao monte de Cabalaqui. A morte devolveu-lhe o mote. O encanto não passara de um autêntico rain-fila.* (Cardoso, 1997: 153–4)

Then the longed-for letter of invitation came from Australia. At his request I took him an English dictionary. He intended to brush up on the language he had learned from the *malae-matam-balanda** – the foreigner with pale eyes. But his memory, so prodigal in restoring to him things he did not require, resisted giving him convenient access to the words. He would get irritated and grind his teeth with rage, punch the air, making moves he had learned in the art of *silat*,** cursing in Mambae**. But the hot, dry days of June soon made breathing difficult for him. Afraid that he would miss this unique opportunity, he wanted to catch an earlier flight. He felt that he had a mission in Australia, the collection of an old debt. He had his hair cut very short, shaved off his beard and bought a new suit. He was dressed like a collector not of taxes but of history. He went into Lisbon to get his passport photos taken. Two different ones, in contrary poses, as if of his front and his back. The point of departure and the end of the journey. When he returned, he could not climb the stairs to the first floor. He waited on the ground floor for the ambulance to come. The repetitive siren announced the end of the dream. In his hospital room, he tried spelling out to me the garbled names of Australian soldiers. He delegated his task to me. He wanted fate to finish the plot: *mate-bandera-hum*.** A white sheet, like a flag bereft of colours and symbols, covered his bare, brown body. Ready to take the road back up Mount Cabalaqui.** Death restored his motto to him. The spell he had been under was nothing but a *rain-fila*.** (Jull Costa, 2000: 151–2)

* = reference explained here or elsewhere in text;
** = reference explained in glossary.
(These asterisks do not, of course, appear in the published text.)

As I floundered in this fascinating other culture, and gradually learned more about it, what was brought home to me was how much the European cultures from which I usually translate have in common. It made me realise the extent to which, as a translator, I can leave cultural concepts and references and even ways of thinking unexplained because I can rely on readers being sufficiently well-read, well-educated and, sometimes, well-travelled to be able to 'translate' these things for themselves. In the first example I give above of the trip to Sintra described in *The Maias*, I do not need to explain what and where Sintra is because Byron and, since him, thousands of British tourists, have been there already. Most readers of the *The Crossing*, on the other hand, would know nothing of East Timor, its geography, its languages, its religions, its history, and so on. The footnotes in that translation are like the answers to the many questions that anyone would need to ask when in conversation with someone from a very different culture. In the European novels I usually translate and in that one East Timorese book, I can also rely on the fact that all of us, however unconsciously, translate and interpret all the time, whether it be the look on someone's face, their use of a particular word, their tone of voice, their gestures, their references, jokey and otherwise. The choices and decisions I make as a translator when faced by the apparently untranslatable are, then, based on my own experiences of the languages and cultures I am translating from and into, and also on my sense of what is 'universal' to those hypothetical readers of the finished translation. Translation is itself a culturally specific activity. Each translated work is filtered through one particular person's imagination and perception and fixed in a particular time. Perhaps this is why 'old' translations seem odd or quaint or dead, and this may explain the need for the periodic re-translation of great works of fiction. Time moves on, the landscape of the past changes, language changes, and all must be re-imagined.

Note
1. In all cases emphasis is the author's own.
2. To those unfamiliar with Saramago's books, I should point out his rather unusual approach to capitalisation and punctuation. He tends not to capitalise proper names, for example, here 'providential', which is the name of the insurance company. In dialogues, he does not use quotation marks, question marks or exclamation marks, and only uses full stops to signal the end of a conversation. A capital letter indicates a new speaker. For obvious reasons, most dialogues, although not all, involve only two speakers.

References
Byron, Lord G.G. (1902) *Childe Harold's Pilgrimage*. Boston: Francis A. Niccolls & Co.
Cardoso, L. (1997) *Crónica de Uma Travessia: A época do Ai-Dik-Funam*. Lisbon: Publicações Dom Quixote.
Eça de Queiroz, J.M. (1888) *Os Maias (23ª edição)*. Lisbon: Livros do Brasil.
Jull Costa, M. (trans.) (1991) *The Book of Disquiet*. London: Serpent's Tail.
Jull Costa, M. (trans.) (2000) *The Crossing: A Story of East Timor*. London: Granta Publications.
Jull Costa, M. (trans.) (2006) *Seeing*. Harvill Secker: London.
Jull Costa, M. (trans.) (forthcoming) *The Maias*. Sawtry: Dedalus Books.
Patterson, C. (2006) Interview with Javier Marias. *The Independent*, 25 July.
Pessoa, F. (1982) *Livro do desassossego*. Lisbon: Publicações Europa-América.
Saramago, J. (2004) *Ensaio sobre a lucidez*. Lisbon: Editorial Caminho.

Chapter 10

Alice in Denmark

VIGGO HJØRNAGER PEDERSEN AND KIRSTEN NAUJA ANDERSEN

Introduction

One of the most stimulating books on literary translation of the 1990s was Romy Heylen's *Translation, Poetics and the Stage* in which she describes six French Hamlet translations from the 18th century onwards and tries to account for the reasons for their differences. In her introduction, she outlines a 'cultural model of translation'. The thinking is in the tradition of Toury (1980). One may not agree with all of it, but a convincing case is made for seeing literary translation as a case of negotiation between two literary systems rather than as simply a linguistic operation:

> A descriptive, historical model of translation goes beyond questions of whether and to what degree a translation matches an original; it investigates the underlying constraints and motivations that inform the translation process. Translation is a teleological activity of a profoundly transformative nature. Therefore, normative models of translation based on the absolute concept of equivalence need to be replaced by a historical-relative and socio-cultural model of translation. (Heylen, 1993: 5)

Perhaps 'supplemented by' rather than 'replaced by' would be more appropriate when comparing the relative merits of the concepts of equivalence and cultural correspondence. But Heylen's point of view is valid as far as it goes and the comparative study of the six translations is an eye-opener – so much so that it has stimulated us to undertake an analogous study of certain aspects of the work of the Danish translators of *Alice in Wonderland*.

However, in addition to describing the translation strategies of the translators, we have ventured into the dubious territory of 'the limits of translation'; for there is no denying that none of the translations is as good or as convincing as the original and, in this chapter, we shall explore the reasons why.

Although a very demanding text to translate, *Alice in Wonderland* (1865) has been translated repeatedly into foreign languages, and Danish is no exception. Disregarding revised editions and adaptations including cartoon versions, there are six Danish translations to consider:

- Anon (D.G.): *Maries Hændelser i Vidunderlandet*. Copenhagen: Wøldike, 1875.
- Kjeld Elfelt: *Alice i Eventyrland (till 1964: Æventyrland) og Bag Spejlet*. Copenhagen: Gyldendal, 1946.
- Eva Hemmer Hansen: *Alice i Eventyrland*. Copenhagen: Lademann, 1972.
- Mogens Boisen: *Alice i Eventyrland*. Copenhagen: Mallings, 1982.
- Franz Berliner: *Alice i Eventyrland*. Risskov: Klematis, 1999.
- Ejgil Søholm: *Alice i Undreland*. Copenhagen: Apostrof, 2000.

In the following, we shall give a brief account of all of these. Carroll's text will be referred to as 'LC', the translations by their year of publication.

The Translations

The first, anonymous, translation from 1875 still sees English as a somewhat exotic language from an equally exotic country, which few Danes had visited at that time. Hence 'Alice' is changed to the familiar 'Marie', and the location '*Vidunderlandet*' (the Land of Marvels) is coined for the occasion – no equivalent concept existed in Danish at the time. Altogether, while the translation is self-effacing right down to giving the initials rather than the full name of the translator, and mostly following the English text closely, it does, as we shall see, in quite creative ways try to find Danish equivalents for phenomena in the original that are not easily transferred. Thus it tries to render English sociolects by corresponding Danish ones, and it introduces a parody of a popular Danish poem to render Carroll's parody of an English one.[1] The translation was reissued twice (1912, 1930), the language being modernised in the process.

Kjeld Elfelt's (1946) translation of both Alice books, most recently reprinted in 1977, has come to be viewed as the standard translation. Elfelt (1902–1993) is a painstaking translator, although perhaps not a very creative one. His care for details can be seen in a correction in the second and following editions, where '*Alice havde ikke det fjerneste Begreb om, hvad Breddegrad eller Længdegrad var for noget*' ('Alice had no idea what Latitude was or Longitude either') is changed to '*Breddegrad og Længdegrad*' – 'latitude and (rather than 'or') longitude' – which is the idiomatic Danish solution, whereas his first attempt showed interference from English. On the other hand, Elfelt has limited success with tackling many of the puns and other linguistic difficulties of the original.

The poems in Elfelt's edition are translated by Mogens Jermiin Nissen (1906–1972), whose version is probably the best there is in Danish.

Eva Hemmer Hansen (1913–1983) was a well-known Danish writer and translator with several novels and an almost complete Dickens translation to her credit. As a translator, she is very creative, especially in rendering puns, but for that very reason, at times seems a little too contrived (see the example under 'Linguistic problems' below).

Mogens Boisen's *Alice*, from 1982, in spite of its title, is in fact not a translation of *Alice in Wonderland*, but of *Alice's Adventures Underground* (1865). This means that this text is shorter than the others. However, for the translation of specific words and phrases in the discussion below the source language text is identical with that of the published novel, in so far as Boisen's source includes the item in question. Mogens Boisen (1910–87) was one of the leading translators of his time, with more than 800 translations to his credit. Famed among other things for the three versions of his translation of James Joyce's *Ulysses*, he was anything but anonymous. In a postscript he states that he has felt obliged to leave out some puns, and acknowledges that, like Elfelt, he has not been able to render all the details of the original. The drawback of this strategy, of course, is its defensiveness: if the puns and allusions omitted are not compensated for by the introduction of new ones, the translation will appear poorer than the original.

Franz Berliner (1930–) is a Danish writer and translator. In an introduction to his translation (Berliner, 1999), which is an international co-production with illustrations by Lisbeth Zwerger, Berliner states his intention of keeping as closely as possible to Carroll's text, 'even when curious asides, hidden and distorted quotations, puns, and 'reversed' logic make it difficult'. He adds a Danish pun, and probably an indirect criticism of Hemmer Hansen, that *'Hvis man fordansker for meget, kan det hele blive meget for dansk'* ('if you "Danish" it too much, it may become much too Danish'). Consequently, his text is a fairly literal translation, which means that puns are often lost and whole sequences at times become almost meaningless, as for instance in the description of underwater school life. On the other hand, the text is good, colloquial modern Danish, and Berliner has contributed some good translations of a number of the poems, while choosing an edited version of Jermin Nissen for *You are Old, Father William* and a couple of other prominent poems.

Ejgil Søholm (1936–2002), journalist, writer and translator, brought the text up to date, often choosing quite colloquial solutions. He also invents quite a few compensatory puns, as in *Du er gammel, Far Vilhelm*, where the son asks, *'hvordan ku' du æde en and i et rap?'* ('how could you eat a duck at one go?'), punning on the verb at *rappe* (to quack), and the phrase *i et rap* ('without intermission, quickly'). However, Søholm tries to stay as close to Denmark's coast as possible, leaving out or changing many specific references to things English, and even changing names, such as 'William' to 'Vilhelm'. In some cases, his text seems influenced by Berliner's.

Problem Types: Time, Place, Culture, Language

Hjørnager Pedersen (1980) operates with the parameters of time, place, culture and language when trying to assess the relative difficulty of different translation situations. This model is used in the following, which, however, is also indebted to *Alice i Ingenmandsland* (Andersen, 1993), where the translation problems encountered in Alice are also divided into a number of categories. Andersen's theory derives in particular from a discussion of Reiss's distinction between content-oriented problems on the one hand and time and space-oriented ones on the other (Reiss, 1993: 19ff), Newmark's distinction between 'transference' and 'componential analysis' (Newmark, 1988: 81) and Nida's concept of dynamic equivalence (quoted in Nida & Taber, 1974: 24). This in turn, forms the basis for the attempt, in the following, to split up the problems that a Danish translator of Carroll's work would encounter into a number of different categories, though we are well aware that there is considerable overlap, for example between cultural and linguistic translation problems. Many of the examples are taken from Andersen (1993).

Time

The translations span a period of 125 years from 1875 to 2000; the first is almost contemporary with the original, whereas the last is more than a century later. Needless to say, the first translator had some advantages in that many features of the receptor culture were similar to those of the original, such as insisting on a more restrained behaviour for girls than for boys, and having middle class families with resident servants. On the other hand, as we have observed above, in 1875 England was very exotic to Danes, and here we see the paradoxical situation that the closer we come to the present, the more familiar does the English context become.

One problem that is very dependent on the time aspect is the relationship between the little girl and her nurse (or teacher):

LC:	'Miss Alice! Come here directly, and get ready for your walk!' 'Coming in a minute, nurse!' (p. 56).
1875:	*Naar Barnepigen sagde: 'Frøken Marie! Kom og gjør Dem i Stand til at spadsere!' – 'Jeg skal straks komme'* (p. 35).
1946:	*Naar Barnepgen sagde: 'Alice! Kom her... og klæd dig paa, vi skal ud og spadsere!' – 'Jeg kommer straks!'* (p. 36).
1972:	*'Alice! Kom hjem med det samme og få dit overtøj på, vi skal ud at gå tur!' 'Jeg kommer om lidt'* (p. 13f).
1982:	*'Lille Alice, vil du straks tage overtøjet på. Vi skal ud at gå tur' 'Ja, det skal jeg nok, frøken* (p. 30).
1999:	*'Frøken Alice, kom og få overtøj på til spadsereturen!' – 'Kommer straks!'* (p. 27).

2000:   *'Kom nu Alice, se at få frakken på, vi skal ud at gå tur!' – 'Ja-ja, jeg kommer lige om lidt ...'* (p. 56).

In the 1875 translation, as well as in the original, the nurse addresses the child as 'Miss/*Frøken*'. This is dropped in 1946, and in 1972 the tone becomes more peremptory, whereas it grows milder again in 1982 (*'Lille Alice'*). It is not quite clear in 1982 and 2000 who Alice's interlocutor is. *'Frøken'* of 1982 might indicate a teacher or kindergarten assistant, and in any case the *'frøken'* represents a reversal of roles: now it is the child who is respectful to an adult (in 2000 the respect is somewhat reduced). Thus the only translation offering full cultural (and linguistic) equivalence is the first, 1875, though the 1999 translation comes close by reintroducing *'Frøken'* (Miss) as applied to Alice.

Place

Southern England is basically not very different from Denmark, consequently there are no difficulties of the kind encountered when translators have to convey an impression of arctic or tropical scenery unknown to untravelled Westerners. Moreover, fantasy literature often takes place in a non-descript world that cannot easily be located on a map. Nevertheless, there are some tricky references to England, which is the assumed background if not the actual scene throughout, the more so, because there is a greater tendency to localise literature for children than literature for adults (cf. Hjørnager Pedersen, 2004: 69). One such reference appears in the lobster quadrille, with its longing for foreign parts:

LC: 'What matters it how far we go?' his scaly friend replied. 'There is another shore, you know, upon the other side. The further off from England the nearer is to France – Then turn not pale, beloved snail, but come and join the dance' (p. 134).

1875:   *'Hvad siger det, hvor langt vi gaa?' saa svarede dens Ven, 'Er der ikke en anden Kyst hvor vi ville komme hen? Fjærne vi os fra Sjællands Strand, ville vi jo snart med Glans! betræde Skaanes, derfor kom og faa dig en lille Dans!'* (p. 120).

1946:   *'Hvad betyder dog den lange Vej,'* bedyrede hans Ven, *'for der findes jo en anden Kyst, hvor sagtens man når hen. Er du alt for langt fra vores, gir den næste dig en Tjans – altså ikke blive bleg, min Ven, men kom og faa en Dans!'* (p. 95).

1972:   The text is completely changed, and this stanza is not translated. There are a number of new puns like *'sådan går vor livsens dans alt for tit i fisk'* ('Thus the dance of our lives all too often comes to nothing' – *'gå i fisk'* is an idiom that literally means 'disappear into [or be eaten by] fish').

1982:   Not included.

1999: Almost identical with 1946.
2000: *'Pyt da med, hvor langt vi kommer ud!'* sa' sneglens fiskeven,
'Vi har ovelevet hver gang, og du klarer det med glans!
Der er andre lande, mange steder man kan komme hen.
Kom nu, kom nu, være snegl og træd den vilde hummerdans (p. 167).

As will be seen, most of the translators have chosen a neutral translation that does not necessitate references to the Channel or any other geographical location. 1875, however, substitutes the Sound for the Channel, and Scania for France, thus localising the text.

Culture

There are several subheadings in this category and, as we have seen, it necessarily overlaps with the preceding categories, because culture is dependent on time and place. In the following, we shall discuss some prominent examples of cultural problem areas typical of Alice: the transference (or not) of material and social phenomena, allusions, and stylistic level(s).

Material culture markers: Food

There are several references to food in Alice, and some of the things mentioned are not Danish, and seem – or at least must have seemed – rather strange. When Alice compares the taste of one of her magic potions to 'custard, pineapple, roast turkey, toffy and hot buttered toast' (LC, p. 31) she refers to phenomena well known in England at the time. But custard and hot buttered toast were unknown in Denmark (the former still is), and in the 1875 translation, *flødekage* ('pancake with cream') is no more an equivalent of custard than *ristet Smørrebrød* ('roast bread-and-butter') is for toast; and although *'kalkunsteg'* is a more or less literal rendering of roast turkey, the translation does not refer to something well-known to and liked by children. A true equivalent would rather be *andesteg* ('roast duck') which is a typically Danish dish. At least for toast, the situation has changed. In our international world, every middle-class child knows what toast is, and the English word is frequently used in Danish. But even 1999 keeps the faintly exotic *varmt ristet brød med smør* ('hot roasted bread with butter').

Social culture markers: Schools

The Mock turtle's account of its school days obviously refers to typically 19th century public school education, which is far from the experience of most Danish children, especially today. Some of the problems are linguistic, and will be dealt with below, but some are social. For instance, Danish has no word for 'day school', because this presupposes 'boarding school', which is a very unusual phenomenon in Denmark. 1875 simply translates *'skole'* (school), which gets only part of the meaning of the original.

Allusion

All texts presuppose a certain amount of knowledge on the part of the recipients of the matters they refer to. Needless to say, these presuppositions do not necessarily hold for the recipients of a translated text. In the example below there are two problems, which the various translators have chosen to tackle in different ways. First, there is an allusion to William the Conqueror and '1066 and all that' which a contemporary English schoolchild would know about, and secondly, the frame of reference is English: it is not very meaningful to talk about 'understanding English' (1972, 1999), when the text is in Danish.

LC: 'Perhaps it doesn't understand English,' thought Alice. 'I daresay it's a French mouse, come over with William the Conqueror' (p. 41).

1875: *'Maaske forstaar den ikke Dansk', tænkte Marie, 'det er bestemt en fransk Mus, der er kommen her til Landet med de franske Hjælpetropper'* (p. 21f).

1946: *'Den forstaar maaske ikke, hvad jeg siger,' tænkte Alice. Det er bestemt en fremmed Mus, der er kommet her til Landet...'* (p. 23).

1972: *'Den forstår måske ikke Engelsk,' tænkte Alice. 'Det er måske en fransk mus, der er kommet hertil med Vilhelm Erobreren'* (p. 7).

1982: *'Den forstår måske ikke dansk,' tænkte Alice. 'Det kan være, at den er amerikansk. Der er jo så mange amerikanske turister'* (p. 18).

1999: *'Måske forstår den ikke engelsk', tænkte Alice. 'Det er nok en fransk mus, der er kommet over med Vilhelm Erobreren'* (p. 18).

2000: *'Måske forstår den ikke sproget', tænkte Alice. 'Det er sikkert en fransk mus, der er kommet over sammen med Vilhelm Erobreren'* (p. 34).

As will be seen, early translations substitute 'Danish' for 'English', or leave out the specific reference, whereas some of the more recent ones keep 'English'. 1875 replaces 'William' with a reference to the Napoleonic wars, when Napoleonic auxiliary troops were stationed in Denmark. But in 1946 this reference was no longer felt to be relevant, and more recent translations stay with 'William', although Danish children are not likely to know much about him. An exception is 1982, which substitutes 'American tourists' for 'Norman marauders'.

A special problem is the poems that are parodies of well-known English poems. A more or less direct translation, which most translator's try (such as 'You are old, Father William') obviously loses the allusion to Robert Southey's 'The Old Man's Comforts and How he Gained Them' (see the *Annotated Alice*, Carroll, 1981: 69–70). However, 1875 and 1972 sometimes use a different strategy, modelling their versions (which then cease to be translations, strictly speaking) on popular Danish poems. Thus 1972 translates 'How does the gentle crocodile' with *'se den lille kokodille'*, alluding to a popular Danish children's song, *Se den lille kattekilling* ('look at the little kitten'). (For 1875, see endnote 1.)

Stylistic levels

Hjørnager Pedersen (2004) frequently refers to the fact that the average literary style in Victorian fiction for children was at a higher level than that found in Denmark, and certainly higher than is found in modern Danish texts. Even if the extract from a history textbook in 'The Caucus Race' is not children's fiction, it is still a text to which children might be subjected, and it presents certain difficulties for most translators.

LC: This is the driest thing I know ... 'William the Conqueror, whose cause was favoured by the Pope ...' (p. 46).

1875: Changes the text, so that it no longer deals with history, but politics instead.

1946: *'Dette er noget af det tørreste, jeg kender ... Jeg vil holde et historisk Foredrag om Vilhelm Erobreren – altså, Vilhelm Erobreren, hvis sag fandt støtte hos Paven ...'* (p. 26).

1972: *'så kommer den tørreste beretning. ... Vilhelm Erobreren, hvis sag støttedes af paven ...'* (p. 9).

1982: *'I skal nu høre det tørreste, jeg nogen sinde selv har hørt. ... Det drejer sig om et stykke af Englands historie. Det forholdt sig således, at Vilhelm Erobreren, hvis sag støttedes af paven ...'* (p. 22).

1999: *'Høm!' sagde musen med en vigtig mine. 'Er I klar? Det her er det mest tørre, jeg kender. Må jeg bede om fuldstsændig stilhed! Hør så: Vilhelm Erobreren, hvis sag blev støttet af paven ...'* (p. 21).

2000: *'H-hm!' begyndte musen og så sig om med en vigtig mine. 'Er I klar alle sammen? Det her er det mest knastørre, jeg kender. Ro i lejren, om jeg må bede!' Og så startede musen på sit foredrag. 'Vilhelm Erobreren, som hos paven fandt støtte for sin sag ...'* (p. 42).

It appears that several translators find it necessary to write a little introduction to the paragraph on William. On the other hand, the language in the actual text tends to be less formal than in the English original, for example in 2000, which avoids the passive of the first clause:

LC: 'William the Conqueror, whose cause was favoured by the pope, was soon submitted to by the English, who wanted leaders, and had been of late much accustomed to usurpation and conquest' (p. 46).

2000: *'Vilhelm Erobreren, som hos paven fandt støtte for sin sag, ham underkastede englænderne sig snart, fordi de savnede ledere og på det sidste havde været udsat for gentagne tilfælde af magtmisbrug og erobringsforsøg.'*

However, Carroll also introduces dialect and non-standard speech (the rabbit's servant, the Griffin) for comic effect, something that only 1875 consistently tries to imitate:

LC: 'Sure I'm here! Digging for apples, yer honour! ... Sure it's an arm, yer honour! (He pronounced it 'arrum'.) Sure it does, yer honour, but it's an arm for all that' (p. 60)

1875: '*Nu kommer jeg! Jeg graver Kantøfler op, husbond! Det er min Sandten en Arm, Husbond! ... Ja, så Skam gør den inte, men det er illigeveller en Arm*' (p. 27)

1946: '*Jeg er her – nu kommer jeg! Jeg graver efter Æbler, deres Naade! ... Det er min Sandten en Arm, Deres Naade! Ja, det gør det, Deres Naade, men det er nu lige godt en Arm!*' (p. 38)

1972: '*Nu kommer jeg! Jeg graver efter Æbler, deres Naade! ... Det er min Sandten en Arm, Deres Naade! Det gør jeg ganske vist Deres Naade, men det er nu alligevel en Arm!*' (p. 27)

1982: '*Jamen a er da her og graver efter æbler, Deres Velbårenhed! ... Det er en arm, Deres Velbårenhed! ... Jow, jow, Deres Velbårenhed, men det er nu alligevel en arm!*' (p. 34)

2000: '*Her, Deres Velburenhed! Jeg er ude at grave æbler op!*' ... '*Det er en arm, Deres Velburenhed!*' *(Sådan udtalte han nu det fine ord)* ... (p. 62)

Here, the 1875 translation is good at finding Danish dialect equivalents for the English – and *Kantøfler*, standard Danish *Kartofler* ('potatoes'), is in all likelihood what the gardener is digging for, cf. French *pomme de terre*. But to some extent all the translations try to imitate the gardener's non-standard language, unlike the following example, where only 1875 uses dialect:

LC: 'It's all her fancy, that: they never executes nobody, you know ... ' (p. 125f).

1875: '*Det er nu hendes Kjæphest; de hugge slets inte Hoveder af, nej Skam gjør de ej ...*' (p. 110).

1946: '*Det er noget, hun bilder sig ind – der er ingen, som bliver halshugget!*' (p. 88).

1972: '*Det er alt sammen indbildning – der er aldrig nogen, der bliver henrettet ...*' (p. 40f).

1982: '*Fantasien løber af med hende, for sagen er, at der aldrig bliver henrettet nogen ...*' (p. 62).

1999: '*Det er fantasi alt sammen – de henretter faktisk aldrig nogen*' (p. 74).

2000: ' *... Det er bare noget, hun bilder sig ind. I virkeligheden er der aldrig nogen, der bliver halshugget*' (p. 156).

Linguistic problems

In Alice, precision is insisted upon, although not always achieved. As Humpty Dumpty reminds us, 'When I use a word ... it means just what I choose it to mean – neither more nor less.' But frequently, words in Alice have to carry more than one meaning. For reasons of space, we shall here confine ourselves to one example of a pun and the difficulties it presents for translators.

The Griffin's account of its school days, which apparently resembled those of the typical public school boy at the time, offers several examples. For instance, the Griffin's teacher was called Tortoise (taught us), and the number of lessons 'lessened' (that is decreased) every day.

LC: 'The master was an old Turtle – we used to call him Tortoise – ' (p. 127).
1875: 'Skolelæreren var en gammel Søpadde – vi plejede at kalde ham 'Landpadden' (p. 112).
1946: 'Vores Lærer var en gammel Skildpadde – vi kaldte ham for Sildesnuden...'[2] (p. 90).
1972: 'Da vi var børn [...] blev vi sendt på Sorø Akvademi hos doktor Dermatycholos Coriacea – vi kaldte ham Gamle Læderpadde – '[3] (p. 41).
1982: Leaves out most of this and also the following speeches (p. 64).
1999: Like 1982 (p. 76).
2000: 'Vores lærer var en gammel havpadde, som vi drenge plejede af kalde Landpadden' (p. 158).

Generally, Danish translators give up when they come to the joke about lessons lessening; and the favourite solution to the 'Tortoise problem' is either to leave it out or to substitute a different word like 'landpadde' for 'søpadde', explaining that otherwise it would not be a nickname – true, but not really satisfactory in the context.

Conclusion

The above cursory investigation unfortunately yields a fairly negative result: none of the Danish translations really lives up to the original. It is our assumption that this is due to at least two factors. The first is a basic difference between the conventions governing the use of 'nonsense' in English and Danish, perhaps most clearly seen in the substitution in the first Danish translation, of a pointless parody of 'Konen med Æggene' for the original's wicked crocodile (see endnote 1). The second factor is an unwillingness in practice to live up to the demands of cultural adaptation. To succeed as works of art, the Danish texts would really have needed to depart much more drastically from the English than they do, consistently substituting Danish situations, jokes and puns for the English ones of the original; but then, of course, they would no longer have been about Alice but Marie, a strategy that only 1875 employs, and that only in part.

Notes

1. It replaces 'how doth the little crocodile' with *'Konen med Æggene'* (about a woman taking a basket of eggs to market) where the lines are garbled, but without the malicious undertone of Carroll's original.
2. *Sildesnuden*, literally 'the Herring Snout', prepares for the pun with which that of the original has been replaced. The reason for the name, we are told, is that *'vi fik paa Snuden, naar vi kom for silde'*, i.e. they were beaten when being late; *'få på snuden'* and *'komme for silde'* are idiomatic Danish phrases (though the latter is dated).
3. This puns on *'Sorø Akademi'*, one of the very few Danish public schools. *'Læder'* (leather) in the nickname should be pronounced *'læ'er'*, thus becoming indistinguishable from a rapid pronunciation of *'lærer'*, teacher.

References

Andersen, K. (1993) Alice i Ingenmandsland. Prize-awarded thesis, Copenhagen University.
Anon (D.G.) (1875) *Maries Hændelser i Vidunderlandet*. Copenhagen: Wøldike.
Berliner, F. (1999) *Alice i Eventyrland*. Risskov: Klematis.
Boisen, M. (1982) *Alice i Eventyrland*. Copenhagen: Mallings.
Carroll, L. (1960/1970/1981) *The Annotated Alice: Alice's Adventures in Wonderland & Through the Looking Glass* (M. Gardner, ed.). Harmondsworth: Penguin. (Reference is made to the 1981 edition.)
Elfelt, K. (1946) *Alice i Eventyrland (till 1964: Æventyrland) og Bag Spejlet*. Copenhagen: Gyldendal.
Hemmer Hansen, E. (1972) *Alice i Eventyrland*. Copenhagen: Lademann.
Heylen, R. (1993) *Translation, Poetics and the Stage*. London: Routledge.
Hjørnager Pedersen, V. (1980) Towards a theory of literary translation. In S. Hanon and V. Hjørnager Pedersen (eds) *Human Translation: Machine Translation. NOK 39* (pp. 7–18). Odense University.
Hjørnager Pedersen, V. (2004) *Ugly Ducklings? Studies in the English Translations of Hans Christian Andersen's Tales and Stories*. Odense: University Press of Southern Denmark.
Newmark, P. (1988) *A Textbook of Translation*. Hemel Hempstead: Prentice Hall.
Nida, E.A. and Taber, C.A. (1974) *The Theory and Practice of Translation*. Leiden: Brill.
Reiss, K. (1971) *Möglichkeiten und Grenzen der Übersetzungskritik*. München: Hueber.
Søholm, E. (2000) *Alice i Undreland*. Copenhagen: Apostrof.
Toury, G. (1980) *In Search of a Theory of Translation*. Tel Aviv: Tel Aviv University.

Chapter 11

Little Snowdrop and The Magic Mirror: Two Approaches to Creating a 'Suitable' Translation in 19th-Century England

NIAMH CHAPELLE AND JENNY WILLIAMS

Introduction

In this chapter we demonstrate how two translators in 19th-century England adopted very different approaches to bridging the same cultural divide. They both translated the Grimms' fairy tale *Sneewittchen* (*Snow White*) into English, using the 1857 edition of the tale, and their translations appeared within no more than 11 years of each other. Both were translating for young people and in the prefaces to their translations they each emphasised the pains they had taken to ensure that their translations were suitable for their audience in terms of both style and content. Yet despite the similarity of their aims and intended readership, the translators produced two very different translations: *Little Snowdrop* (1863) and *The Magic Mirror* (1871/1874). The reasons for this must be sought in two radically different definitions of 'suitability' which, in turn, can be explained by the different approaches to writing and translation adopted by the two translators concerned and their very different attitudes towards their target audience.

The Translations

Little Snowdrop is one of 12 Grimm tales included in *The Fairy Book. The Best Popular Fairy Stories. Selected and Rendered Anew by the Author of 'John Halifax Gentleman'* first published by Macmillan in London in 1863 and re-issued in various editions up to 2003. The author of *John Halifax Gentleman* (1856) was Dinah Maria Mulock (1826–1887), known after her marriage in 1865 as Mrs George Lillie Craik, a very popular novelist and writer in mid- to-late Victorian Britain. Given her prominence as a writer, it is surprising that Mulock's translations of the Grimms' tales are not mentioned in any of the standard works on the translation history of the Grimms' tales in English: Morgan (1938), Alderson (1993) and Sutton (1996). It can be assumed that Mulock was responsible both for re-translating and editing the tales (Chapelle, 2001: 125–126).

The second translation, *The Magic Mirror*, is one of 130 translations of Grimm tales published by Frederick Warne and Company under the title *Grimms Fairy Tales*. The publishing date is most likely to have been between 1871 and 1874 (Chapelle, 2001: 144–5). The title page informs the reader that the collection is 'a new translation by Mrs H.H.B. Paull'.

Mrs Paull's translations of Grimms' tales have received negative evaluations from the critics. Morgan (1938: 181) accuses her of taking 'unwarrantable liberties'. Alderson (1985: 5) describes Paull's translations as 'inaccurate and stilted'. Sutton (1996: 255) criticises her work as 'a blatant distortion of the Grimms' own narrative'. However, Mrs Paull's translations have proved to be one of the most popular Grimm collections in English, having appeared in different editions for over one hundred years since their first appearance, most recently in 1996 (Owens, 1996).

The Translators

Dinah Mulock, later Mrs Craik, wrote more than 20 novels, 12 children's books and more than 150 short stories and essays. Her poems were collected in four volumes, including one of children's verse. She also produced three volumes of travel narrative and translated three French novels. She was a personal friend of the publisher Alexander Macmillan who published *The Fairy Book*, her second book for children. Her first, *Alice Learmont* (1852), was one of several original fairy tales and fantasies she wrote for a young audience. Between 1849 and 1855, she also wrote five moral stories for children (Mitchell, 1983).

While very little is known about Mrs Henry H.B. Paull's life, her output as a children's writer was prodigious: the British Library Catalogue lists some 50 publications which appeared under her name between 1855 and 1890. The title page of her 1855 publication reveals that she was also the author of at least two school books. In addition to these she translated a selection of Andersen's Danish tales, *Hans Andersen's Fairy Tales* (1867) and J.D. Wyss's *The Swiss Family Robinson* (1888).

Dinah Mulock and Mrs Paull adopted two very different approaches to writing for children. Mulock's tales were not overtly moralistic or cautionary. Rather, they sought to impart morals by appealing to children's feelings and imagination. In 1860, Mulock published an essay in *Macmillan's Magazine* entitled 'The Age of Gold' in which she discusses 'the character, tone and manner most suitable for children's books' (Mulock, 1860: 295). Mulock believed that 'no preaching should be admissible' in a children's book and criticises the 'flood of moral and religious literature with which our hapless infants are now overwhelmed'. Mulock expresses disdain for tales in which the narrator is constantly present to point out the moral and she underlines the importance of cultivating children's imaginative capacities. In Mulock's view (1860: 298), morals should be imparted 'by implication rather than direct admonition'. If a tale has imaginative appeal, children will naturally absorb lessons of 'heroism, self-denial, patience, and love'. She viewed fairy tales as ideal reading matter for young children: 'the general tenor of old-fashioned fairy-lore ... furnishes as much moral teaching as can well be taken in at the age of six or seven'.

Mrs Paull was undoubtedly part of the wave of children's authors Mulock criticised in her 1860 article. She very clearly moulded her children's stories around the morals she wished to impart. The titles of her books often reveal the lesson to be learned, for example *Mary Elton; or Self-Control* (1869) and *Schoolday Memories; or 'Charity Envieth Not'* (1876). The narrator is also ever-present to provide moral instruction, and Paull frequently addresses her readers directly to provide unambiguous moral interpretations of events. The morals in her tales were usually based on biblical authority and several were published by the Religious Tract Society and the Sunday School Union. Most of her school stories and domestic dramas are thinly-disguised allegorical warnings against pride, envy, vanity, conceit and jealousy, which must be overcome by strong faith, piety and salvation through punishment. Paull viewed her readers not as Mulock's 'hapless infants' but rather as naturally having 'naughty, spiteful tempers' and needing to be taught self-control (Paull, 1890: 82).

According to Melrose and Gardner (1996: 44) 'Two main views of the child co-existed throughout the 19th century: either children were naturally naughty and so in need of reform; or they were pure, and therefore required protection from evil influences; either way guiding and teaching were considered necessary'. Kane (1995: 45) similarly divides Victorian attitudes to children into the view of the child's soul on the brink of damnation, and the view that a child's soul should be kept innocent and untouched. Paull clearly subscribes to the first of these two views. Mulock, meanwhile, would appear to fit more into the second category of writer, viewing children as 'hapless' and in need of protection. However, she seems to have been less concerned with sheltering children from evil than from the huge wave of moralistic fiction that was part of the religious publishing boom that took place in England in the middle of the 19th century. She was also concerned with feeding rather than stifling children's imaginative capacities.

The Prefaces: Definitions of 'Suitability'

In the prefaces and paratextual material of the translations, both are presented as suitable reading material for children. An advertisement at the front of Mulock's *The Fairy Book* states that it 'will be found *peculiarly adapted* for presents and school prizes'. The title page of Paull's collection, meanwhile, announces that the tales have been '*specially adapted and arranged for young people*'.

In her preface, Mulock explains that all of the 'foreign' tales in the collection have been 're-translated, condensed, and *in any other needful way made suitable for modern British children*'. In the first paragraph of Paull's preface, she expresses the hope that her translations will be 'approved' by her readership. In the final paragraph, she expresses the hope that her Grimm translations will not only be 'a *suitable* companion volume to those of Hans Andersen, but also *really acceptable* to households, as their title of "Household Stories" seems to imply'.

In both cases, suitability refers to appropriateness of style, content and moral tone. Both translators explain that stylistic improvements were necessary. Paull states explicitly that she has been 'most careful to [...] render the English phraseology simple and pure both in style and tendency' (Paull, 1871/1874: iv). Mulock, meanwhile, states that, unlike the 'foreign' tales she translated, she was unable to improve upon the few 'real old English fairy tales' in the collection and she praises their 'charming Saxon simplicity of style'. Interestingly, Paull similarly praises 'good simple Saxon English' in her preface to her translation of *The Swiss Family Robinson* (Paull, 1888: v).

Both translators also point out that they have been careful to omit harmful or unsuitable elements of content. Mulock assures adult readers that she has been 'especially careful that the tales should contain nothing which could really harm a child' (Mulock, 1863: viii). Paull, meanwhile, explains that she has omitted 'a very few' of the tales deemed 'not exactly suited to young English readers'. This is quite an understatement, as Sutton (1996: 233) has calculated that Paull omitted no less than 83 tales. This approach was very much in keeping with the policy of Frederick Warne to offer 'wholesome entertainment'. In announcing the publication of the *Arabian Nights Entertainment* in their *Monthly List* for September 1865, for example, the publisher assured potential readers that 'the Editor has been able to expurgate entirely the parts that parents consider objectionable for their children to read' (Golden, 1991: 327–28).

Despite these very similar concerns with suitability, the prefaces also reflect the translators' different attitudes towards their young readers.

Mulock emphasises that the purpose of her translation is to amuse. She describes fairy tales as 'that delight of all children'. Moreover, she points out that the tales are not intended to impart morals: 'in fairy tales instruction is not expected – we find there only the rude moral of virtue rewarded and vice punished'. She expresses her view that 'the tender young heart is often reached as soon by the imagination as by the intellect' and so the tales make no 'direct appeal to either reason or conscience' (Mulock, 1863: viii).

Paull, meanwhile, points out that the Grimms' tales have some moral value. While she appeals to young readers by describing the tales as exciting and full of adventure and magic, she appeals also to the background authority of parents by hinting that the characters also provide suitable role models. She explains that the 'escapes from danger into which the heroes and heroines fall are not always attributed to supernatural causes, but to their own tact and courage' and that the characters also display an admirable 'spirit of enterprise' (Paull, 1871/1874: iii).

The translators' comments regarding the moral content of the tales they translated are indicative of the position occupied by fairy tales in the canon of English children's literature in the 1860s and 1870s. Mulock's view of fairy tales is not unlike the views expressed by the first anonymous translators (now known to be Edgar Taylor and David Jardine) of the Grimms' tales into English almost 40 years earlier, in 1823. Like Mulock, Taylor and Jardine believed that fairy tales provided ideal nourishment for children's imaginations. However, Taylor and Jardine's views and translation can be seen as radical because fairy tales were excluded from the canon of children's literature in the early 19th century and regarded almost unanimously as useless or even potentially harmful. By the 1860s, however, fairy tales and other imaginative literature were accepted as a staple part of children's literature, partly due to the success of the first translation of Grimms' tales (Zipes, 1987: xviii).

As Green (1956: 70) explains: 'No longer was it thought wrong for children to read fairy stories, or books of which the chief or only object was simply to amuse'. However, he goes on to say that the moral element had not disappeared entirely from children's literature and was 'unpleasantly stressed, or delightfully concealed according to the character of the author'. As a writer, Mulock belonged to the second category. Nevertheless, the comments in her preface regarding the potentially harmful content of her source texts also illustrate the fact that some element of concern persisted among parents that fairy tales could harm children through their lack of morals or morally confusing content (Townsend, 1990: 69).

Meanwhile, the first approach described by Green was taken by moralistic writers who had, by the 1860s, 'captured fairy tales for their own' (Bratton, 1981: 150) in order to compete with the growing range of imaginative children's literature that was becoming available. Many now viewed the genre as an ideal vehicle for teaching readers to become model children. This view is hinted at in Paull's preface (Paull, 1871/1874: iii).

Translation Comparison

A suitable moral tone

The difference in moral tone between the two translations is very much in keeping with the translators' different approaches to writing for children. In Mulock's translation, the 'rude moral' of the source text, conveyed 'by implication rather than direct admonition' (cf. Mulock, 1860: 198), is simply preserved. In Paull's hands, meanwhile, the story becomes an explicitly moralistic one.

The most immediately obvious difference between the two translations, apart from their titles, is their length. At 2955 words, Mulock's translation is not much longer than the source text's (ST) 2819 words, which is in keeping with her aim of rendering fairy tales without embellishment. In a small number of cases, she clarifies the action in the ST by means of explicitation and specification. Meanwhile, Paull's translation, at 3714 words, is considerably longer than both the ST and Mulock's text. In most instances, Paull's additions serve to underline the moral message of the ST or to draw out the secondary morals implied.

This is most obvious in Paull's handling of the ending of the tale. In the ST, Snow White's evil stepmother, the Queen, who believes the heroine is dead, receives an invitation to her wedding. Having donned her finery, she asks the magic mirror for the seventh time who is 'the fairest in the land'. On being told that Snow White is still a thousand times fairer, the Queen is shocked and frightened but compelled by envy to see her with her own eyes. Mulock renders the final three ST sentences as follows – material added by Mulock is indicated in italics:

> When she came, and found that it was Snowdrop *alive again*, she stood petrified with terror and despair. Then two iron shoes, heated burning hot, *were drawn out of the fire* with a pair of tongs, and laid before her feet. She was forced to put them on, *and to go and dance at Snowdrop's wedding* – dancing, dancing on these red-hot shoes till she fell down dead. (Mulock, 1863: 298)

This is one of the few passages where Mulock adds information; here it is clearly in order to make the rather short and abrupt ST ending more comprehensible to young readers.

Paull, in contrast, translates the final three sentences as follows (material added by Paull is indicated in italics):

> But *what was her astonishment and vexation* when she recognised *in the young bride* Snow-white herself, *now grown a charming young woman, and richly dressed in royal robes?* Her rage and terror were so great that she stood still and could not move *for some minutes. At last she went into the ballroom*, but the slippers she wore *were to her as* iron bands full of coals of fire, in which she was obliged to dance. And so in the red, glowing shoes she continued to dance till she fell dead on the floor, *a sad example of envy and jealousy.* (Paull, 1871/1874: 213)

Paull replaces the Queen's death by cruel physical punishment with death by self-inflicted pain and self-destruction. In her translation, the Queen is not forced to don a pair of red-hot shoes that have been heated in preparation for her punishment. Instead, *her own* shoes begin to feel like red-hot iron bands. The shoes thus become a metaphor for the Queen's all-consuming feelings of rage and envy, which finally overpower her and she literally dies of envy. Paull addresses readers directly, pointing out that the Queen is 'a sad example of envy and jealousy'. In this way, she renders the ending of the tale more explicitly moralistic than the source text. The transgression/punishment model of implicit moral instruction used in the source text is replaced by an explicit transgression/self-destruction model, which imparts more clearly the moral that vanity and envy will lead to one's own downfall. It serves also to exonerate the good characters from any implication in an act of cruelty and vengeance. Furthermore, the use of 'sad' here also invites readers to pity the Queen's sinful soul rather than condemn her.

Paull also makes the secondary morals implied in the German text more explicit. Firstly, she emphasises the point that vanity can lead an innocent girl astray. In her translation, Snow-white is shown to be prone to vanity when she is beguiled by the beautiful trinkets that the Queen in disguise offers her when she visits the dwarfs' cottage: 'Everything that is pretty ... laces and pearls, and ear-rings, and bracelets of every colour', in a basket 'lined with glittering silk'. Snow-white is also attracted by the 'bright tortoiseshell comb', which will make her hair 'wonderfully smooth and glossy' (Paull, 1871/1874: 210). None of these details are present in the source text. The reader is clearly intended to understand that all that glitters is not gold.

Paull also reinforces the moral that children should follow the advice of their elders. She reminds readers on two occasions that the heroine puts herself in danger by forgetting to obey the dwarfs. In the poisoned comb episode, 'she opened the door and let the woman in '*forgetting the advice of the dwarfs*'. When the dwarfs warn her again after this, Paull adds '*but Snow-white was not clever enough to resist her clever wicked stepmother and she forgot to obey*' (Paull, 1871/1874: 210).

Paull adds subtle details in various other parts of the translation that serve to draw out the moral dimension of the tale. For example, she alters the hunter's motivation for taking the child into the woods with the intention of killing her. In the source text, it is implied that the hunter is simply following orders, while in the target text, the hunter is led astray by the promise of a generous monetary reward. Later, Paull adds that the Queen hurries away from the dwarfs' cottage after her handiwork with the lace, '*fancying she heard footsteps*', which serves to emphasise the unappealing, cowardly nature of the Queen. Paull also adds the detail that, as the Queen prepares to attend the wedding, she stands in front of the mirror '*to admire her own beauty*', again underlining her vanity (Paull, 1871/1874: 209).

The choice of title is a further indicator of the difference in the translators' approaches. Mulock's *Little Snowdrop* recalls the first English translation of the tale by Taylor and Jardine in 1823, entitled *Snow-drop*. Paull chooses a completely new title, *The Magic Mirror*, which is attractive in its alliteration and its promise of magic. At the same time, it also points to the moral of the tale for the mirror symbolises the sins of vanity and envy, embodied in the villainess and her obsession with her mirror.

The diametrically-opposed views of the two translators to what Mulock termed 'preaching' in children's literature can be illustrated with reference to their handling of the value adjectives attributed to Snow White and the Queen. In the source text, negative value adjectives are applied to the Queen on seven occasions. Table 1 shows the strategies adopted by each translator (the number of occurrences of each word is shown in brackets).

Mulock inserts an additional 'wicked' in the warning: 'Beware of thy *wicked* stepmother'. Paull, on the other hand, doubles the number of negative value adjectives applied to the Queen, leaving the young reader in no doubt about the Queen's wickedness.

A similar picture emerges from an analysis of the two translators' handling of the six positive value adjectives attributed to the heroine in the source text (Table 2).

Mulock's translation remains close to the German source text. Paull, on the other hand, more than doubles the number of times positive value adjectives are applied to her heroine. She doubles the number of instances where she is described as 'poor' (*'arm'*), thus portraying her as more deserving of the reader's sympathy. Paull uses an additional 'innocent'; she adds the details that the heroine thanks the hunter 'sweetly' for sparing her life and that she is 'a charming young woman' on her wedding day. She also praises her housekeeping skills: 'she was a clever little thing. She managed very well' (Paull, 1871/1874: 207). However, she points out that the girl is not clever in the same manipulative sense as her stepmother: 'not clever

Table 1 Translation of negative value adjectives

Sneewittchen	*Mulock*	*Paull*
böse (2)	cruel (1), evil-hearted (1)	wicked (2)
boshaft (2)	wicked (2)	wicked (2)
gottlos (2)	wicked (2)	wicked (2)
grausig (1)	barbarous (1)	horrible (1)
	Added:	*Added:*
	wicked (1)	wicked (6)
		evil (eye) (1)
Total: 7	**Total: 8**	**Total: 14**

Table 2 Translation of positive value adjectives

Sneewittchen	Mulock	Paull
arm (3)	poor (3)	poor (3)
lieb (2)	poor (1), darling (1)	dear (2)
unschuldig (1)	innocent (1)	innocent (1)
		Added:
		sweet[ly] (1)
		poor (3)
		innocent (1)
		clever (1)
		charming (1)
Total: 6	**Total: 6**	**Total: 14**

enough to resist her clever wicked stepmother'. In Paull's translation the reader is left in no doubt with whom their sympathies should lie and the heroine is portrayed as an even more innocent victim than in the source text.

The Magic Mirror, from its title to its altered ending, is an allegorical warning about the sinfulness of envy. The source text could be said to have been moulded in several ways to conform to Paull's preferred model of instruction, with the narrator ever-present to pass judgement on the characters, sentimentalised descriptions of good characters, and sinfulness leading to suffering and self destruction. This is in direct contrast to Mulock's preservation of what she saw as the 'rude' but sufficient moral implied in the source text (see Mulock, 1860).

Suitable content

As we have seen, the translators pointed out in their prefaces that they had taken care to omit any potentially unsuitable or harmful content from the tales they translated. Their different views of 'suitability' can also be illustrated by their handling of content such as cannibalism, the female body and references to death in this tale.

In the source text, the Queen orders her hunter to kill Snow White and to bring her the lungs and liver as proof; she subsequently eats the cooked lungs and liver of a wild boar, believing them to be those of her murdered stepdaughter. Mulock retains all four references to lungs and liver. Paull, on the other hand, omits the Queen's cannibalistic intentions altogether and avoids any mention of innards. The Queen in her translation simply demands 'some proofs' from the hunter, who takes 'part of the inside of a young fawn', which the Queen believes to belong to the child but does not eat. Interestingly, Mulock was the first English translator of *Sneewittchen* to provide a literal translation of the innards in the source text (see Chapelle, 2001: 139).

Mulock and Paull also take different approaches to the subtle but potentially problematic reference to female nudity. Following the third 'temptation episode' in which the Queen persuades the heroine to eat the poisoned apple, the dwarfs in Mulock's translation behave as follows:

> ... [they] searched whether she had anything poisonous about her, unlaced her, combed her hair, washed her with water and with wine. (Mulock, 1863: 296)

As in the source text, this implies that the seven men probably undressed the young girl and washed her naked body. Paull clearly considered such 'content' unsuitable for young readers and specifies that it is only her hair that they wash:

> ... they tried to extract the poison from her lips, they combed her hair, and washed it with wine and water. (Paull, 1871/1874: 211)

Mulock and Paull differ once again on the subject of death-related references in this tale. According to Mallet (1985: 165), *Sneewittchen* contains more references to murder and death than any other Grimm tale. In addition to the lexical items directly related to killing and dying, the source text also has the hunter slit the throat of a wild boar ('*stach ihn ab*'), states that the apparently-dead heroine looked as 'fresh' as a living person and that her body did not decay ('*verweste nicht*'), and refers several times to her coffin. Again, the translators' handling of this issue differs significantly (Table 3).

There is less emphasis on death and murder in Mulock's translation than in the source text as she omits two references and softens several others. In

Table 3 Translation of death-related references

Sneewittchen	*Mulock*	*Paull*
töten (2), *umbringen* (2)	killed (3)	killed/killing (3)
	taking her life (1)	get rid of (1)
Zugrunde richten (1)	destroy utterly (1)	get rid of (1)
abstechen (1)	killed (1)	[omitted]
tot (8)	dead (2)	dead (11)
	lifeless (3)	
	motionless (0)	
sterben (3)	die/d (2)	die/d (3)
	death (1)	
Sarg (7)	coffin (7)	coffin (10)
sah noch frisch aus (1)	still looked so fresh (1)	her face was as fresh (1)
verweste nicht (1)	unchanged (0)	decay/ing (2)
Total: 26	**Total: 22**	**Total: 32**

one case, she softens *'töten'* (kill) somewhat to 'taking her life'. The slitting of the boar's throat *'stach ihn ab'* is rendered as the less graphic 'killed'. On three occasions, she uses the less final 'lifeless', rather than the literal 'dead' to describe the appearance of the heroine after her stepmother's attempts on her life. When the dwarfs discover her after the final, successful attempt with the poisoned apple, Mulock uses the much less final 'motionless', even though the source text states most definitely that the girl is dead. After the dwarfs place her body in a glass coffin, the source text relates that she lay for a long time without decaying (*'verweste nicht'*). Mulock eschews mention of decay for the less disturbing 'unchanged'. She seems to have viewed death as one topic from which young people required some degree of protection.

As illustrated by Table 3, Paull takes a different approach and actually increases the total number of death-related references in the tale. She omits only one reference – the mention of throat-slitting, which is connected to her omission of the 'cannibalistic' episode in the source text. She adds the word 'dead' and 'coffin' three times each in her explicitation of the source text, provides a literal translation of *'verwesen'*, and even includes an additional reference to decay: she explains that the dwarfs place the heroine in a glass coffin because it will allow them to 'watch for any signs of decay'.

Paull's avoidance of the gory elements of cannibalism and innards and of the sexual undertones of the dwarfs' handling of the heroine's body are no doubt related to her concern with suitability and acceptability as expressed in her preface, as well as to the publisher's reputation for offering wholesome reading. Mulock's retention of these elements is perhaps surprising, given that she claimed to have excised potentially harmful elements. Her inclusion of these elements may perhaps reflect her desire to provide a definitive collection of genuine tales and to improve on earlier translations. Or perhaps the publisher Alexander Macmillan's children 'took to' these elements when he carried out his plan to 'test' the translations on them prior to publication, as mentioned in an unpublished letter to Mulock in 1862 (see Chapelle, 2001: 126). In any case, it seems that Mulock did not consider that these elements could 'really harm a child'. For her, repeated references to murder and death were potentially much more harmful for 'tender young hearts'.

This, again, is in direct contrast to Paull, who had no problem with the subject of death, while considering cannibalism and nakedness unsuitable elements. The subject of death was in fact fairly commonplace in children's books in 19-century England and frequently occurred in association with the themes of punishment and reward in moralistic tales (cf. Avery & Bull, 1965: 212). Indeed, it often makes an appearance in Paull's own stories, either as a reward for an angelic hero or heroine, or as a means of testing their faith.

A suitable style

Where Mulock's and Paull's approaches more or less agree is in relation to the style in which the tale is written. The Grimms' process of editing their tales, which they claimed had origins in oral tradition, produced a distinctive and standardised style. The Grimm 'genre' can be described as 'leading an uneasy double life as literature and folklore' (Tatar, 1987: 32). Both translators consciously or unconsciously moved the tale further from the oral and closer to the literary pole. They did so by cancelling lexical repetition; by rendering the episodic action less formulaic; by avoiding repeated use of diminutive forms (-*chen* and -*lein* in the source text), contracted verb forms and parataxis (the juxtaposition of clauses without explicit subordination or coordination); and by reducing other spoken language signals. However, Paull retained and indeed enhanced one of the 'oral' features of the Grimm genre in her translation: the use of spoken language signals (And, But, Now, So, Then) in initial sentence position. This produces a smooth, fast-flowing narrative and this feature of Paull's text may possibly be linked to her considerable experience of writing for children. Mulock's translation reflects this feature to a much lesser degree.

Both translators also introduce archaisms in the rhymes and dialogue. While this was in keeping with the tradition of English translations of the Grimms' tales since Taylor and Jardine in 1823, Mulock uses archaic pronouns and verb forms (thou, thee, thy, thyself, wilt, art, canst, lettest) in the dialogue to a much greater degree than Paull or any previous translator. This may be related to her desire to present the text as a 'real old' tale and perhaps also to make it sound more 'charming' and 'Saxon' and less 'foreign'.

In any case, it is perhaps not surprising that both translators should have given their source text a literary polishing. Both were writers used to producing texts that would be considered 'well-written' rather than reflecting folk poetry. Neither translator mentions the folk aspect of the Grimms' tales in her preface and both state their preference for a 'simple' and domesticated style. It was not until 1884 that an English translation was produced in which the aim was to reflect the style of the original tales. This was Margaret Hunt's translation (Hunt, 1884), aimed not at children but at students of folklore which had then only recently been established as a discipline in England. Mulock and Paull would have been much more concerned with ensuring that their young readers had before them an example of 'good' English style.

Conclusion

Dinah Mulock and Mrs Paull set out to bridge the same cultural divide with their translations of *Sneewittchen*, and yet produced two very different English texts. This study confirms Bassnett's (1998: 26) assertion that 'the signs of the translator's involvement in the process of interlinear transfer will always be present, and those signs can be decoded by any reader examining the process'. Our examination of this process has demonstrated that both Mulock and Paull constructed texts that could be considered 'suitable' for children within their culture, as there was no one prevailing view of children, of the best way to impart moral instruction, nor of what constituted acceptable literature for young readers in England at that time. Coming from their different viewpoints and based on their different experiences of writing for children, the translators played an active role in aligning their translations with two conflicting but co-existent norms in the target culture.

References

Alderson, B. (1985) *Grimm Fairy Tales in English: British Library Exhibition Notes*. London: The British Library Board.

Alderson, B. (1993) The spoken and the read: German popular stories and English popular diction. In D. Haase (ed.) *The Reception of Grimms' Fairy Tales: Responses, Reactions, Revisions* (pp. 59–77). Detroit: Wayne State University Press.

Avery, G. and Bull, A. (1965) *Nineteenth Century Children; Heroes and Heroines in English Children's Stories 1780–1900*. Chicago: University of Chicago Press.

Bassnett, S. (1998) When is a translation not a translation? In S. Bassnett and A. Lefevere (eds) *Constructing Cultures: Essays on Literary Translation* (pp. 25–40). Clevedon: Multilingual Matters.

Bratton, J.S. (1981) *The Impact of Victorian Children's Fiction*. London: Croom Helm.

Chapelle, N. (2001) The translators' tale: A translator-centred history of seven English translations (1823–1944) of the Grimms' fairy tale 'Sneewittchen'. PhD thesis, Dublin City University.

Craik, D.M. (2003) The Fairy Book. In R. Gilbert, *Victorian Sources of Fairy Tales, Part II* (Vol. 3). Bristol: Thoemmes.

Golden, C. (1991) Frederick Warne and Company. In P.J. Anderson and J. Rose (eds) *Dictionary of Literary Biography* (Vol. 106): *British Literary Publishing Houses 1820 – 1880* (pp. 321–27). Michigan: Thomson Gale.

Green, R.L. (1956) *Tellers of Tales: Children's Books and Their Authors from 1800 to 1964*. London: Edmund Ward.

Grimm, J. and Grimm, W. (1857) *Kinder-und Hausmärchen gesammelt durch die Brüder Grimm. Grosse Ausgabe. Siebente Auflage* (2 vols). Göttingen: Dieterichs.

Hunt, M. (1884) *Grimm's Household Tales: With the Author's Notes. Translated from the German and Edited by Margaret Hunt. With an Introduction by Andrew Lang* (2 vols). London: George Bell and Sons.

Kane, P. (1995) *Victorian Families in Fact and Fiction*. London: Macmillan.

Mallet, C-H. (1985) *Kopf ab! Gewalt im Märchen*. Hamburg: Rasch und Röhring.

Melrose, R. and Gardner, D. (1996) The language of control in Victorian children's literature. In R. Robbins and J. Wolfreys (eds) *Victorian Identities. Social and Cultural Formations in Nineteenth Century Literature* (pp. 143–62). London: Macmillan.

Mitchell, S. (1983) *Dinah Mulock Craik*. Boston: Twayne Publishers.

Morgan, B.Q. (1938) *A Critical Bibliography of German Literature in English Translation: 1481-1927. With a Supplement Embracing the Years 1928–1935* (2nd edn; completely revised and greatly augmented). London: Humphrey Milford.

Mulock, D.M. (1852) *Alice Learmont*. London: Hurst and Blackett.

Mulock, D.M. (1856) *John Halifax Gentleman*. London: Hurst and Blackett.

Mulock, D.M. (1860) The Age of Gold. *Macmillan's Magazine* 1 (4), 193–304.

Mulock, D.M. (1863) Sneewittchen. In *The Fairy Book. The Best Popular Fairy Stories. Selected and Rendered Anew by the Author of 'John Halifax Gentleman'* (pp. 289–98). London: Macmillan.

Owens, L (ed.) (1996) *The Complete Brothers Grimm Fairy Tales*. Fully illustrated. New York: Gramercy Books.

Paull, Mrs H.H.B. (1855) *The Doctor's Vision: An Allegory*. London: Bell and Daldy.

Paull, Mrs H.H.B. (1867) *Hans Andersen's Fairy Tales: A New Translation by Mrs Henry H.B. Paull*. London: Frederick Warne and Co.

Paull, Mrs H.H.B. (1869) *Mary Elton, or Self-Control*. London: Jarrold and Sons.

Paull, Mrs H.H.B. (1871/1874) The Magic Mirror. In *Grimm's Fairy Tales: A New Translation by Mrs H.H.B. Paull. Specially Adapted and Arranged for Young People* (pp. 204–13). London: Frederick Warne and Co.

Paull, Mrs H.H.B. (1876) *Schoolday Memories, or 'Charity Envieth Not'*. London: Jarrold and Sons.

Paull, Mrs H.H.B. (1888) *The Swiss Family Robinson, or The Adventures of a Shipwrecked Family on an Uninhabited Island near New Guinea*. London: Frederick Warne and Co.

Paull, Mrs H.H.B. (1890) *Clever Cats*. London: Routledge.

Sutton, M. (1996) *The Sin-Complex: A Critical Study of English Versions of the Grimms' 'Kinder und Hausmärchen' in the Nineteenth Century*. Kassel: Brüder Grimm Gesellschaft.

Tatar, M. (1987) *The Hard Facts of the Grimms' Fairy Tales*. Princeton: Princeton University Press.

Taylor, E. and Jardine, D. (1823) *German Popular Stories: Translated from the Kinder – und Hausmarchen. Collected by M.M. Grimm from Oral Tradition*. London: C. Baldwyn.

Townsend, J.R. (1990) *Written for Children: An Outline of English-language Children's Literature* (6th edn). London: The Bodley Head.

Zipes, J. (1987) *Victorian Fairy Tales: The Revolt of the Fairies and Elves*. New York: Routledge.

Chapter 12

From Dissidents to Bestsellers: Polish Literature in English Translation After the End of the Cold War

PIOTR KUHIWCZAK

Introduction

In the densely-written paragraph below, Itamar Evan-Zohar talks about a major shift in literary sensibility and the role translation may play during the periods when such shift is becoming conspicuous:

> The dynamics within the polysystem creates turning points, that is to say, historical moments where established models are no longer tenable for a younger generation. At such moments, even in central literatures, translated literature may assume a central position. This is all the more true when at a turning point no item in the indigenous stock is taken to be acceptable, as a result of which a literary 'vacuum'occurs. In such a vacuum, it is easy for foreign models to infiltrate, and translated literature may consequently assume a central position. (Evan-Zohar, 1990: 48)

In literary history Evan-Zohar's 'moments' are often represented as long periods of transition that eventually lead to the formation of a new literary convention and a new period in the history of literature. But such transitions are never autonomous – they are closely connected with other, often turbulent, changes in the social, economic and political life of whole countries and nations.

Critics differ as to the reasons why these changes come about,[1] but no critical school has managed to work out a paradigm that would allow us to predict how literary taste is going to develop in the future (Besserman, 1996). Traditionally, literary criticism suggests that a substantial change in literary taste follows a major political upheaval, and Evan-Zohar's views on the role of translation in the formation of literary styles seem to have developed along similar lines. So, for instance, there is a wide-ranging agreement that in the 18th century it was the French Revolution that served as a turning point in the history of European literatures. Considerable importance is also attached to the Franco-Prussian war of 1870. In the 20th century the major turning points for European literatures coincided with the end of the two world wars. Within national literatures, periodisation was linked to local events such as the Civil War in England, the revolutions of 1848 in France and Hungary, the Russian Revolution of 1917, or the 1968 student protests in France.

The 'Velvet Revolutions' and the End of an Epoch

It is very likely that that within this familiar paradigm the 1989–1991 changes in Eastern Europe and Russia will also be perceived as a significant turning point for literature (Hammond, 2005; Rosslyn, 1991). It may be too early to decide whether this transition to democracy in Eastern Europe can be regarded as a major caesura in literary studies, or as a turning point of only local significance. There is no doubt, however, that if we take a systemic approach, as advocated by Evan-Zohar and his followers (Toury, 1995; Hermans, 1999), we shall have to agree that in the former Eastern Bloc countries the place of literature in a social system, and the relationship between original and translated literatures, have changed dramatically since 1989 (Wachtel, 2006). It is already the case that, in everyday discourse in Poland, 1989 is used as a metaphor for a whole variety of phenomena that have developed since the Communist Party lost power.

It would be difficult within this short space to give a full account of the changes that have taken place in all the countries of the region. But space is not the sole problem here. Another, and perhaps more important, source of difficulty is precisely the fact that 1989 marked a collapse of what was perceived as one region, or a political unit that used to be conveniently known as either 'the Soviet Bloc', the 'Warsaw Pact' or 'Eastern Europe'. This collapse is reflected even in the very fact that the old labels used to describe the Soviet sphere ceased to fit the new political reality. The early 1990s were marked by a desperate search for new terminology that could reflect a multitude of transformations – political, religious, economic and military. The East–West divide was beginning to give way to the North–South paradigm, and the forgotten notion of 'the Balkans' made a swift comeback as wars swept the territory of what used to be called Yugoslavia (Rosslyn, 1996). The expansion of NATO and the European Union introduced further complications. Suddenly, there was a dilemma with the newly emerging Baltic States – were they still 'Baltic', a part of cultural zone called 'Scandinavia', or just three countries with distinctive names, languages and cultures? The terms eastern and western Europe, which used to be so neat and convenient are now fuzzy terms, and the fuzziness is reflected in the uncertainty with which we now use capital letters to describe the parts of the old continent.

The Usefulness of the Polish Case

Many of the semantic, cultural and political dilemmas will have to wait longer for a satisfying resolution. Here, I want to look only at Poland, the largest country of the region, and for historical reasons perhaps the most familiar to English-speaking audiences. Some issues in Poland's cultural transitions have been unique, and are linked to the specific turns in Polish history. But in many cases the recent developments in Polish publishing, and specifically in literary translation from and into Polish, will parallel what happened in other countries of the region when the major political change took place in the last decade of the 20th century.

One can make a safe generalisation today, that prior to the 'Velvet Revolutions', political change, politics and ideology affected the perception, selection and translation of Polish and other East European literature (Kuhiwczak, 1989).

Although it does not mean that, in order to be translated, a book had to fit the Cold War paradigm, there is no doubt that politics played an important role in the process of selection. However, while thinking about the impact of politics, we must not imagine that it was a matter of attention-grabbing headlines and commercial cynicism, as is often the case today. Literature in Eastern Europe used to be political not so much because all writers deliberately chose to oppose the Communist regime, but because the publishing was entirely controlled by the state apparatus. The Marxist–Leninist dogma considered literature as an important part of ideology; it was a tool that should help to convince the populations that socialism and communism were the only viable ideologies (Luker, 1992). It is obvious, then, that any writing that fell outside this requirement was already politically suspect, although with the weakening of the communist system, there was progressively more tolerance for 'non-committed writing'. Writers who were deliberately questioning the ethics of the socialist–realist framework even without making any allusion to politics, were considered, if not as political enemies, at least as 'unreliable elements' that needed to be treated with supreme caution. It is not surprising that the restrictions on what was and what was not acceptable to the political establishment pushed the ethical questions to the fore. In characterising Zbigniew Herbert's poetry long after the end of the Cold War, the Polish critic, Jerzy Jarniewicz wrote:

> Yet whether Herbert is read as a political poet, history's witness, a metaphysical or an existentialist poet, he remains the poet of moral examination, affirming (however anachronistic it may seem) that art cannot exist outside the realm of morality. Perhaps he will turn out to have been the last great poet who explicitly eclared the ethical duties of art. During the long communist night poets were expected to fulfil these duties; in today's climate, where moral debates are conducted in

public without censorship, poets have been assigned a different, humbler role. (Jarniewicz, 2001: 362)

Further on, Jarniewicz (2001: 359) states that it is this ethical stance, not only in poetry but also in film, that made Polish art so attractive to British writers and readers in the years of the Cold War. The imported works filled in the metaphysical gap that existed in the country where ethics and art did not have to live under the same roof and were not expected to share the same intellectual space. Further evidence that British writers were aware of this useful influence of East European writing comes from Seamus Heany, who wrote extensively about the impact East European poets had on the native literary scene:

> What translation has done over the last couple of decades is not only to introduce us to new literary traditions but also to link the new literary experience to modern martyrology, a record of courage and sacrifice which elicits our unstinted admiration. So, subtly, with a kind of hangdog intimation of desertion, poets in English have felt compelled to turn their gaze East and have been encouraged to concede that the locus of greatness is shifting away from their language. (Heaney, 1988: 38)

The 'Golden Age' of Polish Poetry

Indeed, while looking through the lists of authors translated from Polish, we can clearly see that poetry was a dominant genre. This conclusion is based not only on statistics but the prestige of publishers and magazines that published Polish literature. Faber and Faber, Carcanet Press, Bloodaxe Books, PN Review, Modern Poetry in Translation are just few household names that took a strong interest in poetry coming from Poland and other East European countries.

An additional factor that privileged poetry over other genres was the award of the Nobel Prize for Literature to Czeslaw Milosz in 1980, and several prestigious European distinctions awarded to Zbigniew Herbert and Wislawa Szymborska. In the same decade two other East European poets were awarded the Nobel Prize for Literature: Jaroslav Seifert in 1984 and Joseph Brodsky in 1987. This helped to keep the interest in the region's poetry going for a bit longer.

It would be perhaps unjust to claim that politics and prizes were more important in the promotion of Polish poetry than its intrinsic quality. Many Polish critics are inclined to admit that the quality of Polish literature is reflected much better in poetry than in the novel. But this is not only the view of the Poles. The towering figure of German literary criticism, Marcel Reich-Ranicki arrived at a similar conclusion after having read extensively Polish literature in the 1950s:

In fact, next to the works of Chopin, poetry is the Poles' finest contribution to European art. I still believe this. Unfortunately Europe was never much concerned about Polish poetry. This is as regrettable as it is understandable, but it is a misfortune for Polish literature. Because Polish novels, with few exceptions, do not rise above mediocrity and the same is true of Polish drama, unless it is verse drama. Polish poetry, however, stubbornly resists attempts to translate it into another language. While we have respectable German translations, really good ones are exceedingly rare. (Reich-Ranicki, 2002: 115)

Reich-Ranicki bemoans the fact that German translations do not give justice to Polish poetry. It would be hard to provide textual evidence that translations into English were better than the ones into German, nevertheless it is certain that from 1960s onwards Polish poetry attracted the attention of major British writers – first Ted Hughes and then Seamus Heaney. In the United States the poetry of Czeslaw Milosz in English translation became so important that it began to have close followers in Britain (Davie, 1986).

The Changes in the Polish Polysystem

This good patch for Polish poetry lasted a bit longer than communism, mainly due to the fact that the 1996 Nobel Prize went again to a Polish poet, Wislawa Szymborska. But if we look at a wider context, then we can clearly see that the times for Polish literature and its translation into other languages were already changing. The change did not come from outside Poland but from inside the country.

The 'historical moment' as defined by Evan-Zohar (1990) arrived in 1989 and not only changed the position of literature in the Polish polysystem, but radically altered the polysystem itself (Marody, 1991, 2004). The most radical change, which had triggered a whole chain reaction, was the end of the state monopoly on publishing. This meant not only the end of censorship and micro-management of publishing houses, but also the end of the extensive but politically-motivated support system that publishing and other cultural institutions had enjoyed in the whole of post-1945 period.

The end of subsidies led in turn to the privatisation of publishing and bookselling and the creation of the market. Now the publishers were free to choose what they wanted to publish, as well as what they wanted to translate from other languages. But this long-awaited freedom also had another face – competition, staff redundancies, bankruptcies and mergers. Like the rest of the state-controlled economy, publishing was subject to the rigorous rules of what is now known as the 'Polish shock therapy' (Sachs, 1993). The changes were so unexpected, paradoxical and far reaching that they were immortalised in literary works. At the peak of painful economic reforms,

Zbigniew Machej wrote a poem about the impact the 'shock therapy' had on the hierarchy of Poland's cultural values:

> Dignity and desire shall find refuge under the same
> roof, and the wolf shall lie down with the black sheep
> and the ugly duckling. Dreams of a wholesale business
> selling exotic fruits shall eclipse the longing
> for pure art. The Messiah of the Lithuanian prophets will find no
> refuge, not even in a waxworks museum. (Machez, 1991: 150)

Although this is a poetic text, it encapsulates very well what happened not only with the Polish economy, but also with the system of values. Market rules, irrelevant under communism, are now of primary importance, and art as well as artists have to adapt to the new economic realities. Sell or perish, rather than publish, or perish became the dominant motto of Polish literary scene after 1989.

The Market and Translation into Polish

Although the transition was painful, there is no doubt that after 1989 translation into Polish began to flourish (Korzeniowska & Kuhiwczak, 1994) The UNESCO statistics (*Index Translationum*),[2] indicate that, after the initial collapse of the Polish publishing market in 1990, the next five years were marked by a steady growth of translations from English into Polish. After that year the numbers fluctuate slightly, which means that a natural saturation of the publishing market must have been reached. The statistics also tell us that English became a dominant language from which Polish publishers were buying translation rights. In contrast, the translations from Russian, which collapsed from 90 in 1989 to 19 in 1990, never reached the pre-1989 level. This is also the case for all the former 'Eastern Bloc' languages, including German because the official policy before 1989 was to subsidise the publishing of books from the 'fraternal countries'.[3] Translations from French, although recovered from the low point of 42 in 1989, fluctuated widely in the same period and reached 116 in 1995. The general trends remained unchanged in the second half of the decade and in the early years of the 21st century. In the most recent set of statistics provided by *Insyutut Ksiazki* (Polish Book Institute) for 2004 the gap between translations from English (1602 titles) and the second largest translated literature, German (116 titles) remains very substantial.[4]

But numbers alone do not provide a full picture. In the pre-1989 Poland, publishers were obliged to supply data about the number of copies printed, and statistics about sold number of copies was easily obtainable. This is no longer the case – yet another symptom that Polish publishing has caught up with the rest of the developed world. The most recent available independent research (*Polityka*, 2006) reveals that between August 2005 and August 2006 the eight largest publishers published 1267 novels. Only 121 of these were by Polish authors, and only one publishing company had a substantial proportion of Polish authors (40%).

While discussing the systemic changes, Evan-Zohar (1990: 48) states that when the literary system evolves the 'established models are no longer tenable for a younger generation'. When applied to the particular situation in Poland, Evan-Zohar's statement implies that the wider social changes may have led to the change of public taste, and then perhaps to the change of literary style. The question about public taste is not hard to answer. The liberation of the market meant an instant influx of popular literature, particularly from the USA and the UK. The evidence for this is not only in statistics and titles, but also in Polish language, where a generic new term for low-grade popular literature is 'ludlum' coined from the name of Robert Ludlum – a master of popular fiction. This sudden influx of popular literature caused a major change of proportions between the genres, favouring narrative prose at the expense of poetry and drama.[5]

The Polish language itself underwent a major change (Pisarek, 1999). From the schizophrenic situation before 1989, when a gap between the language used in the private and the public spheres was enormous (Glowinski, 1990), Polish was plunged straight into the situation when the two registers merged with a vengeance. To prevent the side effects of such an explosion of 'private languages' and 'free for all', in 1999 the Polish parliament passed a law protecting the appropriate use of Polish in the public sphere.[6] What the law did not tackle was the overwhelming influence of English on the Polish language in private and public spheres both in a written and a spoken form (Kwiecinski, 1998). This influence is conspicuous not only in translated literature from English, but also in literary texts written in Polish.[7]

It would be difficult to prove whether, as Evan-Zohar claims, all these changes have led to the 'vacuum' and the dominant, or even central position of translated literature within the Polish literary system. Perhaps this is true of popular literature, because before 1989 popular literature in the Western understanding of the term was actively discouraged by the authorities and constituted a marginal phenomenon in the official sphere (Kloskowska, 2005). The sudden influx of inexpensive paperbacks available in large numbers in Polish hypermarkets did certainly mean that they began to occupy a central position within this genre. In general, however, the urge to reject the old models as an intentional action was a matter of the formation of small new literary groupings such as a literary group *BRuLion*. In the mid-1990s there was also a brief period of wide-ranging media discussion about the demise of what was called 'traditional Polish cultural paradigms' and an emergence of new attitudes and styles in creative writing (Janion, 1996), including women's writing and gay literature. However, all these symptoms do not constitute sufficient evidence to suggest that the transformations in the Polish polysystem caused a radical and permanent change in literary taste. Foreign models have 'infiltrated' some aspects of the Polish literary system, but it is too early to state that they changed the prevailing taste.

What has certainly changed is the mechanism by which books are marketed and sold. In the absence of modern marketing tools and the absence of the very word 'marketing' in the Polish vocabulary, books in pre-1989 Poland were neither promoted nor advertised. Bestsellers were created by word of mouth, or by the simple fact that books that were in demand were not available in a sufficient numbers. A queue in front of a bookshop used to be as common as a queue in front of any other shop. Now, the bestsellers are manufactured in the same way they are manufactured in other countries and the Polish bestseller lists are not different from similar lists elsewhere. Although Poland is perceived as a deeply Catholic country, *The Da Vinci Code* dominates the bestseller lists in Poland in the same way that it does anywhere else.

The Impact of Change on the Translation from Polish

So far polysystem theory has not been preoccupied with the question of how far the major changes within one social and literary polysystem influence other literary polysystems. In this particular case, the question is whether the major changes in Poland had any impact on the translation of Polish literature into other languages. The question has two aspects. The first one concerns textual matters, that is whether the new linguistic and stylistic features of post-1989 Polish literature are a challenge for translators, and whether the new Polish idiom is reflected in the English versions of translated books. The second aspect of this question is about the selection of what gets translated and why. To answer the first question one would have to undertake a systematic corpus research with a sample of representative texts. However, since the period under consideration is short and the selection of literary texts from 'small' literatures is always idiosyncratic, the outcome of this kind of research would not be neither particularly useful nor incisive. Perhaps at this stage in the evolution of the Polish literary polysystem, it is more important to ask how the response to the Polish changes is reflected in the change of book selection for translation in relation to the period before 1989.

The first response to the changes in Poland was an expectation on the part of British and also American[8] publishers that the change will either reveal something that was hidden from the public view by censorship, or generate a wave of new and exciting writing. In 1993 the now-defunct

Forest Books published a collection of Polish poetry with an emphatic title *Young Poets of a New Poland*. In the introduction to the volume, the editor Donald Pirie claimed:

> Though this selection of poems may reflect a period of transition rather than a new poetic aesthetic that is the expression of a very different Polish society, it is surely also true that authentic, convincing poetry is always located in the transitional and unstable, rather than confined by the predictable. (Machey: 1993: XIII)

Ten years later, an anthology, *Altered States* (Mengham *et al.*, 2003) was very similar in tone. In fact, the subtitle of the volume, *New Polish Poetry*, implied that Poland had a generation of new poets to be discovered. In both volumes separated by exactly a decade, *new* was a buzz word, very much in the spirit of how Poland and the whole of Eastern Europe was represented in the media. However, when we try to assess the impact of both volumes, we shall see that it was not substantial. Neither of the two publications generated either individual volumes for the poets included, or a follow-up interest in the whole generation of these poets. In fact, the mainstream publishers, if they published Polish poetry at all, remained committed to the poets of the older generation: Czeslaw Milosz, Wislawa Szymborska, Zbigniew Herbert, Tadeusz Rozewicz, Ewa Lipska, Adam Zagajewski and Piotr Sommer. Even if we take into consideration publications in small literary magazines, we can clearly see that Polish poetry ceased to be in demand and that the *novelty* of Polish literature had to be discovered in other genres.

In contrast to poetry, the Polish prose, not very well represented before 1989 (perhaps with the exception of Stanislaw Lem's science fiction and Ryszard Kapuscinski's literary reportage) began to be noticed abroad, and in a different way from before. In the absence of political criteria for the selection of texts, the UK publishers began to apply the same criteria to Polish literature as to literature from other countries. There is now a clear correlation between the translated texts and their reputation in Poland. This reputation is based on three sets of criteria: an award of a prestigious literary prize (such as Nike Readers' Prize), the long-term reputation of the writer in Poland, or the media publicity around a book, usually written by a previously unknown author.

In the first category, that is books awarded prizes in Poland, we have Olga Tokarczuk's *House of Day, House of Night*, Joanne Olczk-Roniker's *In the Garden of Memory*, and Antoni Libera's *Madame*. Pawel Huelle's short stories were published in 1991, so his novel *Mercedes-Benz* had an easier entry into the market, although the sponsorship by Mercedes-Benz for this novel created a lot of media and marketing publicity for the author in Poland. Tomek Tryzna's *Girl Nobody*, and Dorota Maslowska's *White and*

Red are good examples of a new Polish phenomenon of authors and books whose reputation is created by publicity and media manipulation.[9]

What Can the 'New' Polish Literature Offer?

Despite the fact that the number of publications is small, it is possible to identify the kind of writing that can count on the publishers', and perhaps readers', interest. There is no doubt that Polish literature connected with the Holocaust that was translated, albeit in small doses, before 1989 has remained popular. As well as Joanna Olczak-Ronikier's memoir (2004), in recent years we have seen the publication of Roma Ligocka's memoir (2003), Hanna Krall's short stories (2006) and Bohdan Wojdowski's novel (1997). Krall is of particular interest here, because her works have been translated in to all major European languages, but have had limited luck with translation into English. It may be the case that the publication and a subsequent filming of Wladyslaw Szpilman's memoir *The Pianist* (1999) helped other authors in the same way that Steven Spielberg's film *Schindler's List* helped to revive the interest in the Holocaust literature in the United States.

An entirely new interest is the Polish writing that is trying to explore the complicated ethnic and political dilemmas of Poland's past. Peppered with a good dose of the 'old world' nostalgia, these books touch on subjects that before 1989 were taboo in Poland. Huelle, Libera, Chwin and Tokarczuk fit neatly into this paradigm. Few reviews that have been written on these writers draw attention to the affinity, or contrast with Gunter Grass, or evoke a general impression about the Central European quality of prose. Such was the view of Marek Kohn on *Mercedes-Benz*:

> Huelle's wit and his subtle gift for measuring absurdity stand comparison with Hrabal or any of the other great central European ironists. Even so, it fell to commerce rather than art to add the finishing touch. By the time the book appeared, capitalism and culture had developed in Poland to a point where Mercedes-Benz felt able to take the hint from the Citroen anecdote and sponsor the publication. Time had turned another of its circles. (Kohn, 2005)

Similarly Michel Hoffman in *The Guardian* of 5 March 2005 called attention to Grass and then Sebald:

> Stefan Chwin is a new name to me, and *Death in Danzig* is his first book in English. It reminds me a little of Rushdie and Grass (himself a native of Danzig, after all), and perhaps a little more of Sebald, in the way it deploys a damaged individual at a crux of history. (Hoffman, 2005)

There is no doubt that this kind of writing finds keen readers in the UK, perhaps more than in mainland Europe, where Max Sebaldis is nowhere near as popular as here. It is sufficiently familiar stylistically to be accepted, and it provides an acceptable dose of otherness that fits into the existing notion of what is seen as 'Eastern' or 'Central' European.

While taking this necessarily cursory look at what kind of Polish writing is translated into English, one can clearly see that on one hand there is an expectation that the creative energy released after 1989 should produce something new and unexpected. On the other hand, there is a longing for what is essentially defined as 'East European' literature – a specific, personal account of the region's troubled history. This dual and rather incompatible set of expectations does not concern Poland alone. In the recent review of Czech short stories, the author Maya Jaggi began by laying down the dilemma that all literatures from the region are facing when they hit the desk of foreign publishers:

> The Cold War guaranteed a readership in the West for dissident Czech writers after the Soviet invasion of 1968, and among Czechs who queued for their books when the Velvet Revolution of 1989 put an end to censorship. Yet, just as the bookshop queues have long since disappeared, writers have found that their international appeal has ebbed away. The most feted Czech novelists today, including Michal Viewegh and Jachym Topol, are scarcely known in the English-speaking world. *Gargling Tar*, Topol's latest novel, is *A Czech Tin Drum* set during the crushing of the Prague spring of his boyhood. But who will publish it in Britain? As I heard one local critic ask despondently at May's Prague Book Fair, 'What is the selling point of post-communist literature?' (*The Guardian*, 8 July, 2006)

It seems that only time will help to bring such historical comparisons to an end. As A. Alvarez (1966) and then Seamus Heaney (1988) stressed, the quality of East European literature came out of innumerable historical pressures. The post-1989 writing from Eastern Europe is bound to be different, perhaps based much more on individual than collective experience. In this respect, the fiction translated from Polish in the last few years gives a true picture of what East Europeans experience, write and read, although those who remember pre-1989 Europe may be disappointed that this new, liberated Eastern Europe does not provide extraordinary literary talent as it used to in the past.

Notes
1. In the late 20th century, comparative criticism uses Thomas Kuhn's theory presented in his *The Structure of Scientific Revolution* published in 1962.
2. On WWW at http://portal.unesco.org/culture/en/ev.php-URL_ID=7810&URL_DO=DO_TOPIC&URL_SECTION=201.html. Accessed 17.03.97.

3. Pre-1989 figures for German were boosted by a substantial number of translations from the German Democratic Republic.
4. On WWW at http://www.instytutksiazki.pl/. Accessed 17.03.97.
5. The immediate impact of this change on translation was conspicuous. The influx of popular literature meant that publishers were engaging more translators, often poorly qualified for the job.
6. On WWW at http://ks.sejm.gov.pl/proc3/ustawy/10_u.htm. Accessed 17.03.97.
7. A similar situation exists in Italian. See Ray, Leslie (2004) Italian lies dying ... and the assassin is English. *The Linguist* 43, 34–37.
8. Because of massive take-overs and changes to book distribution over the years, it is difficult now to determine separate identities of UK and US publishers and publishing markets.
9. Andrzej Wajda's film based on the novel did not turn out to be either an artistic or a commercial success.

References

Alvarez, A. (1965) *Under Pressure: The Writer in Society: Eastern Europe and the USA*. Harmondsworth: Penguin.
Besserman, L. (1996) *The Challenge of Periodization: Old Paradigms and New Perspectives*. New York: Garland.
Davie, D. (1986) *Czeslaw Milosz and the Insufficiency of Lyric*. Knoxville, TN: University of Tennessee Press.
Evan-Zohar, I. (1990) Polysystem studies. *Poetics Today* 11 (1), 48.
Glowinski, M. (1990) *Nowomowa po polsku*. Warszawa: Pen.
Hammond, A. (2005) *Cold War Literature*. London: Routledge.
Heaney, S. (1988) *The Government of the Tongue*. London: Faber and Faber.
Hermans, T. (1999) *Translation in Systems: Descriptive and System-oriented Approaches Explained*. Manchester: St Jerome.
Hoffman, M. (2005) What life after linden blossom tea. *The Guardian*, March 5.
Huelle, P. (2005) *Mercedes-Benz*. London: Serpent's Tail.
Jaggi, M. (2006) Povidky: Short stories by Czech women. *The Guardian*, July 8.
Janion, M. (1996) *Czy będżiesz wiedział, co przeżyłeś*. Warszawa: Sic!
Jarniewicz, J. (2001) Poetry and the cogwheels of history. *The Cambridge Quarterly* 30, 358–63.
Kloskowska, A. (2005) *Kultura masowa: Krytyka i obrona*. Warszawa: PWN.
Kohn, M. (2005) Fiction roundabout. *New Statesman*, October 3.
Korzeniowska, A. and Kuhiwczak, P. (1994) *Successful Polish–English Translation*. Warszawa: PWN.
Krall, H. (2005) *The Woman from Hamburg and Other True Stories*. New York: Other Press.
Kuhiwczak, P. (1989) Before and after the burning forest: Modern Polish poetry in Britain. *The Polish Review*, 1 57–71.
Kwiecinski, P. (1998) Translation strategies in a rapidly transforming culture. *The Translator*, 2, 183-206.
Kuhn, T. (1962) *The Structure of Scientific Revolution*. Chicago, IL: University of Chicago Press.
Libera, A. (2000) *Madame*. London: Canongate Books.
Ligocka, R. (2003) *The Girl in the Red Coat*. London: Hodder and Stoughton.
Luker, N. (1992) *From Furmanov to Sholokhov: An Anthology of the Classics of Socialist Realism*. Ann Arbor: Ardis.

Machej, Z. (1991) Old prophecy. In D. Pirie (ed.) *Young Poets of a New Poland* (150) London: Forest Books.
Marody, M. (ed.) (1991) *Co nam zostało z tych lat: Spoleczenstwo polskie na progu zmiany systemowe*. London: Aneks.
Marody, M. (ed.) (2004) *Zmiana czy stagnacja?* Warszawa: Scholar.
Maslowska, D. (2005) *White and Red*. London: Atlantic Books.
Mengham, R., Pior, T. and Szymore, P. (eds) (2003) *Altered State: The New Polish Poetry*. Todmorden: Arc Publications.
Olczak-Ronikier, J. (2004) *In the Garden of Memory*. London: Orion Books.
Pisarek, Wa. (1999) *Polszczyzna 2000*. Krakow: Uniwersytet Jagiellonski.
Polityka (2006) Kram z powiesciami. *Polityka* 38, 64.
Reich-Ranicki, M. (2002) *The Author of Himself*. London: Orion Books.
Rosslyn, F. (1991) Over the wall: East–West perspectives at the end of the Cold War. *The Cambridge Quarterly* 20, 285–303.
Rosslyn, F. (1996) Balkan affair. *The Cambridge Quarterly* 25, 61–81.
Sachs, J. (1993) *Poland's Jump to the Market Economy*. Cambridge: MIT Press.
Tokarczuk, O. (2003) *House of Day, House of Night*. Evanston: Northwestern University Press.
Toury, G. (1995) *Descriptive Translation Studies and Beyond*. Philadelphia: John Benjamins.
Tryzna, T. (1999) *Girl Nobody*. London: Fourth Estate.
Wachtel, A. (2006) *Remaining Relevant after Communism: The Role of the Writer in Eastern Europe*. Chicago: University of Chicago Press.
Wojdowski, B. (1997) *Bread for the Departed*. Evanston: Northwestern University Press.

For Product Safety Concerns and Information please contact our EU Authorised Representative:

Easy Access System Europe

Mustamäe tee 50

10621 Tallinn

Estonia

gpsr.requests@easproject.com

www.ingramcontent.com/pod-product-compliance
Ingram Content Group UK Ltd.
Pitfield, Milton Keynes, MK11 3LW, UK
UKHW021834140426
5217IPUK00021B/1450